ERIC GILL

ERIC GILL

Man of Flesh and Spirit

MALCOLM YORKE

TAURIS PARKE PAPERBACKS
LONDON • NEW YORK

Published in 2000 by Tauris Parke Paperbacks
an imprint of I.B.Tauris & Co Ltd
Victoria House, Bloomsbury Square, London WC1B 4DZ
175 Fifth Avenue, New York NY 10010
Website: http://www.ibtauris.com

In the United States and Canada distributed by St. Martin's Press
175 Fifth Avenue, New York NY 10010

First published in 1981 by Constable and Company Limited

ISBN 1 86064 584 4

A full CIP record for this book is available from the British Library
A full CIP record for this book is available from the Library of
Congress

Library of Congress catalog card: available

Printed and bound in Malaysia

Contents

Illustrations

*

The initial letters used as tailpieces on pp. 47, 72 and
131 are taken from *Autumn Midnight* by Frances
Cornford, printed by St Dominic's Press and
published by the Poetry Bookshop, London (1923)

Border decorations 'Woman supporting
Cupid' and 'Sleeping man' from
Chaucer's *Troilus and Criseyde* (1927),
Golden Cockerel Press, 17.6cm × 3.4cm
and 17.8cm × 4.4cm

Acknowledgements

Many people helped me to write this book, though only I
am responsible for the views expressed in it and any errors
it may contain.

I am grateful to the late Joan and the late René Hague
for their help in the initial stages of the research, and to
Petra Tegetmeier, now Eric Gill's sole surviving daughter, for her kind permission to reproduce so many of his
graphic works. Walter Shewring, Gill's literary executor,
was also most generous.

In America, the staff at the Humanities Research
Centre, University of Texas in Austin, were most helpful
and hospitable. In the William Andrews Clark Library of
the University of California in Los Angeles I was made
similarly welcome. Albert Sperison showed me over the
Gill collection he had donated to the Donahue Rare
Books Room in the Richard A. Gleeson Library of the
University of San Francisco. The librarian there, Steve
Corey, extended a cordiality which went well beyond the
calls of duty.

Nearer home I had helpful correspondence from David
Kindersley and Edward Johnston's daughter, Priscilla
Roworth, and some enjoyable chats with Douglas Cleverdon (who incidentally owns the copyright of Gill's St
Dominic Press wood-blocks and the famous self-portrait
of 1927). Mr James Mosley of St Bride Printing Library
assisted with the illustrations to the section on printing
and typography.

Manchester University Department of the History of
Art generously made all its Gill negatives available to me,
and in Newcastle Rik Walton worked hard to prepare my
photographs and slides. Finally Elfreda Powell edited my
typescript, and my wife supported me through it all.

M.Y.
1981

For Mavis, Rachel and Jonathan

Preface

Between the wars Eric Gill was one of the best-known and most controversial artists in England. Today his name is only current amongst connoisseurs of rare and fine books, or to specialist admirers of his typefaces. His sculpture, once the main source of his public fame, has been overshadowed by the works of later, more aggressively modern artists, and his drawings and engravings on wood and metal are rarely exhibited or reproduced. This book is an attempt to redress such neglect and to introduce the man, his ideas, and his works to a wider audience.

Gill was not just a versatile artist but a wide-ranging polemicist in a way no other British artist of this century can match. His art and thought are inter-dependent so that some understanding of his political, aesthetic and religious ideas is essential before one can fully appreciate the sources of his graphic and sculptural works. As he entitled one of his essays: 'It All Goes Together.' He was a voluminous writer all his adult life so that in a book this size one cannot trace all the influences, false trails, contradictions and minor developments of his ideas. I have therefore concentrated on what I take to be the central beliefs of his mature years and have tried to retain Gill's own words and tone wherever possible. As this is intended to be primarily an art book I have omitted the writings on Catholic theology and other specialist topics about which I am unqualified to speak. Similarly his typography receives briefer mention than it deserves as this has been adequately dealt with elsewhere by specialists.

The questions Gill raises on the nature of our industrial society and the place of art within it still need answers. We may not like or accept the ones he offers but we shall find them truculently and often humorously expressed. I have refrained from imposing my own judgements on Gill's ideas even when I have found them wrong or downright absurd, partly because it would need several volumes to do so, but mainly because I believe the reader will be provoked by what he reads into his own reactions and replies.

It would be a mistake to stress Gill the controversialist and make him sound only strenuously intellectual and pedantic. He did indeed strive always to be rational, to force the logic of a situation as far as it would go, and like a medieval Schoolman to define all his basic terms (Beauty, Truth, Prudence, Art, etc.). However, constantly breaking through all this tidy categorizing is a very human delight in the flesh and all its pleasures. One motive for his intellectual quest was to find a doctrinal justification for his own strong erotic feelings and actions. He found much comfort in the Catholic Church's tolerance of the body and its precept that 'Man is composed of matter and spirit, both real and both good'. We must take this earthier side of Gill into account, as well as his spiritual strivings, if we are to judge his art aright. It is from this struggle to fuse the erotic and the divine that his most typical works take their start, and this book its broad central theme.

Previous writers on Gill such as his brother Evan, Robert Speaight, Donald Attwater, Walter Shewring, Conrad Pepler, David Jones, and David Kindersley have all been personal friends and usually fellow-Catholics. Their accounts and those of surviving friends I have spoken to glow with the admiration and affection Gill seems to have inspired in all who knew him well.* My approach has been very different. I came to the man and his ideas through the works, and this long after his death. As Gill was remorselessly self-revealing in his published and unpublished writings it is largely from these that I have reconstructed my picture of the man. I have endeavoured to restrain any impulse to offer glib psychological analyses of the strong but often contradictory character which emerges. It was the difficulty I encountered in tracing the drawings and sculptures (now

* The only hostility to Gill as a man that I have found is in Graham Greene's spiteful little article 'Eric Gill' (1941) in his *Collected Essays*, London 1977.

largely in America), as well as the obscure pamphlets and out-of-print books in which Gill's essays and engravings appeared which drove me to collect as many as possible together in this one volume. Obviously to do justice to Gill's vast output in all media several large volumes would have been more appropriate.

Since a book needs some kind of plan I have chosen to deal with Gill's life, beliefs, and artistic activities in separate chapters, but this is obviously untrue to the way Gill actually lived his crowded days. He might sculpt in the morning, draw in the afternoon, engrave in the evening, and still find time for prayers, teaching, love-making, writing and discussion. Someone remarked that he was not so much eccentric as concentric, and this is surely true. It is part of my purpose, therefore, to demonstrate the unity of belief beneath all this seeming diversity of activity, and to see why he impressed so many people by his integrity and consistency. He was also human enough to fall below his own high standards sometimes, and these occasions need mentioning when they have some bearing on his art.

I think now, the centenary of Gill's birth, an appropriate time for a new generation of artists and readers to encounter his ideas and works, and to appraise their continuing relevance to modern society and modern art.

Biographical details

Eric Gill wrote at the beginning of his *Autobiography* that 'nothing very particular has happened to me – except inside my head', and that he would write an 'auto-psychography', a record of mental experience, instead. The following brief outline fills in those events and 'accidents' he omitted.

1882
Feb 22
Born Arthur Eric Rowton Gill at Brighton. Father Assistant Minister in a chapel of the Countess of Huntingdon's Connexion and receiving £150 per year. Mother former professional singer. Eric second child and eldest son of their thirteen children.

1897
Father joins Church of England and re-trains at Chichester.

Jan 18
Eric's favourite sister Cicely dies aged 14. Family move to Chichester where father has curacy. Eric leaves school. Becomes day-student at Chichester Technical and Arts School. Learns decorative lettering. Develops taste for church architecture and music.

1899
Apprenticed to W.H. Caroë (1857–1938) architect to Ecclesiastical Commissioners in Westminster. Father moves to curacy at Bognor at £90 per year. Eric attends LCC Central School of Arts and Crafts to learn lettering from Edward Johnston. On advice of the Principal, W.R. Lethaby, also learns masonry and stone-cutting. Period of agnosticism and disillusion begins.

1901–2
Begins to receive inscriptional and tombstone

work. Shares rooms with Edward Johnston in Lincoln's Inn.

1903   Meets Ethel Moore, daughter of the head verger at Chichester Cathedral. Engaged 22 June. Finishes at architect's office and becomes professional stone-cutter.

1904   Marries. Sets up home in Battersea. Receives
Aug 6   first commission for engraved headings and titles from Count Kessler.

1905   Birth of daughter Elizabeth. Moves to Hammersmith. Johnstons living nearby. Teacher of monumental masonry and lettering at LCC Paddington Institute. Attends Fabian Society. Befriended by William Rothenstein and meets other famous artists and writers.

1906   Wins £20 prize for inscription and takes Ethel to Rome. Takes on Joseph Cribb as apprentice. Begins to wood-engrave. Birth of daughter Petra.

1907   Brief love affair with woman in Fabian Society. Takes part in political demonstration which is strongly broken up by police. Visits Belgium.

Oct   Moves to 'Sopers' in Ditchling village, Sussex.

1910   Birth of daughter Joanna. Carves first figure in stone and is praised by Roger Fry and Count Kessler. Kessler finances trip for Eric to meet Aristide Maillol, but Eric runs away. Plans to make colossal sculpture park with Epstein, but fails to raise money.

1911   Ethel has miscarriage and is unable to have more children. He begins to move towards Catholicism, especially after visit to Abbey of Mont-César in France and hearing plainsong for the first time.

1912   Exhibits eight sculptures in the Second Post Impressionist Exhibition which opened in October at the Grafton Gallery and continued until January 1913. Edward Johnston settles in Ditchling.

1913
Feb 22   Eric and Ethel (now to be known as Mary) received into the Catholic Church. Move across Ditchling village to bigger 'Hopkins Crank'. Desmond Chute comes to Ditchling.

1914   Gill is not deeply involved in war issues and is exempted from war service to work on Westminster Cathedral Stations of the Cross.

1916   Hilary Pepler moves to Ditchling and sets up printing press. Pepler also joins Catholic Church. The 'Ditchling Community' begins to take shape.

1917   Receives commission for Leeds University War Memorial. Gordian Gill adopted.

1918   Westminster 'Stations' completed.

July 29   Eric and Mary Gill, Pepler and Chute invested as novices in the Third Order of St Dominic.

August   Gill called up into RAF transport at Blandford. For most of his 4 months' service he is ill.

1919   Many commissions for war memorials. Visits Ireland with Pepler.

1920   Founder member of Society of Wood-engravers.

1921   David Jones comes to visit Ditchling and stays for next 4 years. Craft Guild of St Joseph and St Dominic formed by the Ditchling Community. Philip Hagreen joins community. Chute leaves to study for priesthood.

1923   Gill helps publish Jacques Maritain's *Art et Scolastique* in limited edition on St Dominic's Press.

June   Controversy over Leeds War Memorial after its dedication.

1924   Quarrels with Pepler and resigns from Guild. Leaves to live at Capel-y-ffin in Welsh Black Mountains. Joined by Jones, Hagreen, Joseph Cribb, René Hague and Donald Attwater.

1925   Pilgrimage to Rome, via Paris.

1926–7   Winter in Salies-de-Béarn near Pyrenees. Meets Zadkine and Maillol. Daughter Elizabeth marries Pepler's son in spite of fathers' estrangement.

1928   Gills move to 'Pigotts', near High Wycombe, Bucks. He works on St James Headquarters commission.

1930   Daughter Petra marries engraver Denis Tegetmeier. Gill visits Weimar and meets Maillol again. Beginning of ill-health. Commissioned to do sculpture on Broadcasting House. Daughter Joan (or Joanna) marries printer René Hague.

1933   Founder member of Artists' International Foundation to oppose Fascism and war. Works on designs for Archaeological Museum of Palestine.

1934   Works in Jerusalem. Son-in-law David Pepler dies.

1935   Awarded Honorary Associateship of Royal Institute of British Architects.

1936   Appointed Royal Designer to Industry. Begins to speak and write for pacifism.

1937   Convalesces in Italy. Awarded Honorary Associateship of Royal Society of British Sculptors. Elected Associate of Royal Academy. Revisits Palestine and Egypt.

Eric and Mary Gill's grave at Speen, near High Wycombe, Buckinghamshire. The inscription, designed by Eric Gill himself, was cut by his assistant Laurie Cribb

1938   Given Honorary Doctorate of Laws at Edin-
            burgh University. His largest work – the
            panels for the League of Nations Building in
            Geneva – is completed and installed.

1939   Designs church at Gorleston-on-Sea, near
            Yarmouth.

1940   Cancer of lung diagnosed. Writes 100,000
            word *Autobiography* between April and July.

Nov 17   Dies, aged 58.

            Buried in Speen Churchyard with own
            epitaph:
            'Pray for Me/Eric Gill/Stone Carver
            1882–1940.'

Dec 20   *Autobiography* published.
            Mary Gill survived at Pigotts until 22 March
            1961 and is buried with her husband.

'Man is matter and Spirit: both real and both good'

What was Gill like? In appearance the mature man was short, sturdy, full-bearded and heavily be-spectacled. Count Harry Kessler, a life-long patron noted, 'his gaze, out of bloodshot eyes, is guileless yet strong-willed and has on occasion an almost fanatical gleam'.[1]* Invariably he was photographed posing with a cigarette in a long holder, in spite of his father's pronouncement that 'smoking a cigarette in a holder is like kissing a lady with her veil on'. However, it was his clothing rather than his figure which attracted most attention once he ventured outside the workshop setting. He used it as a kind of placard for his ideas and to mark his separation from the drably uniform society he despised. He wore a beret because, he said, hats were a tribute to the dignity of the human head (he was also bald), and boots because they were similarly a tribute to the feet. Ideally he would have loved to wear a toga, or the black and gold Arab robes he adopted in Palestine as being 'clothes fit for meditation and the life of thought and gentle occupation', but since stone-cutting is none of these he always wore a drab collarless belted smock to his shins. He thought this the ideal garment for both men and women so long as it covered the genitals, and children should wear a shorter version to 'a few inches below the belly'. Trousers he despised, so under the smock he wore loose scarlet silk underpants, or when working on the scaffold for his BBC carvings he wore a crimson petticoat-bodice with no breeches at all. In hot weather he was inclined to discard underclothes altogether and hang them on the scaffolding.[2] Leg-wear varied, but scarlet socks left over from his Fabian days and bare knees were as likely as anything, and John Rothenstein claims to have seen him in yellow stockings cross-gartered like Malvolio![3] Kessler thought

* References begin on p. 277.

Gill carving a panel of St Mary, St Denis and St George, Manchester Cathedral (1933)

Gill liked to dress in this way to make himself conspicuous, but, as we shall see, this bizarre ensemble was not arrived at without much delving into the nature of man and the clothing most suited to his place in the universal scheme of things.

Gill's character seems compounded of opposites. Donald Attwater notes that in many ways he was a very Victorian person not only in his optimism, solid sincerity and high seriousness (and one might add, his surprising flashes of prudery) but in the way he combined these qualities with the kind of gay frolicsomeness that could be found in Charles Dodgson and Edward Lear. The accounts left by those who knew him speak of his lively laughter and frequently very earthy humour. His sheer friendliness and interest in people shines out of his letters to his enormously varied circle of friends, but he combined this with a decorum and formality so that everybody in the three communities he led knew their exact place. Apprentices addressed him as Mister Gill, no matter how old they were, and in fact continued to refer to him as 'Mr' even when writing of him forty years after his death.[4] David Kindersley, a former apprentice, says their respectful address arose 'because we took a strong objection to young "bloods" from Oxford turning up, worshipping at EG's feet for half-an-hour then coming over to the workshop out of duty before departing, during which time they would invariably refer to ERIC, in their animated conversation. Even amongst ourselves we referred to him as Mr Gill.'[5]

There is no truth, however, in Speaight's claim that Gill in turn referred to his old teacher Edward Johnston as 'Master' all his life, though 'Most dear Master' *is* the title he used in the last letter he ever wrote to Johnston in 1938.[6] On the other hand, he did write to his closest friend and assistant Desmond Chute, 'I would like you to call me Master. It gives me great satisfaction – but what am I to call you?'[7]

Along with these orderly relationships he insisted on order within the workshops, over the entrance to which was written, 'A bad workman blames his tools: because a good workman does not use bad tools'. He taught that a workman's bench should be as neat as an altar. This passion for precision showed early in his schoolboy enthusiasm for mathematics and his meticulous drawings of locomotives, and it carried over into his adult thinking about life, art and society. His art works too are often weakened by excessive 'rounding off' and finishing: he seemed unable to leave any detail unaccounted for whether in stone, or money, or argument, or his life.

Related to this passion for order was his compulsion to record everything in writing. In his earliest diaries this takes the form of lists of sermons and church music heard, masturbations, plays and pictures seen, books read, and an exact account of every coin spent, even down to the single penny paid in a public lavatory. All the hundreds of visits and visitors are recorded, often with a terse comment such as, 'Rupert Brooke and E. Marsh came in morn & stayed to lunch. Atheistical beggars' (13/1/1913). Or, 'Frank Dobson came at noon. Excellent man' (8/3/1921). A few world events are noted, but mostly we get glimpses of a warm family life of evenings with the mirrorscope or stamp collections, Gill's attacks of boils, making toys or Christmas cribs, haircuts, burying Maggie the goat, 'rather a cross argument with Ethel and Enid re women's clothes', the death of his brother Kenneth in a war-time flying accident ('a life thrown away but perhaps the throw was caught by God'), Gill's tumble into a cesspool, tennis parties, family baths, and later the great pleasure with which the births of grandchildren are recorded. Mixed in with these are events which a more prudent man would have left unwritten, such as the exact details of his infidelities. As the head of a workshop it was necessary to log the daily hours worked by himself and his apprentices, and here again the ledgers, worksheets and bills are scrupulously kept. Rubbings were kept of all inscriptional work and small sculptures, and all rough and finished drawings exactly dated, as well as subsequent tracings from them. All notes for his published writings are preserved, carbons of letters sent, and all his childish little books of engine drawings as far back as 1890 are intact. So are the architectural sketches and watercolour paintings of his

Chichester and London periods, and numerous states of his wood-engravings of all periods are labelled and in order. No future cataloguer of his vast output should encounter any difficulties, especially as he was already well served during his lifetime by his brother Evan's catalogue of his inscriptions and his later bibliography. Gill was evidently passionate for order, believing with Aquinas, 'It is only in Order that the mind can find rest'. Unfortunately his life was not so easy to keep as tidy as his workshops, for bursting out from beneath all these self-imposed rules came capricious lusts of the flesh which crept into all aspects of his life and work.

All his life he lived in poverty or near it, but without resentment, as this fitted in with his need for asceticism, and with his hatred of the products of industrial society. His letters and diaries, however, show that money matters weighed upon him as his family and dependants increased, and how he was concerned to get an exactly fair price for his labour. He would charge the stone-mason's daily wage of about £2 for a lecture, but insisted upon first-class rail fare so that he could continue his work on the journey. His resentment of the critics' and dealers' exploitations of the artists' labours was fierce indeed, though his scheme to bypass the men of business which he devised with Augustus John, Jacob Epstein and Ambrose McEvoy came to nothing and he had to continue to use commercial galleries all his life. He loathed the machine-made, but there exists a circular letter dated 7 October 1933 in which Gill exhorts his fellow artists to supply small, cheap works (10 to 60 shillings) for sale with the best machine-made furniture in the showrooms of Whiteley Ltd, London W2. He quotes with approval Le Corbusier's saying that 'a machine-made house is a machine to live in', but insists that cheap machine-made reproductions are not the things to ornament them. The same Cézanne on every wall in every house is 'monstrous and nauseating', and moreover does a disservice to contemporary artists. The only place for reproductions is in a portfolio, for reference. The response to this advertisement is not known.[8]

Sometimes Gill's principles seem flexible where money was concerned, so when an ex-apprentice wrote to him in some moral perplexity over whether to carve a memorial to the Fascist dead in the Spanish Civil War which would also be exhibited in London to raise funds for Franco's cause, Gill, who was a life-long opponent of Fascism and was a member at the time of the Artists' International Foundation, replied by postcard '"Plenty biz no do! No biz. DO!" It was done.'⁹ As W.R. Lethaby wrote in another context, 'It is difficult to maintain an ideal in a deal'. Gill's book-keeping was so precise that he could record, for example, that in 1906 his income was £553 11s 6d and expenditure £478 4s 8d,¹⁰ though in later years the balance sometimes tipped the other way and he had to defer paying the wages of his apprentices. The quarrel with Hilary Pepler which eventually split the Ditchling community was basically over money and the richer Pepler's more careless attitude towards it.

Gill's days were full of hard work on his engraving blocks or plates, type design, sculpture, drawings, lecturing and writing as well as his devotions and serious reading. Nevertheless, he found time for various recreations within the family circle such as singing, playing the clavichord, walking, tennis, swimming, drinking home-made beer, writing occasional verse and talking to anyone who would listen. His energies must have been remarkable, though Speaight records he was not over-robust and needed a lot of sleep as he grew older. He frequented theatres, circuses, music halls and other more dubious places of entertainment on his trips to London and Paris, but permitted no 'wireless' or newspapers in the house – the 'Daily Mail mind' being one of the things he despised most. In spite of this, and his admiration for the self-effacing anonymous medieval sculptors, he was well aware of all the critics' responses to his work. Mary even paid a press-cutting agency and kept volumes of his reviews, though he professed to scorn all critics except Marriott of *The Times* (his remarks were 'most kind and generous, considering that he's not R.C. and depends solely on his own decency of mind').¹¹ There were no cars, or telephones or gramophones permitted either, at least not until the later years at Pigotts. Railway engines he loved all his life and a flight in an aeroplane in Egypt in 1937 gave him immense pleasure. As he kept insisting, it was not machines themselves he hated (many were very beautiful) but he hated the way they demeaned and enslaved the workers who operated them for the profit of others. As far as he could in this imperfect world he would avoid their use and products and the seductive short cuts they offered in art. Nevertheless, he gained at least part of his fame and income by designing typefaces for that 'one particular industry which was the first in history to exemplify our modern way of making things – not single things one by one, but batches of interchangeably alike, because mechanical, copies from master patterns'.[12]

The families who gathered round the Gills at Ditchling, then Capel-y-ffin and finally at Pigotts were similarly motivated to seek artistic independence, simple self-sufficiency and a dignified poverty, but above all they were united by their religious convictions. Several of the men at Ditchling became Tertiaries in the Order of St Dominic which imposed upon them certain duties. They gathered together from their various workshops four times each day to sing the Little Office. Day began at 6 a.m. with Prime and ended with Compline in the Chapel so that work and prayer mingled throughout the day. The Order of St Dominic stressed that worldly frivolities of dress and amusement should be avoided, which suited the side of Gill's nature which sought asceticism and discipline very well, and the Order's call to seek and preach the truth chimed in nicely with his love of debate and belief that 'all art is propaganda'.

Conrad Pepler recalls the fun of growing up in such a varied community as the Ditchling one with human eccentrics mingling with poultry, pigs, goat, Guernsey cows, pony, the excitements of sorting offal after a pig-killing, hot cakes from brick ovens, butter-making, wine-making, family prayers, harvesting, amateur dramatics and home-made music. There also seem to have been a variety of infirm or eccentric priests attached to the chapels in each place the Gills lived in who added to the commotion of work and worship. Attempts were made to establish links with the local community, but as the children were taught, very haphazardly, at home and the adults differed from their neighbours in religion and occupations, these links were never strong, as Pepler admitted. The puzzled locals called Gill 'The Married Monk'.[13]

Some visitors were less impressed by the fun and more by the discomforts of smoky fires, scratchy wooden and pewter plates, the lack of electricity, draughty rooms, water frozen in wash-basins, and the general tumbledown condition of the buildings, especially the remote half-ruin at Capel-y-ffin. Mary Gill explained their choice of this rural wilderness as being because she only wanted 'a bit of land to help with the food, and thus avoid as much as possible recourse to New Zealand mutton and Chinese eggs'.[14] But the farming seems to have been an incompetent affair, as Johnston's daughter Priscilla and David Kindersley admit in their respective accounts of Ditchling and Pigotts. The reading of the Martyrologium before meals, the long Epistles and Gospel of the day, the splashing of holy water, the long graces and frequent services some visitors found 'not a little sinister' and precious.[15] Crueller suggestions were made that here were people in retreat, families of misfits and cranks who would not survive elsewhere in society, and so fled to despise it in safety.

At first even the Catholic hierarchy viewed Ditchling with bewilderment and suspicion. The local priest said, 'I don't go there very often, but whenever I do go Pepler is ordaining Gill or Gill is consecrating Pepler'.[16] Eventually, however, more radical priests began to admire their adherence to religious fundamentals and sent people to learn from them. Soon publicity and the flood of visitors became unbearable for Gill and this, together with his financial quarrel with Pepler, precipitated the move to the inaccessible Capel-y-ffin, ten miles from the nearest station, 15 miles from Abergavenny by pony-cart, and post delivered once a week on horseback.

John Rothenstein recalled, 'It rained continuously, the house was damp – the paper in my bedroom leaned crazily away from all four walls – there was no hot water, no newspapers, spartan food – and I enjoyed every instant of my visit: Gill's sharp-edged genial talk warmed the bleak house.'[17] Such extreme isolation eventually led his womenfolk to rebel and they all moved back to the relatively lush pastures of Pigotts near High Wycombe. Gill would have been happy to have moved back to London or a city, given the right accommodation. He was no fey back-to-the-lander, for the city he believed should be the crown of man's civilization: 'because Babylon is vile it does not follow that Jerusalem is vile also'. Because man has the free will to work with his hands to praise God, a privilege granted to nothing else in the natural world, it should follow that the city is superior to the countryside. 'The countryside exists to support and uphold and nourish and maintain the city',[18] though since we have made our cities places of filth and disease we may *have* to go back to the land to be born again. For all his living in rural retreats Gill showed little artistic interest in landscape and his sculptures take no shapes from his surroundings as Moore's or Barbara Hepworth's do. Even his drawings are confined to architecture and the human figure: Gill is essentially an indoor artist. He enjoyed Paris and London, but claimed he felt closer to smaller communities such as those he found in Ireland, or Salies-de-Béarn where the Gills spent a winter and found the life to be permeated by faith and fully civilized in the way Gill admired.

From his rural homes Gill's work took him away on frequent trips round Britain, Europe and as far as the Middle East. He had no gift for languages, not even for the Latin he used so frequently in his books and carvings, and he had no interest in 'tourism'. The sights of the Vatican, for example, he thought mostly 'swank', and St Peter's 'looks exactly like the Ritz Palace Hotel.' He hoped some enlightened Pope would one day have all the carvings hacked off – but then, as we shall see, the art and architecture of the Renaissance he saw as the beginning of the decadence he saw all around him.

As Gill aged he became surer of his Catholic view of all aspects of life and art and so grew away from various groups of friends who held other ideas. He records these

Mary Gill knitting (1928), pencil
drawing, 34.7cm × 21cm

as 'Escapades' in his *Autobiography*[19] and it is obvious
that his increasingly intractable views made him some
enemies. Speaight comments: 'Like many another man
who knows his own mind beyond the shadow of a doubt,
Eric was not clever at getting inside other people's. He
quite lacked the Shakespearian or the Keatsian capacity
for resting in uncertainty. This was due to the same want
of imagination that prevented him from becoming a great
creative sculptor; he believed in too many rules and he
thought that all one had to do was follow them.'[20]

Only towards the very end of his life did he begin to
accept that truth could have blurred edges and come
from revelation as well as reason. He admitted, 'I had
been misled by the logic of medieval Christian theology,'
and also noted that the fact we know what to love by
intuition 'and not by discursive reasoning and the painful
process of thinking it out step by step by logical
argument, seems to show that reasoning is both unnecessary and absurd'.[21]

One area in which Gill consistently failed to follow the
rules he set himself and where his rationality and will-
power were consistently set aside was in his sexual life. At
school, he tells us, he was abnormally naïve and prudish,
and badly misinformed about the navel being the centre
of female sexuality! The diaries of 1899 and 1900 show
him crushed by the Victorian fears of masturbation so,
'What is a poor chap to do?' and, 'What does God think.
Oh dear I will try again but it seems useless,' he agonizes
on many pages.

He then went to lodge with Mr Moore, florist and
verger at Chichester Cathedral. Ethel Moore (later to be
called Mary on her conversion to Catholicism), his
daughter, was four years older than Gill and sexually more
experienced insofar as she had been previously engaged
and, to Gill's delight, was not shocked at his confessions
about 'Subject X'. When Gill moved to London he
continued to write to her, especially when he lapsed. By
now his curiosity about sex was consuming him and he had
to resort to professional help to satisfy it. His marriage to
Mary did not stop his periodic resort to prostitutes, as a
notebook he and Mary wrote to each other confessing their

sexual pasts makes clear. This book also makes plain,
however, that Mary remained the life-long focus of all his
deepest love and she provided him with a stability and
never-failing source of forgiveness for his many infidelities. He writes: 'It is only necessary to add that though
since marriage I have "known" other women – all
prostitutes with the exception of [...] and a young woman
(since married) with whom I had an affair, very passionate
and serious at the time . . . such things have been mainly
incidental and have occurred during absences from home
as a result of a slack notion of the rights and wrongs of
sexual things. I don't excuse myself I only say it was so . . .
Ethel and I have always been passionately fond of each
other, these moral aberrations have never separated us.'[22]
The affair he refers to is the one he describes in the
Autobiography where he met a girl in the Fabian Society
who gave him Nietzsche's *Thus Spake Zarathustra*.
Just why a female Fabian Socialist should be enthusiastic
about Nietzsche is not clear, but their mutual interests
blossomed far enough to take them to Chartres for Easter
weekend in 1907. There were some fraught encounters
with Mary both before and after this trip, but she seems to
have allowed the girl to become Gill's apprentice in
lettering for a three months' trial, after which she faded
away.

During their early married life Mary frequently
revisited Chichester, and later did the rounds of their
grandchildren or helped Elizabeth with the school she
had established at Capel-y-ffin after the Gills had moved
on to Pigotts. Gill too was frequently away from home on
business or pleasure. These frequent brief separations,
plus Mary's pregnancies, miscarriages and illnesses
meant that the highly virile, and attractive, Gill was
exposed to temptations he could rarely resist. He rejected
the ideas of the 'truly abominable' London art world, but
he could not keep away from its bohemianism and easy-
going relationships. With the Gibbingses he danced and
played tennis in the nude and Moira tucked him up in bed
so affectionately that 'Robert said he would not trust any
other man on earth to enjoy such intimacy' (Diary, 24
January 1925). Gill and the Epstein family spent a day

photographing each other naked. All this fashionable nudity and posing for each other led on naturally to further intimacies with other female artists, models, and fringe figures of the London art scene. Sometimes the diaries show that Gill was brought up short with fear of a disease, or a pregnancy, but the moment always passed safely.

Sometimes the urgency of Gill's inquisitiveness had to be satisfied nearer home. As the family and communities grew, other attractive women came into them and received his attention. The diaries of his last three years reveal tangled sexual manoeuvres with two young women simultaneously: one a school teacher employed at Capel-y-ffin, and the other the beautiful model for all his last and finest life-studies and engravings. This latter relationship seems to have been particularly consuming, on both sides, and it is only in the last few months before his death when he was confined to bed and the girl had been sent to live at Capel-y-ffin that she begins to fade from his diary entries.

Speaight says Gill was neither prurient nor Rabelaisian in sexual matters, but 'he was prey to an obsessive curiosity'.[23] This inquisitiveness, a kind of erotic kleptomania, led him to collect and copy erotic photographs, accumulate an erotic library, study and draw his own and others' genitals, erect a mirror in the studio to watch his illicit love-making, and to watch and draw lovers in Hyde Park. He liked to record in his diaries the matings of the various farm animals. Gibbings introduced him to the works of Havelock Ellis and Gill copied out two case studies at length before writing out his own 'confessions' and getting Mary to do the same. Other unpublished, and unpublishable, works include a 41-page novella (1928) which is naïvely sub-Lawrence and describes only the one act, though the heroine, 'a well-instructed Catholic girl of about sixteen years', thinks of her lover as being like Christ in relation to His Church.[24] This is a theme to which we must return in studying Gill's engravings, for there he gives it graphic form.

All these sexual details would be of no interest or relevance at all if Gill had been a great engineer, or architect, or even a different kind of artist, but it is soon

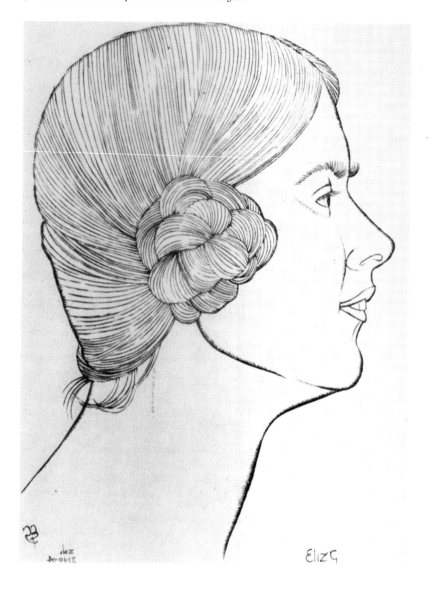

Elizabeth Gill (1924), zinc engraving,
17.5cm × 12.5cm

obvious from a consideration of his subject matter, his treatment of it, and all his views on what it means to be an artist and to work in modern industrial society, that his strong sexuality is one of the two great forces which flow together to make Gill the unique artist he is.

The other great moving force is, of course, his religion. His conversion to Roman Catholicism was simply the most important event in his life, and his claim in the *Autobiography* that all the other happenings after that were mere postscripts is not an affectation.

Gill came from a family of clergymen and missionaries. His own siblings continued the tradition with one sister becoming an Anglican nun and a brother a missionary in New Guinea – only one sister of this generation, Gladys, remained an agnostic and socialist all her life.[25] Gill always knew that 'Life was more than Art'. But what more it was brought him up against the big questions 'What is man, and why?' Fabian socialism does not even approach such questions, but religion does. Gill set out to construct his own faith, only to find all his questions already answered by an old established church, albeit one he had never been in contact with before. His reasoning went like this: 'Religion was the first necessity, and that meant the rule of God. If then there be God, the whole world must be ruled in his name. If there be a religion it must be a world religion, a catholicism. In so far as my religion were true it must be catholic. In so far as the Catholic religion were catholic it must be true! The Catholic Church professed to rule the whole world in the name of God – so far as I could see or imagine, it was the only institution that professed to do so. That fact in itself seemed conclusive, conclusive and sufficient.'[26]

It is not known if he demonstrated this paper-chain of deductions during the week-end he spent with Bertrand Russell! Looking back Gill also noted that medieval Europe where life was 'Christian, normal and human' was entirely Catholic, and the typical modern capitalist countries were not. Other intellectual steps towards his conversion in 1913 are given in the *Autobiography*, but we might expect that a man as sensuous as Gill arrived at this point by other means than logic alone.

At first he thought flesh and spirit, body and soul, were pulling in opposite directions. As he wrote to Rothenstein soon after his conversion: 'The war between the flesh and the spirit is a trial at present. If I wanted either of them to win it would be easier but I don't and that's what makes it more difficult.'[27] He also complained, 'As I am less and less inclined to do what I am by nature best fitted to do (i.e. wicked works) things do not get easier.'[28] Religion, he hoped, would provide an appropriate asceticism by which he might attain to true mysticism, that is close union with God and to 'the tranquillity of order'. This is why he became not just a Catholic, but a Tertiary in the Order of Dominicans. He sought such asceticism as a 'religious astringent' and because, given his unruly sexuality, he must 'seek, ask for and demand a circumscribing discipline if only that he might not be a victim of his own exuberance'.[29] This search for rules to follow, curbs, checks, and the cleansing act of confession (whether to his diary or a priest), is something which runs through all his life and work.

St Thomas Aquinas wrote that 'the senses are a kind of reason', a means not just to sensation but to knowledge and to holiness. After all, 'nothing is in the mind but what comes to it through the senses'. Gill's conversion was only partly through ratiocination, for, as he admits, the sheer beauty of the plain-chant at Mont César played an important part too. He wrote: 'I became a Catholic because I fell *in love* with the truth, and love is an experience. I said, I heard, I felt, I tasted, I touched. And that is what lovers do.'[30]

He soon realized too that many of the priests he knew were tolerant of the flesh and not scornful of its weaknesses. Gill notes in his 1912 diary after hearing a lecture by Abbot Ford, 'He said, "Ideals were more important than morals" – Good', and he frequently quotes his close friend, the Rev. Desmond Chute's saying, 'If naked bodies can arouse a hell-hunger of lust, they can and do kindle a hunger for heaven. May God bring us all thither.'[31] If Chute is right then perhaps Gill's feelings before the nude model are signs of revelation too? 'They bring the thrill and tremble of the heart . . . when for a second (you) seem to know as God knows – sometimes when you are drawing the human body, even the turn of a shoulder or the firmness of a waist, it seems to shine with the radiance of righteousness.'[32] Such things are not there to be grasped or possessed, or to be seen as ministering to us alone – this was Adam's sin in falling from contemplation, and as he knew well, Gill's own. Seen rightly such things are 'beings manifesting Being himself'.

'Have you felt the smooth whiteness of the flesh between her thighs and the dividing roundness? Such thoughts are kindling to our fires. Hasten then to cast them on that Rock – and give thanks, give thanks, above all give thanks.'[33] And, as you do so, he warns, do not be misled by the jargon of Psychoanalysis (as abominable in its way as that of Art Criticism) into thinking this is 'sublimation' for there is no diversion or transformation involved, 'it is plain acceptance of things in their actuality, and reference of them to their Author'. That Author would accept gladly and understand, for was not 'Christ the material manifestation of God'? And if he had been 'every inch a man' would he not have genitals too? For Gill 'the Incarnation was God's seal upon the goodness of the body, a seal which remained ever fresh in the Eucharist'. It followed that if the Eucharist was the blood and body of Christ it should be easily available for the worshipper to see and taste, placed upon the table of the altar in the very centre of the church, not hidden remotely at one end. Then we will really know 'the real Presence which we affirm is the real presence of the man Jesus,' and we can speak directly to Him and thank Him that 'he ordained that our bodily motions should be pleasant and gratifying and that the pleasure of marriage should be beyond the dreams of avarice.'

As we can see Gill's writings are heavily concerned to reconcile any seeming separation between matter and spirit, and given what we know of his temperament and life it was obviously important for him to do so. To do this he over-selected, misread, or ignored, centuries of Christian history and art where this dualism was obvious, and where the body was seen as a source of shame or pathos, a burden holding us 'unwilling exiles from eternity'.[34] He strained contemporary Catholic teachings to accommodate his own views on this matter in both his writings and his art and in doing so offended some of the Church hierarchy, as we shall see. A friend commented that when he became a Catholic he thought of everything in terms of religion, including sex; and that later he thought of all things in terms of sex, including religion.[35] It is true that from the start he always took any theological mention of bodies, brides and marriages very literally. One of the monks at Mont César had impressed upon him that his faith was '*pas symbolique*,' and it was a lesson he never forgot. Here for example is his explanation to Rayner Heppenstall of what it means to be a Catholic: 'I wish I could get you to see the point about Xtianity – e.g. when we 'marry' we don't say to the girl: madam you realize what we are at is the embodiment of an idea (or do you?). We say: darling, we two persons are now one flesh – or words to that effect. It's a love affair first and last. Joining the Church is not like joining the I.L.P. or the 3rd International. It's like getting married and, speaking analogically, we are fucked by Christ, and bear children to him – or we don't. The Church is the whole body of Christians – the bride. Economic implications follow and are very numerous, but they *follow*. They are implications not explications.'[36] The unbelievers, on the other hand, are a dreary uncollaborative lot, 'they are like those virgins who can only be raped'.[37]

Integration then was what Gill was searching for all his adult working life, trying, as he put it, to make the Lion lie down with the Lamb. At the end of his life he tried to summarise this struggle for unity, the attempt to make all things hang together: '. . . if I might attempt to state in one paragraph the work which I have chiefly tried to do in my life it is this: to make a cell of good living in the chaos of our world. Lettering, type designing, engraving, stone-carving, drawing – these things are all very well, they are a means to the service of God and of our fellows and therefore to the earning of a living, and I have earned my living by them. But what I hope above all things is that I have done something towards re-integrating bed and

The plait (portrait of Petra Gill) (1922), wood-engraving, 16.4cm × 9.6cm

board, the small farm and the workshop, the home and
the school, earth and heaven.'[38] All the published
biographies and obituaries seem to agree that Gill
succeeded in this attempt. Those who knew him closely
concur. Conrad Pepler who grew up at Ditchling wrote 'A
Study in Integrity: the Life and Teachings of Eric Gill'[39]
to show the extent of this integration. Donald Attwater
who knew Gill best during the Capel-y-ffin period makes
it plain in his *A Cell of Good Living*[40] that he too thought
Gill lived all he preached to the full and reached a wisdom
and vision beyond most of us. Cecil Gill, his brother,
thought him a wise, great and good man. 'Good? Yes, in
spite of deviations from the moral norms in early life and
the constant tightrope-balancing act of a strongly sexed
and virile man, only with effort and discipline containing
and retaining the motions of the flesh.'[41] Other writers
agree with him in making this one reservation, but fail to
see that this was the one aspect of Gill's life, above all
others, which *had* to be integrated into his world picture if
it was to make total sense to him. Herbert Read who knew
both the man and the works wrote perceptively of the
latter, but concluded nevertheless, 'it is his life, and the
philosophy upon which it is based that will endure even
longer than his art.'[42] Finally, Richard Church made a
telling comparison in a review of the posthumous
Autobiography.

Those complexities, with their surface contradictions
and basic unity, suggest an affinity to William Blake.
Both were artists with a mania for the clean line. Both
were mystics in that special, medieval sense in which
mysticism is the antithesis of wooliness and mushiness.
Blake saw God in every bush. He saw God's love in the
naked body of a woman. So did Gill, and he glorified
what he saw. Blake sitting naked in his garden was a
naïve spectacle. Gill also had his naïvity, a quality
which in the twentieth century is in danger of being
mistaken for archness and pose. Ten minutes conversation with the man would have dispelled such a
suspicion from the mind of the most blasé of critics.[43]

Gill lived a life of unremitting activity and pushed his God-given rationality and his equally God-given body to their furthest limits. From 1931 his health worsened with attacks of heart and chest troubles which sometimes kept him in bed for weeks, though even there he rarely rested from his various labours. He died of complications after an operation for lung cancer, probably caused by inhaling stone dust and a lifetime's smoking. He calmly went through Confession, Holy Communion and recited with Mary the full Litany of the Saints. Before his funeral his doctor brother, Cecil, cut a vein in his wrist as Gill had asked, lest he be buried alive. Cecil also recalls a conversation with the surgeon who tried to encourage the dying Gill just before the operation by saying he had many active years ahead of him, to which Gill replied: 'Oh dear, I wouldn't care to be like old Rodin, at the age of seventy carving ladies' bottoms with marvellous technique – but no inspiration'.[44]

Writing, crafts, clothes, and the modern woman

Gill wrote voluminously all his adult life and towards the end of it, as he saw the world deteriorate around him, he was spending more time with the pen than the chisel or graver. Apart from 55 published books and pamphlets he found outlets for his views on a wide range of topics in such assorted journals as *The Sun Bathing Review*, *The Slough Observer*, *The L.N.E.R. Magazine*, *The Times*, *The Socialist Review*, *The Engineer*, *Music and Liturgy*, *Ireland Today*, *The Schoolmaster & Woman Teacher's Chronicle*, and of course several Catholic magazines of various levels of brow. The *Bibliography* lists 202 books and periodicals to which he was a contributing author.[1] Some of the crankier or more specialist topics, such as Custard Powder, Shorthand, Spelling Reform, Social Credit, Plain Chant, Insurance, Postage Stamps and Nudism, need not concern us here, but it must be admitted that whatever the topic his published works usually reveal what Lady Rothenstein called his 'hard and unsubtle clarity' and his 'abrasively opinionated and aggressive intellect'.[2] Elsewhere her husband Sir John wrote, 'in spite of his Nonconformist origins there was a dry legalistic element in Gill's mind'.[3] Notable exceptions to these strictures are the delightful *Autobiography*, many of the *Letters*, *The Palestine Diary*, and such direct reporting as *On the Flying Scotsman*, but otherwise it is true much of his writing reads rather turgidly today, in spite of the continuing topicality of his subject matter. D.H. Lawrence, in the last piece of writing he ever did, a review of *Art Nonsense*, complained that Gill 'was so bad at the mere craft of language, that he sets a real writer's nerves on edge', and he grew tired of Gill's 'jargon' and 'trick of firing off phrases'. Furthermore, 'Mr Gill is not a born writer: he is a crude and crass amateur. Still less is he a born thinker, in the reasoning and argumentative sense of the word. He is again a crude and crass amateur: crass is the. only word: maddening like a tiresome uneducated workman arguing in a pub – argufying would describe it better – and banging his fist.'[4]

He found Gill's determination to define all his terms (God, Art, Beauty etc.,) tiresome too, but after all these harsh words (too harsh I believe), he did admire Gill's writing in 'Slavery and Freedom':[5]

T HAT state is a state of Slavery in which a man does what he likes to do in his spare time and in his working time that which is required of him. This state can only exist when what a man likes to do is to please himself.

That state is a state of Freedom in which a man does what he likes to do in his working time and in his spare time that which is required of him. This state can only exist when what a man likes to do is to please God.

In spite of the difficulty of Gill's kind of God, Lawrence found here 'more in those two paragraphs than in all Karl Marx or Professor Whitehead or a dozen other philosophers rolled together'. Gill admired Lawrence as a fellow prophet against the emasculation of workers by industrialization and had claimed in a review that *A propos of Lady Chatterley's Lover* 'states the Catholic view of sex and marriage more clearly and with more enthusiasm than most of our text books'.[6] Gill took Lawrence's criticism well. He said humbly 'I agree with practically all of it,' and added, 'I hope it didn't spoil his last hours'.[7] This kind of modesty is everywhere in his private writings and there he admits also he has 'a dictatorial manner' and that 'my writing is inaccurate and insufficiently precise', or that he has not the training or education for it. In public, however, his defence is as trenchant as ever: 'It has been said that I am one of those writers who can only keep to the point by returning to it. I may say in self-defence that there are many readers who can only remember the point if it is repeated often enough.'[8] He wrote because he had important things to say not because he was a natural writer, and if his style and tone irritated a lot of people that does not invalidate the ideas he struggled to disseminate, as indeed Lawrence saw. It is to those ideas that we must turn.

His first published letters were in the *Chichester Observer* (April 1901 and January 1903) demanding that the Chichester Market Cross be repaired, rather than renovated in fake medieval masonry.[9] This stand was obviously derived from his reading of Ruskin ('architecture and painting can be "restored" when the dead can be raised – and not till then'), Morris's Anti-Scrape campaigns and the teachings of W.R. Lethaby. Nevertheless, it is the earliest statement of Gill's abhorrence of sham and 'art nonsense' that was to run through all his writings. Soon after he likened the beauty of modern pylons striding across the South Downs to the aqueducts across the Roman Campagna and said anyone who objected to them on 'aesthetic' grounds while still being prepared to use electricity was 'fundamentally sentimental and romantic and hypocritical'.[10] The new stamps of 1936 are similarly praised for being true to the machine economy and processes which produced them and for being free of the 'banalities of imitation hand-engravings and stupid ornamentation'.[11] On the other hand machinery is not appropriate for producing war graves which should be hand-made by local craftsmen, and the designs kept out of the hands of architects who would mass-produce cheap, drab, uniform slabs.[12]

This topic of the hand-made versus the mass-produced surfaces repeatedly in Gill's thought and appears in its most ruthlessly logical and unsentimental form in his relations with the Arts and Crafts Movement. He was disillusioned with this well before 1910 despite his admiration for its two great leaders William Morris and W.R. Lethaby. This was on the grounds that the fine hand-crafted work was necessarily so expensive only the rich could afford it, and given patrons like that the works tended to become more luxurious and 'emasculated' (a favourite word) to cater for their tastes. This was a trap of which Morris was well aware. Gill soon found himself in it too: 'For stone carving of my sort is only wanted by the few and cultured and I object to being absolutely dependent upon such.'[13] Secondly, 'instead of wrecking commercial industrialism and resuscitating a human world' as Morris's followers hoped, it had the opposite effect of boosting the factory system by enabling firms like Heals, Liberty, and Waring and Gillow to steal ideas and to put an 'artistic' finish on their mass-produced goods and extend their sales to the 'quasi and pseudo educated'. Gill thought the Art and Crafters were essentially genial bumblers: 'What we cannot thank Heaven for is the mass of good intentions which, befogged by the vaguest theories of the nature both of art and craft, becalmed in the absence of any trade wind of the spirit, intellectually muddled and with will decayed – for what is not known cannot be willed – is enrolled under the general banner of the Arts and Crafts Movement. Here is fiddling while Rome burns!'[14] His desertion of the Movement caused some outcry, and W.R. Lethaby accused him of 'crabbing his mother', but as Gill replied, 'I'm no gentleman and I don't understand loyalty to lost causes when the cause deserves to be lost.'[15]

As we have seen Gill had strong views on his own clothing, and as one would expect from so highly sexed a man, strong views on nakedness too. He gave these views in various essays such as *Dress* (1920), *Art and Love* (1927), *Clothes* (1931) and *Trousers and the Most Precious Ornament* (1937). He claims, 'I never could bother to dress smartly or bother about doing so,' but how to dress rationally and with dignity obviously became something of an obsession with him. His basic tenet was that man is by nature clothed, not naked, and here for once he contradicts his beloved St Thomas Aquinas who believed man to be naturally naked and needing to don clothes after the shame of the Fall. Gill did not argue from man's need for warmth, or convenience ('boots, hats, belts and things with pockets in them') but from decency and dignity. It is desirable to hide 'those motions we called irregular in men and regular in women – motions over which we have an imperfect control'. Such exposure of a person's innermost thoughts would be indecent, he claimed. Anthropologists might now agree with him that man is by nature clothed – there is no such thing as a 'naked savage' to be found. On the other hand they would be dubious about his attempt to allocate any one primary, worldwide original function for clothing and adornment. Protection, modesty, identification, allurement, convenience and dignity all seem to play differing parts in different societies and epochs.[16] Only amongst family and friends is nakedness allowable, believed Gill, because there is no shame or loss of control likely. However, as Speaight writes, and the Diaries confirm, he was very happy to shed his own clothes 'where there was no safety in numbers'.

His *Autobiography* and above all his graphic works speak of a frank pre-occupation with the nude female body, yet in writing of clothes he vehemently insisted women should dress decorously at all times in keeping with their God-given roles as mothers, nurses, servant-maids or nuns – so, 'women should dress in uniforms and be thoroughly covered up'. Otherwise they could provoke lust and 'the essence of lust is covetousness and covetousness leads to Theft. Fornication is theft; adultery is theft. Amongst friends such sins may not be provoked; but amongst strangers how could it not be otherwise?'[17] Consequently the Gill womenfolk who posed for many of his nudes were heavily dressed in public. Speaight comments: 'For Eric almost any woman was so overpowering a provocation that in the interests of security she should conceal her charms.'[18] He inveighed savagely against 'scents, paint, closely clothed hips and croups, a swaying walk, immense care of the face and hair, short skirts in the street, diaphanous clinging drapes in the evening, bare backs and chests,'[19] but how susceptible he was to all these! One reason for such display might be 'that there are more females than males and that therefore women are cheap and must advertise', but the real cause is more to do with the reversal of roles brought about by modern industrial society. For vanity in the male is a virtue, but in the female 'vicious – a sign of degradation, a proof of departure from the divine plan, the fruit of irreligion and sexual abnormality and abandon.'[20]

In a letter confessing his faults that he wrote to Clare Pepler (wife of Hilary with whom he had just quarrelled),

Clothes as churches and town halls, from *Clothes, An Essay upon the Nature and Significance of the Natural and Artificial Integuments worn by Men and Women* (1931), wood-engraving, 8.4cm × 7.3cm

Clothes as workshops, from *Clothes* (1931) wood-engraving, 7.8cm × 7.3cm

he lists lack of physical courage, being 'spoilt', thinking himself more right or more intelligent in argument than other people, getting the 'sulks', meanness, obsessive tidiness, but first of all he puts, '. . . My constant tendency to incontinence – immodesty – the physical nature of man and woman seems to me so utterly delightful and good – to see, to hear, to feel, to know in any way – therefore I find it difficult to see uncleanness where most people see it and where Holy Church bids us see it.'[21]

Obviously true, but on the other hand he also saw uncleanness where most people did not. His Victorian primness is aroused by bare arms, dresses displayed in shop windows ('should be punishable at law as an unwarrantable indecency') and by modern body-fitting clothing, particularly for men. Man's clothing now is depressing, drab, and uniform across all classes and professions and 'his undergarments are worse; they might even be called foul'. The modern male's penis is 'tucked away and all sideways, dishonoured, neglected, ridiculed and ridiculous – no longer the virile member and man's most precious ornament'. But then he does not need it in our industrial society where he is emasculated by the lack of responsibility and manly work. He is only a worm or rabbit content to travel by Tube and work in a burrow, to 'scuffle and scoop and nibble and grab for little profits and quick returns'. Only in his sport dress, or the left-over medieval robes of judges, priests and kings does the male now come near to his natural peacock display. In fact his naturally dominant role in this matter of vanity and display has been usurped by modern woman and he would do well to dress more like her. As we have seen Gill did this, even to the extent of using a dressmaker for his smocks rather than the tailors he despised. After all, the sexes are physically very similar in form so that 'we simply point out that the beard is the proper clothing of the male chin, and the all-sufficing garment of differentiation'. It is noticeable that in his art, figures, if clothed at all, are dressed in a simple smock very like his own ('the Christian norm', he called it), and those he portrays in contemporary dress such as those on the Leeds War

Clothes: for dignity and adornment, from *Art and Love* (1928), Golden Cockerel Press, copper engraving, 11.2cm × 6.8cm

Memorial or various early engravings for *The Game* are invariably made to look ugly and ridiculous.

Clothing obviously concerned Gill because it was for him heavily charged with sexual significance. It is not surprising then to find he has very strong views on more overtly sexual issues. On most of these, except the portrayal of the nude in art (as we shall see), he chose to combine the prudery of his Victorian upbringing and the most rigorously orthodox Catholic teaching of the time to thunder against the abuses of the age. So divorce was a 'phantasy of disordered imagination,' female adultery much more reprehensible than male, and homosexuality 'the ultimate disrespect both to the human body and to human love'. As to contraception it was simply 'masturbation *à deux*, and when by means of contraceptive contrivances, a man and a woman seek the same gratifications they make themselves homosexual and earn the same condemnation.' For contraception is 'incompatible with the nature of man and the nature of sex,' and what is more the arguments for it read very like those of art critics who claim that industrialisation has set the artist free from doing anything useful, serviceable, or meaningful and just allowed them to enjoy painting for its own sake.[22] When Gill and Mary married he tells us, ' "Always ready and willing" was our motto with respect to love-making and "let 'em all come" was our motto in respect of babies.'[23] Marriage meant babies, as simply as that. At the end of his life he considered the modern feminist ideal, 'the tired business woman (and tinned food in the cupboard and tailor-made clothes and golf)' and finds that for these factory slaves indeed, 'Barrenness is now a privilege. Babies are a curse. Motherhood is despicable.' These creatures were symptomatic of the modern matriarchal society where the exclusively male role of artist-work*man* is redundant, and even wars are commercially run and feminine now: 'feminine because they are in essence wars betweeen rival boarding house keepers'. The factories are filled with females minding machines which is 'not only a job women can do cheaper than men, but a job they do better because they like doing it. And they like factory life, the routine and the chatter and the escape from the home in the slum,' and of course escape from their inadequate males. ('What's the good of a handle to your belly in Burnley, or Preston or Limehouse or Leeds?'). The woman's is a purely quantitative world: let there be plenty of cheap groceries, houses, food, clothes and 'finery', even if all these are utterly second-rate the women will be happy and look no further. Not, Gill protests, that he is in any way a misogynist for 'the industrial woman is not despicable because she is like a man, she is despicable because she is barren'.[24]

It will be obvious that Gill's views on women would find little popular support today, and he was aware that even in the late 'Thirties the current ideal was not 'the contented housewife and mother of children – mother, bed-companion, helpmeet and comforter, cook, housekeeper, baker and winemaker, seamstress and broideress; and very likely farm manager and poultry and dairy woman as well,'[25] that he expected his own wife to be. They might be men's equals before God, but that was no reason why they should be equals before the Government. Nor had they any part to play in the arts (except as models) for 'women have rarely been even mediocre artists,' and 'the thousands of young women who today cultivate the arts show no talent for anything but the making of pretty imitations of natural scenes or objects'.[26] This equating of creativity solely with male virility is a prejudice he shares not only with Picasso and Renoir ('I paint with my penis'), but with Van Gogh who praised the 'male potency' of Cézanne's works, and Vlaminck who painted 'with my heart and my loins'.[27]

Some visitors to the three communities commented on how unselfishly the women drudged to support the men's artistic, intellectual and spiritual lives whilst being excluded from the central decision-making structure of the Guild. In effect the communities tended to become patriarchies with Gill in authority (albeit benign authority), not just because he was a natural leader but because he was husband, father, father-in-law, employer or teacher to many of the inhabitants as well as being the chief money-earner. Other visitors, however, believed the quiet, unintellectual, but competent Mary was the power behind the throne and all the women actually enjoyed their work. Gill acknowledged that even if it is natural law that the man 'should rule the roost as a sort of king or bishop' once the women become discontented then there is nothing a man can do but to give in, as he had to do in leaving the rugged Black Mountains for the relative civilization of Pigotts.

It is just one more contradictory aspect of this complex man that this patronising view of woman as a rather dim, inferior Jill-of-all-trades finds no place at all in his art, for there she is exotic, idealized and Gill is obeisant before her.

Et mulier, quam vidisti, est civitas magna, quae habet regnum super rege terrae, frontispiece to *Religion and the Modern State* by Christopher Dawson (1935), pencil drawing, 18cm × 13.5cm

Et mulier quam vidisti est cintas magna quæ regnum super repes terræ

'But see how good are my leaders'

When we come to examine Gill's religious, political and artistic views we find they are much less cranky and dependent upon his personal psychological make-up than those outlined in the previous chapter. In these areas Gill was not an original thinker: his talent was rather to synthesize the ideas of several major nineteenth and twentieth-century thinkers into a coherent whole. He then acted as a powerful propagandist and personal exemplar for this new world view.

Gill's formal education in Brighton was brief and unremarkable and, as he wrote with no bitterness, 'I was taught nothing in such a way as to make it difficult to discard'.[1] Though the rote learning of the classroom bored him he did learn on the sports field and from watching Ranjitsinghi bat on the nearby County Cricket Ground that there are ways of doing things with a ball which are 'intensely lovely, intensely illuminating'. The conviction grew that the discipline of technique is at the heart of doing things well, so the technical results in games or penmanship depend not on showing off, or winning, but on 'the improvement of the game as a thing to be done, as a thing to be made and as a thing to be seen and known and enjoyed in the mind'.[2] Any future aesthetic he adopted would have to take that discovery into account.

As a schoolboy of no great sporting or academic prowess he seems to have had a capacity for hero-worshipping others, so much so that he overheard one of his teachers say of him, 'It's a pity he's so easily led'. He took this as a judgement on his moral inferiority, as it was probably meant to be, but gradually realized it was more a matter for self-congratulation if he could retort, 'Yes, but see how good are my leaders'. If the school offered only sporting heroes then at home his father offered literary and intellectual ones in the form of the Gospels, Carlyle, Tennyson, Kingsley, Dean Farrar, and popular writers such as Robertson and Maurice (indeed he named each of his children after them or one of their characters). It is not surprising, therefore, that when Gill left school in 1897 and took up an apprenticeship in London he read Carlyle over his breakfast, looked to Ruskin for his views on art, and turned to 'Omar Khayám' for his sophistication. Soon the salons and lecture halls of London offered even more daring leaders to follow, but before considering where those led him it is necessary to trace, briefly, what Gill brought into his analysis of twentieth-century society and art from his reading of the great nineteenth-century writers. It would be possible to demonstrate that most of Gill's analysis of industrial society was in fact pre-figured by Carlyle (1795–1881), Ruskin (1819–1900) and Morris (1834–1896), though of course all three would have rejected his grafting on of a Catholic solution to the problems they isolated.

From the Thomas Carlyle of *Past and Present* Gill derived his early enthusiasm for the twelfth century when Abbot Samson ruled his monks in Bury St Edmunds and religion spread over the whole of that unified, orderly society like a canopy. He early began to share Carlyle's distaste for the present where because of industrialization 'men are grown mechanical in head and heart as well as in hand'. Now, thundered Carlyle, all accept the Gospel of Mammonism where Hell is not to make money 'and human relationships between individuals, groups and classes are based solely on the "cash nexus".' Carlyle was contemptuous of democracy as an ideal or a solution ('counting the heads of the greedy blockheads in huge majority'), and of the 'Greater Happiness Principle' which made the word 'soul' synonymous with 'stomach'. Gill too as he came out of his Fabian socialist period came to see that more was needed than a full belly and re-distributed wealth to right the ills of the masses. He would also have found a profound response within himself to Carlyle's stern insistence on work: 'noble fruitful labour – the grand sole miracle of man'. *Laborare est Orare* was something they (and Abbot Samson) both believed and Gill later translated this into his saying, 'Work is sacred: leisure is secular.' The nature of work was central to Gill's thinking from his apprenticeship onwards, though he was to go further than Carlyle into the question of what work could be called worth doing. Carlyle's secular religion was obviously something Gill moved far away from and he seemed to share few of Carlyle's 'Heroes' apart from Christ; though he too made a list of writer Heroes upon whom civilization might rest in this century such as Baudelaire, T.S. Eliot, Stephen Spender, W.H. Auden and D.H. Lawrence. However, the whole tenor of the older writer's social criticism, that of a moral rather than a political or scientific analysis, must have impressed Gill as the right kind of direction to follow in his own thought and writing.

Carlyle had nothing to say about art in his scheme of things so Gill turned to Ruskin for leadership here. It is easy to see why the young Gill found *The Seven Lamps of Architecture* and *Stones of Venice* attractive, but the admiration continued throughout his life in spite of later reservations about Ruskin's views on the relationship of architecture and sculpture. In 1934 he wrote that *Unto This Last* was Ruskin's greatest memorial, plus his ability 'to see clearly that the roots of human action, and therefore of human art, are moral roots'[3]. He was reading a book about Ruskin a few days before his death. Ruskin had looked at the material achievements of the Victorian age and concluded: 'Alas! if read rightly, these perfectnesses are signs of a slavery in our England a thousand times more degrading than that of the scourged African, or helot Greek. They may be beaten, chained, tormented, yoked like cattle, slaughtered like summer flies, and yet remain in one sense, and the best sense, free'.[4] This freedom was the kind enjoyed by the medieval sculptors, for example, who may have lived materially harsh lives and served other more powerful men, but they had pleasure in their work. This pleasure sprang from the spontaneous expression of their individual creativity and it shows in every line they carved. True work in this sense is the highest mode of art whilst 'industry without art is brutality: life without industry is guilt'. Today, thought Ruskin, men may be better fed and housed, but the division of labour from which this improvement comes is

Finis operis, finis operantis, design for *Clothes* (1931) wood-engraving, 13.3cm × 7.3cm

really the division of men, not of labour, so they 'are mere segments of men – broken into small fragments and crumbs of life'. They are degraded into tools of the machines they operate. Ruskin saw only two options: 'You must either make a tool of the creature or a man of him.' The rules he suggests to make labour ennobling and healthy are:

(i) Never encourage the manufacture of any article not absolutely necessary, in the production of which *Invention* has no share.

(ii) Never demand an exact finish for its own sake, but only for some practical or noble end.

(iii) Never encourage imitation or copying of any kind, except for the sake of preserving records of great works.[5]

Elsewhere he added truth to the materials with which one is working as another essential for work satisfaction. It can be judged by the reader how far society ignored, and continues to ignore, these suggestions, and also how far Gill took them over into his own analysis of society and into his own artistic practice. Ruskin defined the 'mercantile' economy then (and now) in force as one which results in the accumulation of the nation's power and wealth in the hands of a few. His 'political' economy, on the other hand, is founded on the individual's creative efforts and consists simply in 'the production, preservation and distribution, at fittest time and place of useful or pleasurable things'[6]. This individual creativity is not just the preserve of the artist but is seen in the farmer cutting hay, the shipwright shaping sound wood, the bricklayer laying good bricks, the housewife at her tasks, the singer who disciplines her voice, and so on. All these can be seen as good political economists 'adding continually to the riches and well-being of the nation to which they belong'. Gill later found echoes of this idea in the work of Ananda Coomaraswamy and took as a central dogma the Indian writer's aphorism: 'The artist is not a special kind of man, but every man is a special kind of artist.'

William Morris, Gill's next leader, acknowledged his early debt to Carlyle and thought Ruskin's words in *Stones of Venice* 'are of the few necessary and inevitable utterances of the century'. As a no-nonsense but eclectic writer on art he admired Ruskin because, 'Ethical and political considerations have never been absent from his

criticisms of art; and in my opinion it is just this part of his
work which has had the most enduring and beneficial
effect . . . Ruskin has let a flood of daylight into the sham
technical twaddle which was once the whole substance of
art criticism.'[7]

One can easily see why the young Gill should admire
Morris as one whose character, range of talents and ideas
were so similar to (but greater and less idiosyncratic than)
his own. Both men based their ideas on a sound practical
knowledge of craftsmanship and hard physical work.
Virtually all Gill's criticisms of industrialism are already
implicit in Morris's *Useful Work Versus Useless Toil, The
Decorative Arts*, and Morris's other socialist writings.[8]
Gill would have fitted with little effort into the sunny,
pseudo-medieval world of *News from Nowhere* in which
Morris projects his ideals into the England of 2003 A.D.
Nobody here suffers from 'Mullygrubs' (idleness) because work is creative, so much so that the term 'artist' is
redundant 'for what is an artist but a workman who is
determined that, whatever else happens, his work shall be
excellent'. The rewards are the same God received: the
satisfaction of true creation. Neither Morris nor Gill
believed that the Leisure State was worth pursuing:
happiness for both could only come through worthwhile
work, not the sterile time-wasting of a 'good time'. The
healthy, handsome people of this new Jerusalem looked
back to the late nineteenth century and saw all its mistakes
as coming from a mad commercialism which enslaved the
majority of the population. Their early pioneers, the
socialists, were mistaken to try to ameliorate the conditions of the poor workers, to get improved slave rations,
as only the complete overthrow of the system offered a
long-term solution. Parliamentary reform led nowhere
and the 'Mother of Parliaments' is by 2003 the farmers'
Dung Market. The marvels of nineteenth-century
science were only 'in the main an appendage to the
commercial system' and, as Gill put it later, 'nothing to do
with anything of real importance'.[9] What the nineteenth
(and twentieth) century did well was to make machines and
Morris admitted, 'These were usually quite perfect pieces
of workmanship, admirably adapted to the end in view so

that it may be fairly said that the great achievement of the
19th century was the making of machines that were
wonders of invention, skill and patience and which were
used for the production of meaningless quantities of
worthless makeshifts.'[10] Gill's views exactly. Neither he
nor Morris were ever Luddites: it was the use, control,
and effects on the workers of machines they objected to.

Gill gradually moved away from Morris's Socialism,
and from the Fabianism, Guild Socialism, and Parliamentary Labour Party which came after it – though
Morris himself had little faith in vote-catching or reform
by Parliamentary means either. Gill came to think Morris
and Ruskin had overvalued the architectural products of
the Middle Ages and failed to see the philosophical
achievements from which they sprang. Nor had they
seemed to realize that other societies such as India and
China had reached similar peaks for much the same
religio-philosophical reasons. Basically Morris and Gill
were incompatible once Gill became a Catholic and
wanted to start every political discussion with the
question, 'What is Man?' Morris described himself as
'basically careless of metaphysics and religion', but of
course he was deeply committed to practical politics on
the street in a way Gill never was. Gill summarised their
differences thus: 'the criticism of the nineteenth century
had to begin at a point nearer to the beginning of things
than any criticism advanced by William Morris. That
great man, that most manly of great men, as sensitive and
passionate as he was fearless and hot-tempered, had not
the mind to see the roots of the disorder. For all his
humanity, he did not see at what point it was that
humanity was corrupted. An agnostic in revolt against a
complacent anglicanism, a Socialist in revolt against a
meanly mercantile parliamentarianism, an artist in revolt
against mechanical industrialism, but an unbeliever! He
saw no being behind doing; he saw no city of God behind
an earthly paradise; he saw joy in labour but no
sacrifice.'[11]

Gill never met Morris but he did come directly under
the instruction of his greatest disciple, William Richard
Lethaby (1857–1931) who founded the Central School of

Arts and Crafts and then went on to be the first Professor
of Design at the Royal College of Art. He helped found
the Art Workers Guild in 1884 with the aim of unifying
the arts of architecture, painting and sculpture, and was
one of the chief movers in the Arts and Crafts Movement
(founded 1886) which took its inspiration directly from
Morris. As a trained architect and designer he worked
with Morris' architect Philip Webb, but Lethaby himself
built very few buildings and soon abandoned architecture
as a career. He must have been a remarkable teacher
though, and Beatrice Warde refers to him as 'the towering
figure of W.R. Lethaby the most influential iconoclast of
his day'.[12] It was he who revived the lost art of calligraphy
by appointing Edward Johnston to teach the subject at the
Central School, and it was in Johnston's first class in 1899
that the seventeen-year-old Gill found his artistic
direction. Lethaby insisted that all his students learned a
useful craft so that Gill was encouraged to take up stone-
cutting and masonry.

Lethaby would have no truck with narrow aesthetic
theories about 'art for art's sake' or just going to art to
have your 'nerve ends tickled'. The origins of all the arts
are to be found in utility and even today, he said, 'Artists,
like everybody else, live by common service.' He opposed
implacably the isolation and separation of the so-called
'Fine Arts' from the everyday arts of boot-making,
cookery, football or gardening – in short, from life.
Without this broad base for art we can never expect the
apex of genius to appear. He wrote, 'Art must be
everywhere. It cannot exist in isolation, or only one man
thick. It must be a thousand men thick'. The rise of art
experts or critics who threw up clouds of words and
theories of beauty to confuse the public led only to 'the
blind reporting to the one-eyed'.[13] The education of
these critics had equipped them only for contemplation,
not doing, for believing culture is only found in books,
and to believe that labour is 'low'. With the Royal
Academy in mind he wrote, 'Labour, work, art, really
make up what should be one body of human service, but
"fine art" has been trained to turn round and revile the rest
for not being "aesthetic" – whatever that may be – and

then it gathers itself together in shilling bazaars for the annual amusement of country cousins in town.'[14] Art is never just an ornament to life and it does not appeal to some special separate 'aesthetic faculty', for, 'Properly, however, art is all worthy productive work; and, looked at in this way, it seems to me that art is about the most serious thing there can be.'[15] Let us forget all the critics' theorizing, for 'Beauty, like breathing, is best solved by doing it, not by this everlasting argument,' or, as Gill called one of his books, *Beauty Looks After Herself*. Like all of Gill's other 'leaders' Lethaby looks back nostalgically to pre-Renaissance times when the craft guilds had the will and power to make their cities into great organic works of art.* The modern trade unions however, are in danger of seeing their task as finished when they have achieved better wages and conditions of labour. Why, suggests Lethaby, do they not train their own apprentices and concern themselves with the quality of the goods their members produce? 'They have, in a word, to find a way in which beautiful craftsmanship will once again become so common that it will reach the homes of their members.'[16] Ultimately, however, this problem of combining quantity with quality defeated the Arts and Crafts Movement, and Gill, as we have seen, parted company with both it and Lethaby.

Gill, by now a Dominican Tertiary, naturally turned for his next 'leader' to the greatest Dominican thinker, St Thomas Aquinas (c.1225–1274). Gill was no academic scholar, and knew it, but he had the wit to pick up what he could where he could. As Shewring writes: 'In Thomism he saw the general lie of the land, knew one stretch well and made one plot his own. Some distinguished Thomists were his friends; he discussed things with them and invited correction of work in progress. He learned much from them; they learned something from him.'[17] In the theory of art itself, however, Aquinas has only scattered insights to offer according to M.D. Kirk.

* Yet, like Gill, he came to be regarded as one of the early advocates of 'functionalism' and 'machine architecture'.

In the 20th century it has become fashionable to
think that Aquinas had a specific and comprehensive
esthetic and that Joyce [in *Portrait of the Artist*]
Maritain, Gilby, Calahan and others, as well as Gill
himself were working and building upon an object as
perfect and well formed and typical of the Middle
Ages as Chartres Cathedral. The plain facts are that,
with the exception of Augustine and Boethius, there
are no treatises devoted specifically to esthetics by
Christians in the first millennium or by later schoolmen; that esthetic teaching is generally incorporated
into a more comprehensive philosophy and needs
extraction; that medieval esthetic is essentially
Neoplatonist in its acceptance of the objectivity of
the world and the harmony between man and nature
and the God of nature; that beauty in the Neoplatonist oriented system was objective; that Aquinas'
contribution to esthetic theory was (with Augustine)
the giving to his simplest definition of the beautiful a
subjective accent; and finally that Aquinas' pertinent
remarks are to be found mainly in the following three
places in the *Summa Theologiae*: I 5,4 ad im (quae visa
placent); I 39,8 (tria requiruntur); I – II 27 ad 3m
(sensus maximi cognoscitive)[18]

Gill attempted to imitate Aquinas' method and style in
his *Id Quod Visum Placet* (a re-statement of Aquinas'
'Pulchra enim dicuntur quae visa placent') and here and
elsewhere tended to use the saint's pronouncements as
starting points for his own speculations. It took the
French Thomist writer Jacques Maritain to extract a
coherent aesthetic theory from the writings of the
schoolmen in his *Art et Scolastique*. Gill helped to
translate and publish this on the St Dominic Press in 1923
and this experience obviously helped clarify many of his
ideas on the relationship of art and religion as well as
confirming his medievalism. In his Introduction to the
book Gill praised it because, 'Its aesthetic is based four-
square upon the Rock of a philosophy wholly philosophic,
wholly Christian, and therefore wholly Catholic.'[19]

Another 'leader' who was in turn influenced by

Maritain, was Ananda Coomaraswamy (1887–1947), undoubtedly the greatest contemporary thinker whom Gill encountered.[20] Coomaraswamy had a Ceylonese father and English mother and, after abandoning a promising career as a geologist, he took it as his mission to explain Eastern art, music, architecture, history, theology, and metaphysics to the West, which by his parentage, learning, and gift for languages he was uniquely qualified to do. Morris's ideas formed the basis for much of his thinking about society, medievalism, crafts and art, and at one point he even owned Morris's old printing presses and had his first influential book, *Medieval Sinhalese Art* (1908), hand-printed on them. When Gill first met him in 1908 Coomaraswamy was busy popularising traditional Ceylonese and Indian art (particularly Rajput painting) by collecting, writing and lecturing as well as later joining with Lethaby, Fry, Rothenstein, and others to found the India Society in 1910. Gill helped this campaign by writing the Preface to *Viśvakarma*, Coomaraswamy's picture book of Indian art published in serial form.[21] However, in 1917 Coomaraswamy left England under a cloud because of his pacifist views on the war and he and Gill never met again, though they continued to correspond regularly until Gill's death. Coomaraswamy became a curator of the Boston Museum's Oriental Section where he slowly moved away from art history, and what he called 'the literature of indictment' on industrial society, into a wider study of the religious and metaphysical ideas which the arts of both East and West embodied. He sought 'the perennial philosophy' or underlying samenesses beneath Buddhist, Hindu, Muslim and Christian thought and arts without himself being a votary to any single faith. As he said, 'I am too catholic to be a Catholic'. Gill shared his early interests in socialism, Nietzsche, Blake, Aquinas, Ruskin and the radical analysis of the human condition. They also shared a deep concern with the erotic in art, as we shall see in considering this aspect of Gill's work. In his *Autobiography* Gill wrote generously and sincerely of his admiration for Coomaraswamy, and concluded, 'I dare not confess myself his disciple; that would only embarrass

Book-plate for Ananda Coomaraswamy
(1920) wood-engraving, 6.3cm × 6.3cm

him. I can only say that I believe no other living writer has
written the truth in matters of art and life and religion and
piety with such wisdom and understanding.'[22] As Attwater put it: 'Coomaraswamy became the Eastern pole of
the Chartres-Ajanta axis.'*

All the modern 'leaders' we have mentioned who
contributed to Gill's own analysis of society looked back
with admiration to the Catholic Middle Ages. This was
also true of other men who influenced Gill at crucial
periods such as Edward Johnston the calligrapher,
Stanley Morison who asked him to design typefaces, and
his patron the dynamic Count Kessler whose Cranach
Press was run by one of Morris's apprentices. All saw it as
a time unsmirched by today's rabid commercialism,
industrialization, competition, humanism, self-seeking
and the cult of self-expression. They all noted that the
disastrous separation of the artist and the artisan had not
yet taken place. None of these writers, or Gill, were really

* Gill refers often to Ajanta in his writings, though he never saw it. It
is a place in Southern India where there are a series of halls excavated
in the side of a ravine. The interiors are filled with religious murals and
carvings dating from 200 B.C. to A.D. 650.

sentimental neo-medievalists or unaware of the blemishes of those ages. William Morris might have spoken for them all when he wrote: 'We cannot turn our people back into Catholic English peasants and Guild craftsmen, or into heathen Norse bonders, much as may be said for such conditions of life; we have no choice but to accept the task which the centuries have laid upon us of using the corruption of three hundred years of profit-mongering for the overthrow of that very corruption.'[23]

Yet, despite their disclaimers, there is a feeling when reading all these writers, especially Gill, that in their admiration for medieval art and the supposed simplicity of the people's spiritual lives they were prepared to gloss over the nasty short and brutish physical lives the majority of medieval people must have endured. For all his determined anti-Romanticism, there are hints that Gill still saw the twelfth century through a Pre-Raphaelite or Tennysonian haze which obscured the excesses of the often corrupt and simoniacal Church which had to resort to a brutal censorship and Inquisition to impose the social and religious unity he so admired. For all his nostalgia it is doubtful if Gill himself could have long survived in such a society, except by repressing his rationality, outspokenness, pacifism, near-anti-clericism, pride in his own body and love of other people's and that sheer individualism which made him Eric Gill.

Attwater tells us that Gill's reading was wide rather than deep or systematic.[24] His library, now in the William Andrews Clark Memorial Library in Los Angeles, would confirm this. Apparently he thought History at best 'a sort of highly interesting hobby'. He blandly admits, 'as to my lack of historical sense: it is true I have none. The world is for me the same – today, yesterday, and tomorrow – there is neither ancient or modern'.[25] This is because the basic emotions of love, grief, and cruelty are always the same, just taking on temporary local dress. In a letter he says explicitly that he tries to avoid the historical bases as much as possible in all that he writes and thinks, for 'it doesn't touch the spot – there isn't a spot to touch,' and much nearer the truth, it was 'beyond my competence, anyway to judge the value of documentary evidence'.[26] So, 'though one knows there must be true history or false, the discovery of which is, compared with the knowledge and love of God, unimportant.' As Attwater comments, 'This is surely an odd line of thought for a Christian, whose religion depends on the truth of certain historical events. It is an example of Gill's tendency – a tendency which lies in wait for all of us – to dismiss as unimportant those things which did not particularly interest him.'[27] It might also show his tendency to take over only evidence to support a position in which he was already firmly entrenched. This makes a little shaky some of his generalizations and comparisons between, for example, the medieval builder and the modern architect, or the cathedral mason and the modern sculptor, especially as more recent discoveries have tended to show the medieval cathedral builders to be quite a *corps d'élite* within their own societies. Yet, even if we can quibble about some of the historical evidence he uses to support his arguments about the untypical and isolated place of the modern artist in his society that does not necessarily invalidate the conclusions, nor the solutions, as we shall see.

The artist in modern society

In writing about art Gill began, as usual, with his basic question about the nature of man. What all ages, civilizations, peoples and individuals have in common is a need to discover and grasp the 'real' – though other names have been used for it in the past such as happiness, the good, the true, safety or repletion. Traditionally, he claimed, there have been two extreme routes to the discovery of the real: first by the evidence of the senses alone (materialism), and secondly via immediate interior knowledge (idealism). The first denies the reality of the spirit and the second of matter. Between these two extremes there are all manner of compromise notions of reality. By our 'notion of reality' we simply mean our religion or philosophy, and as these differ so will the life-styles and products of the people who hold these views because our works reflect our minds. As Gill explains, 'Religion and Philosophy are as necessary to the produc-tion of such monuments as the Forth Bridge or the Aqueduct at Nîmes as they are to the production of such monuments as the Cathedral of Chartres, the Pyramids of Egypt, or the Temples of Ajanta.'[1] Without a philosophy or religion no works would be made because we make only what we believe to be worth making. For the artist or workman, 'whether it be a church or only a tooth-pick he must know what it *is*; he must have it in his mind before he can begin, before he can even choose his material or lay his hand on a tool. And what a thing *is*, what things *are*, and inevitably whether they are good or bad, worth making or not, these questions bring him without fail to the necessity of making philosophical and religious decisions.'[2] If we do not admit this then the Forth Bridge or Venus de Milo are merely caprice or the product of purely animal instinct like a beaver's dam.

Post-Renaissance and Post-Reformation thought has hardened into the current philosophy of materialism with its concomitant denial of spirit and the stress on power.

This belief finds its highest and most typical expression in our engineering and science rather than in our art – in our aeroplanes, locomotives, dams, bridges, dynamos. Our monuments are those which increase our control over matter. Alongside this goes the necessary subordination of the individual into the mass work force so we can see in Russia already 'the worship of men in the communal collective sense,' and, he warns, the West is following close behind.

In other, mainly Eastern, societies where the primacy of the spirit is affirmed, the most representative works are works of love not power, temples not banks, and only secondarily and incidentally do works of convenience get developed. So in these countries, thought Gill, sanitation, transport, communications and tools tend to be 'primitive' because the society stresses the reality of the spirit rather than seeing the control of the visible material universe as the prime objective in life.

Of the two extremes Gill obviously sympathizes with the idealists, for the materialists' philosophy 'is merely a mushroom growth upon the face of the earth' and its tools the telescope and the microscope 'both alike disclose at last nothing but blank walls enclosing a finite universe', for beyond is nothing a materialist could grasp or measure, and therefore know. However, the idealist also distorts and denies in his view of reality. Only the Christian (Catholic) Church embraces both extremes and affirms that 'matter and spirit are both real and both good,' claimed Gill. Though the spiritual predominates the material is neither evil in itself, nor an illusion. It is this doctrine which gave Gill most comfort, and as we shall see, lay behind the production of his own work.

In looking for a society which embodied this balanced view Gill could find none in Europe nearer than the Middle Ages. Then craftsmen and artists were not differentiated as both were seen as skilled, responsible workmen and the customer went to the best available accordingly whether he wanted boots or a crucifix. Art was merely the making well of whatever needed making. The painter or sculptor then did not strive selfconsciously to fulfil some aesthetic programme, or to create Beauty, only to make his product as well as possible. In so doing he unwittingly embodied in his work the collectively held values or 'philosophy' of the society to which he belonged and almost by accident arrived at Beauty. He had no need or wish to strain after personal expression or novelty in materials or theme; rather he manipulated, or added to, traditionally held symbols and was honoured for doing so. The same function is still performed by poets, potters and painters in tribal societies today. Bad work may have been produced, whether boots or crucifixes, but since each workman-artist was solely responsible for his work the customer knew whom to blame in a way one cannot with a mass-produced car or radio. For the larger communal monuments of the period such as cathedrals the artist-workmen co-operated rather in the manner of a football team where individual talents were used but subordinated to a common plan and objective – in this case the glory of God.

This medieval unity was eventually destroyed and the dominant philosophy changed. Gill cites as possible causes for this the Black Death, the 'Great Schism', the rise of merchants and money-lenders to political power, and the worldliness of the ecclesiastics, but whatever it was he insists money was at the root of it. Under the new philosophy works became 'decadent – fanciful, vulgar, pretty, elegant, extravagant, grandiose' – in short we had reached 'that glorious attack of high fever, the Renaissance'.

Gill's judgements on this period are severe, as we can see in his reply to his friend G.K. Chesterton who had seen Giotto as the beginning of Christian art. 'Giotto, alas! was the end, not the beginning. But he is hailed as the beginning because he was the first great illustrator, and illustration, portraiture, criticism are the only functions of art honoured in an age in which men are no longer "partners with God in the *making* of beauteous works," in which artists are a class apart, spoiled and petted so long as they are able to purvey the lovable to their employers.'[3]

Gill acknowledges Giotto's greatness in spite of his talent for story-telling but claims: 'The painting of Cimabue is upon a higher plane, a more exalted plane, a

The artist: man's peculiar and appropriate activity, from *Art and Love* (1928) copper-plate engraving, 6.8cm × 11.2cm

plane more removed from representation and one upon which the painter finds himself face to face with God. It may well be maintained that the great Byzantine school deserves even greater honour for here was not simply one individual bathing in the vision of God, but, as it seems, a whole people and for several centuries, filled with the Holy Ghost. Their works are indeed the evidence – to the Jews a stumbling block, to the Gentiles foolishness, and to Mr. Chesterton and Sir William Orpen ugliness and dullness.'[4] Similarly in architecture Gill saw the medieval inspiration as long dead 'when such a jew-jaw as Henry VII's Chapel at Westminster could popularly be supposed a suitable house for the relics of a saint,' and of course the frivolous and commercial Gothic of the fourteenth and fifteenth centuries he condemned out of hand.

The change of focus at the Renaissance was from God to man, even when the subject matter of the artists might appear to be religious. Now the artists are exalted above the craftsmen and proudly sign their works. Gill writes: 'They were admired, and are still admired, for the completeness with which they made the conquest of nature, for the perfection of their humanism, for the success with which, like clever comedians in a theatre, they reflected and enshrined man's admiration for himself.'[5] It is no coincidence that artists became suddenly concerned with anatomy, chiaroscuro, perspective and new techniques and materials which would enable them to achieve greater verisimilitude. Now they were striving to copy Nature, or to express their admiration for or criticism of it, rather than to work as Nature works – and the logical outcome of that endeavour, says Gill, is the picture-postcard and the photograph. Such a trend was inevitable for 'there is no doubt whatever that portraiture and naturalistic painting, sculpture and music are always found concurrently with the decay of dogmatic religion'.

Gill had little enthusiasm for any art between Giotto and 'the last dying flare of the idolatrous Impressionists'. In this he took support from Coomaraswamy, and from Maritain who wrote – (if somewhat disjointedly!) of post-Renaissance musicians and painters:

If they load their art with exotic riches too heavy for any but themselves to bear, the most potent of them are the most pernicious. Rembrandt is a bad master; would any man refuse him his affection? Even at the risk of painting's being wounded, it was better that Rembrandt should have played and won, made his miraculous breach in the invisible world. It is perfectly true that there is no necessary progress in art, that tradition and discipline are the true nurses of originality; and that the feverish acceleration which modern individualism, with its frenzy for revolution in the mediocre, imposes upon the succession of art forms, abortive schools, and puerile fashions is the symptom of a far-spread intellectual and social poverty. Novelty, nevertheless, is fundamentally necessary to art, which, like nature, goes in seasons.[6]

To many readers these writers' seeming dismissal of five centuries of art must seem perverse and to be taking a theoretical position to absurd practical conclusions. Gill shows his awareness of this in a letter to an American magazine in 1939 in which he says, 'this argument, like so many others in the world, is one in which neither side accepts the other's premises and, what is worse, there is not only an antagonism of minds, but also one of wills'.[7] Gill's (and Maritain's) art judgements begin well away from the whole subject of art in a way which is foreign to most modern art criticism other than Marxist. The picture can only be judged when it is embedded in a whole universal system of values.

Gill is not an aesthetic snob *starting* from an *idée fixe* that certain types or periods of art are always superior to other types, though he admits this might turn out to be one of his conclusions. What moves him is 'something much deeper and more primary than an aesthetic emotion'. It is 'a notion, conception, intuition as to the real nature of man – his nature and therefore his destiny and meaning'. Free will, knowledge, hope and love are all implicit in that nature, and above all, a responsibility for his own actions. Such a notion has not been a dominant one since the Renaissance, Gill would claim. Having arrived at a conception of man's nature one must then try to discover how far he is helped or hindered in fulfilling his nature by this kind of society or that, what kinds of work result in these circumstances or those, and what value, social or otherwise should be placed upon them. 'And possibly we shall discover that, remarkable as they are and almost heartbreaking in the poignancy of their effects upon us, the great works of our "masters" old or new, are, after all, more pathetic and tragic in their quality than either holy or salutary, and that, however deep and terrible, they are essentially barren. God knows. But let us not allow the argument to descend to the level of art criticism. It is *man* we are talking about – man in his millions and not only man in his studios, drawing rooms, and art galleries – and how to contrive that he shall see himself as child of God – and heir also'.[8] Aesthetic emotion, the shiver of the senses before a work of art is 'only a more or less useful handmaid' in such a wide view of things. By this view he was prepared to sacrifice the Sistine Chapel, Rembrandt, Brahms and most post-Cimabue works until the onset of the Cubists as 'more or less presumptuous criticism (even if appreciative criticism) of creatures rather than a worship of the Creator'.[9]

All the foregoing reads like a very one-eyed view of art history if you do not happen to share Gill's stance. However, when he comes to look at the position of the twentieth-century artist and his relation to his society then the points come sharp and provocative whatever one's creed. The modern artist is either a lap-dog to the rich – the only patrons for his work beyond the museums, or he has retreated to his studio to cultivate his private eccentricities or indulge his emotions in 'self-expression'. Lethaby had also pleaded that, 'the art of picture making must be studied from the human and communal points of view and not left to breed in and in to the point of insanity'.[10] Gill thought the ultimate degradation of the artist now is to be freed from all necessity of making anything useful. Though the sense of beauty is common enough (it is 'the very stuff of our minds') there is no longer any call for its exercise in everyday life, in the making of chairs or tables for example, because of the factory system of production and the profit motive. The man who cares for the well-making of ordinary things and has a desire to create beauty is forced either to starve, join the Arts and Crafts Movement and thus pander to the luxurious tastes of the rich, or to become an artist and create not everyday useful things at all but 'fine art'. The modern artist's work is divorced from prophecy, ritual, daily life, common work and from service, but at least he *is* responsible for it from design to execution, unlike the man working on the conveyor belt. Inevitably his work will bear the impress of his personality, and equally inevitably he will be envied for this by those whose working conditions allow no scope for the expression of their individuality. Because of this people tend to seek and over-value the signs of his unique individuality in his works, and again the artist is tempted to over-emphasize it, and of course the dealers are only too eager to exploit it. But, as the rather patrician Coomaraswamy wrote, 'The healthy patron is no more interested in the artist's personality than he is in his tailor's private life; all that he needs of either is that they be in possession of their art'.[11]

Soon, as the artist's work becomes more extreme, rare and expensive, we find 'painting and sculpture are for us mere fal-lals, curiosities suitable for museums. There is no public place for them. They mean nothing to anybody but to their makers and a coterie of aesthetes'.[12] If the artists do reach a wider audience it is at best as entertainers catering for the workers' leisure time. Museums are now the only places an artist and a workman might meet, and there are no shortages of museums as the capitalists and governments of our industrial nations are willing to finance any amount of this kind of cultural charity to salve their consciences for robbing the worker of any outlet for his sense of beauty in the course of his daily work. If you are to regard a nation's culture as something made and consumed in its leisure time, then, writes Gill, 'to hell with culture as a thing added like a sauce to otherwise unpalatable stale fish'.

Gill looks round the contemporary art scene and finds the isolated, avant-garde artist is no longer embodying in his work the commonly held 'philosophy' of his whole society because it does not have one, so that he is often unintelligible unless interpreted to the public, or at least the intellectual classes who might care about such things. This interpretation is the job of a man who neither makes a work – nor buys it – the critic. As Gill said bitterly, 'The artist does the work, the critic has the inspiration.' These

The Lord's song, frontispiece to *The Lord's Song* (1934), Golden Cockerel Press, wood-engraving, 14cm × 7cm

5/25   Eric G

critics have done untold damage by harping on about 'feelings' or 'emotions' in either artist or beholder. 'That ridiculous old man', Tolstoy, for example says, 'the business of the artist is to find a form to fit an emotion,' and Clive Bell that, 'The question is not what a work represents but what it makes you feel'.[13] Either is at best a half-truth and makes the artist a mere pedlar of delights or uplift to the spectator, or following Tolstoy's route it drives him to believe his own emotions are the sole concern of his art. That way lie the excesses of Expressionism on the one hand, or the total abandonment of rationality in Surrealism on the other. Either way the artist begins to cultivate his artistic temperament, to set himself up as a seer and to see his rightful position as upon a pedestal – a position the hangers-on of the 'art world', the critics and dealers, are all too anxious to preserve for him. Gill himself might be charged with adopting the role of seer, but at least he used the position to preach, ironically enough, that the artist was really just a workman like everybody else.

Another half-truth raised to the status of dogma by the critics – and here he had Roger Fry and Clive Bell in mind – was the belief that the artist was distinguished by his 'profound sense of form'. This enabled the critics to avoid encountering the subject matter or meaning of a work of art. He might also have had in mind the cult of the 'primitive' amongst his fellow sculptors, none of whom were interested in the uses, or origins, or anthropology of their African masks or Pre-Columbian statues, but were indulging in a kind of cultural plunder to renew the vitality of a jaded European art and to enlarge its repertoire of forms. Hence the critics and artists could claim: 'they like the sculptures of Sanchi but know nothing of Indian philosophy – that they like the windows of Chartres but loathe the Christian religion. They say they know a good Chinese ivory when they see one, but care nothing for the ideas of Chinamen. They say that they like Westminster Abbey better than the Albert Memorial, but that they are very sure that the ideas of Prince Albert were in every way more enlightened than those of Edward the Third. Therefore they hold it to be clear that philosophical ideas or religious beliefs have little to do with works.'[14] Gill thinks such arguments help very little: since *everything* necessarily has a form we have to talk about good or bad form, right or wrong, and that can only mean that the thing has the form proper to it if it is really what it purports to be. To know that involves us asking after its significance and purpose, the place where it is to go and the material of which it is to be made.

'If we deny that the forms of things owe anything of their quality of beauty, that is their power to please him who sees them (for the beautiful thing is that which being seen pleases, *id quod visum placet*)* to the possession by their makers of some knowledge of what they were making and some good will in the execution; if we deny, that is to say, that good sense and good will have any part in the production of beautiful works; if we say that a thing can have good form and yet this good form, at least as regards its *goodness*, have nothing to do with what the thing is, then we are, in effect and in fact, denying that the thing we call beauty has anything to do with the mind, and therefore that beauty is simply a kind of visible or audible sugar, if we like things sweet, or a kind of visible or audible salt if we prefer them savoury. In such a view a beautiful man is not 'a man as he ought to be' (i.e. a man deprived of nothing that he ought to have – ugliness being simply privation), but is, as a thing of beauty not a man at all, but simply a contraption of shapes and colours causing a charming physical excitement in the same way as does the light reflected in spilt petroleum.'[15]

Not that physical sensations of this kind are to be condemned, especially by the highly sensuous Gill, for 'the visual relations of things, are, of course, the inevitable occasion of pleasure or displeasure'. But if they are *all* we mean by beauty then we must deny the name of beauty to

* Gill is quoting Aquinas here, but cf W.R. Lethaby's 'Beauty is that which when seen we should love.'

things which strike the mind (not the senses alone) by the obvious perfection of their functional adaptation such as locomotives, flying buttresses, flowers, and the bodies of women. Further we should have to make 'good taste' in pictures exactly the same kind as a healthy animal taste in food.

Gill is not claiming here that the production or expression of beauty depends solely upon ratiocination, but that the appreciation of beauty is basically an appreciation of the rational and it requires man's intelligence. Maritain also said, 'Art abides entirely on the side of the mind.' Obviously Gill's works take their start from both his mind and his senses, and he endorses Renoir's claim to have painted his pictures with his penis by saying that organ obviously played a large part in the genesis of his own work. What he is trying to do is apply a corrective to those who believe it is the artist's main concern to gush out in two or three dimensional works his private narcissistic emotional concerns, or to divorce himself from what was once the highest function of art, to express and communicate ideas. As Coomaraswamy regretted, 'It is long since sculpture was thought of as the poor man's book.' Even Picasso disliked such inward looking artists – 'All they're trying to do is make the world a present of their personality. It's horrible.'[16]

Gill, like so many of Europe's art theorists before him was determined to pin down in words and rational explanations the big absolute terms, in the belief that once we have our terms logically defined both the artist's and the spectator's tasks will be enormously simplified. I doubt this, and even his friend G.K. Chesterton in reviewing *Art Nonsense* had to admit, 'even I who sympathize with so many of his primary principles, find them almost too primary to be reduced to any secondary terms. He begins so very much at the right end, that is he begins so very much at the beginning, that there is no getting behind him or treating his absolutes as relative to anything else.'[17] Too much of his writing is concerned with this painstaking definition, often in near metaphysical terms, but a concise statement of what he means does occur in the essay, *Quae Ex Veritate et Bono*: 'Truth

– not science or philosophy but definition, clear headed-ness, good sense. Goodness – not morality or sanctity but patience, perseverance, good will, Beauty – not ornament or "likeness to nature" but order, unity, clarity.'[18] From this comes Gill's motto for all artists and workmen:

Specimen of Monotype Joanna (1930)

'Look after GOOD-NESS and TRUTH, and BEAUTY will look after herself.'

Beauty is the resplendent, though unsought, reward after we have discovered what the thing to be made *is* (its Truth), and then made it as well as it is possible to make it (its Goodness). Lethaby too had warned that Beauty, like wisdom, 'has to come by the way'.

Holding beliefs like this what could Gill find to admire in twentieth-century art? First he gives the useful reminder to the art world that the Picassos and Marinettis of this world are *not* typical of modern art if we think of all the so-called art being produced and bought this century – 'as if *they* made any difference to the manufacturers of Birmingham and Bradford'. Not only the rich industrial patrons but their workers still have debased nineteenth-century views on what constitutes art and so look for flattery, illusionist effects, 'trade finish' and sentimentality. The courageous few, and here he meant the Cubists and Post-Impressionists, have the guts to stand up against the tyranny of Mammon and 'at best they are honest and intensely unworldly experimenters who think that form in the abstract is more important than veri-similitude, that creation is more worthwhile than photo-graphic effects, and that God is more to be worshipped than Man.'[19] This last clause might have surprised the Cubists, Futurists and Post-Impressionists themselves, but then we must remember Gill's stipulative definition: 'All art properly so called is religious, because all art properly so called is an affirmation of absolute values. If we allow the name art to anything irreligious (i.e. affirming relative values) then such art is not, therefore, secular, it is merely paltry.'[20]

The Post-Impressionists, for example, had dared to proclaim that worship should be given to that which is beautiful in itself, not merely that which entertains, or which is merely lovely, so that at its best and 'in its essence [it] is more a return to primary things than pre-Raphaelitism ever was, and as we may contrast Cimabue with Sassoferrato – the godly with the ungodly – so we may contrast Matisse with Orpen.'[21]

While he insisted on the essentially religious basis of the best of modern avant-garde art he denied any religious content to the kind of art commissioned by the Catholic Church itself. This seeming perversity in-furiated many, especially the clergy whose ignorance of modern art, and taste for the vulgar and commercial repository art, he roundly condemned. Though he himself tried to provide plain good sculpture for the church which would work as 'propaganda', he knew this was unlikely to have much effect when he could no longer draw upon an unbroken tradition and a whole unified society's faith as the medieval sculptor could. Such art should be functional and must be judged by its effects, and by this test a medieval crucifix would be better than a modern repository one because, just as good bread nourishes the body better than inferior bread (though inferior bread is better than none at all), so a good crucifix will nourish the soul. The artist working for the church must subordinate all his individuality and 'run on rails' if he is to help the Church fulfil its teaching role and direct

SIMON OF CYRENE HELPS JESUS
TO CARRY THE CROSS

Station V of the Cross, Westminster
Cathedral (1914–18) low relief carving
in Hoptonwood stone, 170cm × 170cm

man towards his last end. Good taste in this sphere, as in all art is mortified taste and the highest periods of artistic achievement had always been those of austerity. If only the Church would apply the same strict insistence on self-denial to its church buildings and the art works it commissioned as it did so unrelentingly to morals then there might be some hope of art once more being the handmaiden of religion.

As we have seen, Gill is basically pessimistic about the place of art in our modern industrial society. The artist is under constant pressure either to sell out or become merely self-indulgent. What then should the person determined to be an artist do to avoid these snares? Gill has several things to teach him, both by precept and example.

Predictably the first requirement is that the would-be artist seeks a coherent viewpoint. Modern art lacks a binding idea, unless it is the feverish seeking for novelty, and so it flounders in a morass of eccentricity. The artist cannot be a slave because his first concern is with the good life and the slave's priority is security. Nor must he be a business man because his next concern is with good work, not the profit the business man seeks. The artist does not have a 'job' where he works for ulterior motives, but a 'vocation', earning only in order to go on working at that which he is by his very nature. Gill knows full well these are difficult rules to follow in a modern society and writes, obviously with himself in mind: 'Except therefore, in the case of rare individuals, good life and good work are impossible in England today. And the individual rebel, however unspotted from the world he may keep himself, is bound to be tainted by idiosyncracy and eccentricity; he is likely to be both a prig and a faddist. He will set up for himself a standard of his own making unless he first ally himself to Truth, and Truth is a "who" and not a "what"!'[22] We already know the unity of belief which inspired Gill's work, though that is obviously not going to be the answer for everyone.

On a more practical level we are advised to flee the 'truly abominable' art world. Gill knew well nearly all the eminent British artists and critics of his day and for a time enjoyed the London art whirl as much as anybody. However, he never involved himself deeply in the Café Royal set and his brushes with Bloomsbury were only intermittent. He was isolated by choice, and also because British art moved on towards things he could not approve of, but even before this happened he had come to realize: 'their whole business of salons and picture galleries [is] symptomatic of all that seems most deplorable in the world and a lot of it not even genuine – no, I don't mean dishonest, I know nothing about that, but just "phoney" and "boloney" and horribly expensive too.'[23]

Ultimately Gill withdrew because he saw that the intellectual giants of the art world were mere aesthetes. They played in a superficial way with religion and philosophy and labour politics, but what they were really seeking was an 'aesthetic emotion' – a thing Gill could not believe in. There were no definite beliefs, all truths were relative, no smell of burning boats, no sense of direction, and no sense that Art related to human life. The whole was a hot-house culture in the midst of an inhuman and anti-human industrialism. 'They seemed oblivious of the precariousness of their position – the lap-dogs of the wealthy with no reason of being but the vapourings of art-critics whose whole position depended upon the 'art-prices' obtainable by the machinations of the art dealers. What a world!'[24]

So Gill followed his own advice and withdrew from Babylon and went, literally in the case of Capel-y-ffin, into the mountains. He took with him the determination to begin again at the beginning, to apply himself to achieving a good life and good work, and to ask himself as he worked the test question: 'Am I doing this because it is right, good and beautiful in itself, or because thus it pleases me or my customers that I should do it?' It helped him to apply this difficult test and to avoid 'struggling in the pot of self doubt' or 'the fire of self-justification' if he could turn to works of the past where such a test was applied 'almost without thought'. He obviously had in mind medieval, peasant and Eastern religious art which, 'owes whatever value it has to its intrinsic merits, and not to its subject matter, its cleverness or its mimicry of nature'.[25]

While drawing strength from various non-Christian religious periods of art he rejected the currently fashionable art of Africa. He was not unsympathetic to its subjects, sensitivity, and physical beauty and he could see why younger artists 'for whom Rodin is something of a mountebank' should turn to it. However, echoing Coomaraswamy, he thought: 'The blatantly phallic art of Central African tribes is no more a degradation than is the blatantly photographic art of modern Europe – no more and no less.* Both are departures from the norm of human understanding; both are the product of mental decay. The norm is seen in the early art of Greece, in the early art of medieval Europe, in the peasant art of all the world, in the plain chant of the Roman Church and in all such music and, pre-eminently in Rajput painting and the sculptures of India and China. But to all these arts the photographic is abhorrent. All are hieratic arts; all are the arts of peoples for whom religion is the main motive and of whose religion love is the beginning and the end.'[26]

After selecting his touchstones of the true from the art of the past the artist must next resign any idea of himself or his work as special. The true artist is not the maker of things 'curiously beautiful but entirely useless', rather he is 'in harness to the community' and his job is to supply what is needed as well made as he is able – just like all other workmen. His love of his neighbour dictates that they be made to an absolute standard of serviceableness. Forget about art as an 'extra' which caters only for the consumer's leisure. Art works are commissioned, just like suits or boots, and the artist is similarly obliged to listen to his customer's needs and has the additional advantage of meeting those customers face to face. It is noticeable that Gill's best sculpture is that for church commissions where he worked on traditional subjects in specific settings and for definite uses. The only drawbacks are when the customer wants the sentimental or the flattering, or does not clearly know enough about what he wants to be specific in his instructions to the artist. 'In actual practice, as things are he (the artist) is expected to supply not only the carving, but also the ideas.'[27] Gill himself was very business-like and unfussy about his work. Speaight records how when he was asked to cut the cost of

---

* We must later consider whether Gill's own drawings are not 'blatantly phallic' – see Chapter 5.

some architectural work Gill replied matter-of-factly, 'Oh, certainly. You can just cut out a leaf here – that will be £10. A whole branch would cost you 25 guineas.'[28] Nor did he object if people chose to alter the work once they had purchased it – though as we shall see his friends protested loudly when this happened after his death to his Sir Thomas More carving in Westminster Cathedral.

It also helps the artist's humility to remember that the division between 'Fine' arts and the 'Servile' Arts is a recent one and not so easy to make in practice as it seems in theory. For, 'All free workmen are artists. All workmen who are not artists are slaves'. The mind's delight and physical usefulness constantly overlap as the maker of poems and the maker of chairs are reminded that the poet has a physical body and the chair-maker a spiritual soul. While there may be cases at the extremes which fall clearly into opposed categories (writing a symphony and dentistry) it might be better, in view of the enormous number of things it is difficult to place definitely, to drop the distinction and judge each case on its merits. 'We should thus perhaps get the picture painters and sculptors, musicians, architects and men of letters off their pedestals and, on the other hand, raise the engineers and crossing sweepers and dentists to a higher level of self-respect.'[29]

How curiously that reads today when there is little sign of the public erecting pedestals for anyone but pop-stars!

Gill wished to revert to an earlier use of the word 'artist' which until the late seventeenth century largely overlapped with the word 'artisan' to mean a person having 'arts' or 'skills'. Coomaraswamy pointed out that in medieval times, 'the product of their work was not called 'art' but an 'artefact', a thing made by art; the art remains in the artist'.[30] Only in the nineteenth century did 'Art' gain its capital letter and such terms as 'artistic', 'artistic temperament' and 'artistic sensibility' come into use. Similarly the distinctions between 'arts' and 'sciences', 'arts' and 'industry', 'fine arts' and 'useful arts' or 'technology' all begin in this period of vast changes in the division of labour and the social uses of skills. As Raymond Williams points out: 'It can be primarily related to the changes inherent in capitalist commodity production, with its specialization and reduction of use values to exchange values.'[31] By this period the artist can be seen as simultaneously producing work which is non-utilitarian, and yet capable of being treated as a commodity on the art market. Gill's analysis seems to be historically and etymologically correct, but it shows an ignorance of how language actually works and changes to hope that we can re-establish usages that have already been cast aside by social change.

The would-be artist might ask where he is to learn his craft. Certainly *not* in the art schools, replies Gill, as these seem to exist only to pay the wages of the so-called art teachers. These Godless institutions, overrun with women, merely teach the cult of the individual and the commercialism that has ruined art since the Renaissance. True to these principles he turned down invitations to teach at the Royal College, and also because he would 'not be able to keep God out of it'. The best thing that could possibly be done would be to scrap 'art' education before the working classes became infected with the intelligentsia's ideas of art as self-centred, self-indulgent and all about aesthetics. Artists should join the revolution and after that has been achieved, if there is still a need for painting and sculpture, then they can be taught just like other craft skills such as boot-making or brick-laying, by demonstration. The apprenticeship system is the best form of education as Gill showed in his own workshops. Coomaraswamy went further and wanted people to produce 'masterpieces' once more, that is those special pieces of work made at the end of an apprenticeship to prove their fitness to be admitted alongside a body of practising experts. Let us forget the search for genius for, 'Works of genius are of very little use to humanity, which invariably misunderstands, distorts, and caricatures their mannerisms and ignores their essence.'[32]

Gill's idea of art education was to get one or two children together and let them each have a sharp pencil, tell them not to smudge or scribble and then let them draw absolutely anything they like for one hour or less three days per week. The adult merely does more but can profitably avoid life models at least until late in life.

Whatever we do we need not call this drawing and painting in schools 'Art'. 'Art must be abolished – it must, it must, it must.'[33] As part of the search for reality and truth, and on a lower level of serviceableness, there must never be any faking in technique. Verisimilitude is not of course the aim – nature is to be collaborated with, not copied, so the sculptor is creating figures conceived and made in stone rather than trying for pieces which look like recently dead corpses. Gill quotes Maurice Denis with approval: 'The first thing I ask of a painting is that it should look like paint.'

This concern to root out the fake in art led him to praise machine-made reinforced buildings, without however deviating from his belief that 'Industrialization whatever the grandeur of its products is ultimately incompatible with the nature of men'.[34] His own experiences in an architect's office had been of providing scale drawings of fake Gothic ornaments, and once for *both* sides of a wrought iron gate! No wonder then that he, like Lethaby, said it was more honest to be true to our machine society to make buildings, furniture and utensils that are un-adorned, functional and true to their materials. 'Plainness is a negative virtue, it is a privation, an asceticism,' but there was something in Gill which constantly sought the curb of asceticism and thought it appropriate for his age. He approved of skyscrapers, aircraft hangers and the Aswan Dam.

The trouble is, he pointed out, that plain taste is sophisticated taste and the bulk of the population still expect jam with their bread – in short, entertainment of the most vigorous and animal kind such as football, lovemaking, noisy sweet simple music, beer, and coach tours, and certainly not lectures on Goethe and trips round art galleries. It is the artists, architects and manufacturers who must be educated (since the public cannot) to avoid fake ornament. The decoration they provide on buildings, for example, is mere veneering, stage scenery and not the natural exuberance of the free workmen as it was on medieval buildings. If then the people's instinct and need for ornament is so strong as he believes it to be they can either pay real artist-craftsmen to provide it for them, or better still win the right, by revolution if necessary, to make beauty for themselves. After all beauty is 'the love of God made visible in man's work' and it is inconceivable that a man should hire another man to love God for him. Meanwhile, as he never tired of repeating,[35] the only thing to do is to have buildings as austerely plain and honest as possible and for them not to be ashamed of their machine origins. This austerity has happened in the past, 'even in the most boisterously unindustrial times,' notably in Roman Viaducts and the Romanesque churches and it should be achievable now until the normal appetite for the painted and decorated can re-assert itself without compromise. Ironically, Gill is perhaps best known for his sculpture on Broadcasting House and the St James Underground Station, both otherwise perfectly austere modern buildings. Nevertheless, his own venture into architecture, the church he designed at Gorleston-on-Sea near Yarmouth, did fulfil his own severe functional code.

Gill, himself the most decorative of sculptors and engravers, preached this stripped and purged style in art and applied art in the optimistic belief that people's need for beauty would re-assert itself. Towards the end of his life he had begun to realize that people in their pursuit of material comfort and the 'Leisure State' were not in fact bothered about making or designing their own things, or coming anywhere near fulfilling his hopes that every man would become a special kind of artist instead of leaving the artist isolated as a special kind of man. They did not give a damn about art or artists.

He had prophesied the inevitable doom of industrial society (in 'Architecture and Sculpture' 1927)[36] through the breakdown of international finance when 'internal strife and international war' will break those in power because their only route to the top has been 'their superior powers of acquisitiveness.' He was partly right about the events, but not their consequences. He was wrong too in seeing an alternative revolt coming from below when the generations of the servile state begin to notice that the artists ('lap dogs who supply the ornamental knick-knacks and idols for which there will always be a demand') are exempt from the mindless general drudgery. The industrialised masses would then revolt and demand the right to creative work themselves. It is still a pious hope. Like Morris, Gill was under the illusion that all one had to do was describe the perfect state and the good life for all to desire it instantly and work for its appearance. That the majority of workmen actually wanted a life more like that of their capitalist masters did not occur to Gill (who knew no factory workers at all) until towards the end of his life. His later writings therefore take on an anger and frustration as his own idealism is lost on the indifferent and passive public. He knew it too: 'I know my position sounds puritanical and over-strict, but in a world gone wrong, as I think it has done in this matter, reformers must always appear puritanical'.[37]

As always, Gill sought to see the wider picture. The perverted role of the artist was only one symptom of a whole sick society, and to right that strong actions as well as faith were needed. If the revolution would not come then war was surely inevitable, and in the face of that bitter storm Gill could not wrap himself up aloof in his creative work as he had done in the First World War. There must be Catholic politics, as well as aesthetics and economics, if only one went back to fundamentals.

Already by the end of the First World War he had moved away from his red tie and red socks Fabianism into demanding that every worker, not just the privileged artist, should own his own tools, work, workshop, land, and home because, 'we say that man cannot be free without property'. Without it he is in the hands of the bankers, unable to exercise his free will, and above all not responsible for what he makes – 'of no factory hand can you say So-and-So made this bloody thing; let us kick him.' Gill's May Day Message to the *Left Review* of 1938 was, 'In order to make things well [the worker] must control and in order to control he must own.' In necessarily co-operative work, such as mining, the workers should again be owners, not working for the profits of non-owners, but bound together in a real personal ownership which could never degenerate into 'bureau-

The purchaser, from *The Devil's Devices* by Hilary Pepler (1915), St Dominic Press, wood-engraving, 13cm × 8.6cm

cratic socialism', of which he had seen enough. For these views he cited the authority of Pope Leo XIII. He also became, under the influence of his friends Fr Vincent MacNab and G.K. Chesterton, a Distributist – a member of the Catholic movement wishing to decentralise, re-humanise society, and move back to the land away from industrialism. The Ditchling Community was an attempt to make this real.

In his later years Gill was accused of favouring Communism, or the 'beehive state' as he called it, as being the only appropriate system for the machine-dominated society everybody but he seemed to want. At least it was preferable to Fascism, which is where big business led, insofar as Communism vested collective ownership 'in men as workmen rather than in men as men of business'. He saw the Roman Catholic Church in Europe begin to align itself with Fascism, and his fiery letters of warning to the *Catholic Herald* only made him enemies within the English church hierarchy. As Speaight comments, 'For the first time, in his polemical writing, a note of shrillness can be heard which reflects the exasperation of his solitude. Eric Gill, now in his early fifties, was no longer a young man, but he was very angry indeed.'[38] The support of certain priests for Franco's side in the Spanish Civil War added to his indignation, as did their opposition to his exhibiting with Artists International in 1934; their shock at his being quoted in *The Daily Worker* and *Left Review*; and later in 1939 their disapproval of his involvement in the Peace Pledge Union, and his helping hand in founding The Pax Society, a Catholic group which believed a just war was impossible in modern circumstances, and that the bestial kind of conflict it was likely to be could only be a remedy worse than any disease. He also edited *The Gallery*, a short-lived, very virulent, anti-clerical magazine dedicated to printing 'what the Catholic Capitalist press dare not'.

By the mid-Thirties Gill was disillusioned with all the traditional political groupings – even the rightful king, Edward VIII, had been ousted by 'the powers of money behind the Cabinet puppets,' and as for Democracy, it merely means England 'is ruled by its richest men, who, as they control the "press" and the "wireless" and the armed services, have little difficulty in arranging that their willing instruments shall be elected and re-elected to Parliament.' In the approaching war what were we being gulled into defending? Not the really English things such as the English climate, nor the English love of fair play, nor English reticence, nor the South Downs, nor the Cumberland Lakes – all these would survive Hitler's attacks. Rather we were being pushed into preserving Capitalist-Industrialism, a manufacturing country devoted to cheap trading because it had destroyed its own agriculture, some of the ugliest factory towns and slums in the world, the banks, the Leisure State (i.e. unemployment and amusement supplied by the BBC and the 'pools'), religious toleration (i.e. total indifference), and 'democracy' or rule by financial cliques.[39] Given these to defend would Hitler be so much worse? Gill took the trouble to read *Mein Kampf*, and found some things in it to admire such as Hitler's rejection of contraception as 'unworthy of Germans', and also his views that 'land' and 'craft' were 'man-making' and factories 'man-killing', fit only for 'factory coolies' and inferior peoples.[40] In spite of these published views Gill remained an Anti-Fascist to the end and continued to belabour his fellow-Catholics, or anyone else who would read or listen, with his increasingly strident and unheeded views. His most direct piece of writing at this time (1939) is his *Social Justice and the Stations of the Cross* which interprets each painful step along the Via Dolorosa as a direct warning against the iniquities of the bankers, warmongers, and our whole industrial society.[41]

Gill died secure and comforted in his faith; less happy with the political drift he saw many of his co-religionists taking; and most bitter in the knowledge that very few were moving down the road to health and sanity that he had clearly pointed out to them. As a political thinker he was unrealistic and naïve, which is perhaps to his credit rather than otherwise, but in this, as in all else he turned to, he was wholly and passionately committed to trying to see the whole picture and preaching the truth as he saw it.[42]

'The excess of amorous nature fertilizes the spiritual field'

Apart from his train drawings as a child and early
architectural works Gill's sole pre-occupation as an artist
is with the human figure. This is not unusual of course,
especially for a sculptor. Where Gill differs from, say,
Henry Moore, or Giacometti, or Zadkine, or Chadwick, is
that the sexuality of the figures he creates in line or stone
provokes the looker to remember his or her own sexuality
in a very direct way too. This seems true even to a new
generation brought up with a much freer attitude
towards, and easier access to, erotic works in all media. It
is noticeable that even now museum authorities are still
reluctant to display Gill's more overtly sexual works, and
most of them never see the light of day. Nevertheless, this
aspect of his work needs to be encountered frankly if we
are to understand both the man and his total artistic
production.

Gill himself is quite open about the part played by sex
in his life, especially in the *Autobiography* where he
speculates from his own experience: 'How many times a
day do men think, perhaps only momentarily, of the shape
and attributes of female flesh? How many tiny interstices
are thus filled? How often and how vehemently do we look
forward to going to bed – but not to sleep? And is it the
same with women, or are they mostly cold as fishes and as
unconcerned and incurious, or only concerned as victims
. . .? They won't or can't tell you. And the few who can
and do can only speak for themselves; they don't seem to
know what other women think. I must leave it thus. I can
only confess that, judging from my own experience and
having no reason to think that others are different from
me, the thought or memory of that activity of our bodies
which is only acknowledged openly between lovers (or
alas! when illness gives doctors a polite entry into our too
secret life) and which reaches its fulfilment in physical
union and orgasm, does in fact occupy, in greater or lesser
degree, very many of the interstices of our waking lives

Model with arms raised (1938), from
Drawings from Life (1940), Hague and
Gill, pencil drawing, 43cm × 17.5cm

and thus colour and inform and perfect or, it may be, mar our doings.'[1]

It was this curiosity about sex and what it must be like for women which drove him to his first experience after seeing a photograph which showed, 'the adult female has a bush of hair on its belly!' 'The final cause, as I thought then and as I think even now, was not so much sensuality as curiosity, the desire to *know* even more than the desire to experience – to know rather than to feel. And the curiosity aroused by the ignorance which I have disclosed on an earlier page in the matter of human hair, strange as it may seem to some readers, was by now a *burning* curiosity.'[2] This matter of pubic hair 'filled all the nooks and crannies of thought, both day and night, for several months – and added a lot of fuel to the fire'.[3] This fetish seemed to persist all his life and many of his life drawings are of poses contrived to show that pubic hair to advantage. Back views are rare in Gill and hair is always treated decoratively and lovingly no matter where it is situated. In the Prefaces to *25 Nudes* (1938) and *Drawings from Life* (1940) he returns to the topic again but now, at the end of his life, he can treat it with a little less intensity and fervour. 'Don't let's be too solemn about it (drawing the nude). Hair on the belly is certainly very becoming but it is also extremely amusing – quite as amusing as hair on the head. Man is matter and spirit, both real and both good, and the funny is certainly part of the good. The human body is in fact a good joke – let us take it so.'[4]

In his Preface to *Drawings from Life* he hopes his works 'will not be judged simply by what might be called *boudoir* standards'.[5] However this frank interest in depicting the female genitals in his drawings *did* shock, even people like Kessler and John Rothenstein, when Gill displayed his drawings 'of a girl with a fine figure who had assumed poses of a startling impropriety' to a gathering of friends 'with all the candour of a child'. Rothenstein to break the shocked silence asked weakly, 'Who was your model?' Gill replied matter-of-factly. 'Oh she was the Deputy Librarian at High Wycombe.'[6] It could just as easily have been any of the many female guests he persuaded to pose. Kessler was outraged at their display in mixed company.

Gill was equally interested in the male sex organ. He draw numerous sheets of studies of his own penis, as will be described later, and even made a carving of it.[7] One of his patrons, André Raffelovitch, was also a friend of that other black-and-white artist of the Phallus – Aubrey Beardsley, and Gill may well have seen some of Beardsley's erotic works in his collection. There are hints in his writings of a certain vanity about his own physique and most of the male nudes he depicts have slight, strong frames similar to his own, more like Apollo than Hercules. Again this curiosity and interest began early, and he recalls the rapture of his first experiments to discover: 'What a marvellous thing was this that suddenly transformed a mere water tap into a pillar of fire – and water into an elixir of life.'[8] The male nudes whether sculptured or engraved, whether called Christ or Mellors, are all sexually well endowed. Heppenstall recalls a visit to Gill in his sculpture studio. 'Man's proudest ornament', said Gill and touched part of the standing Christ-child above the Virgin's elongated hand on his thigh. 'After all, since in his physical nature he was every inch a man, Jesus must have had proper genitals.'[9]

Another well-developed youth is the Ariel on Broadcasting House which one MP, Mr G.G. Mitcheson, thought lewd and offensive to public morals and decency and demanded that the Home Secretary have it brought down even two years after its unveiling. While Gill was still putting the finishing touches to it behind a tarpaulin the BBC Governors were invited to a preview. D.G. Bridson takes up the story. 'They were startled by what seemed to them a palpable exaggeration in the size of Ariel's pudenda. A meeting was called to discuss the matter. As one of the governors happened to be the ex-headmaster of a famous public school, he was held to be better qualified than the rest to express an opinion as to whether the figure was in any way abnormal. After careful thought, he is reported to have given his verdict thus: "I can only say from personal observation, that the lad is uncommonly well hung." Like Michelangelo before him, Gill was tactfully asked to remount his ladder and cut things down to size.'[10] Andrew Boyle who repeats this

Crucifixion (1918), pencil drawing, 16.5cm × 11.5cm

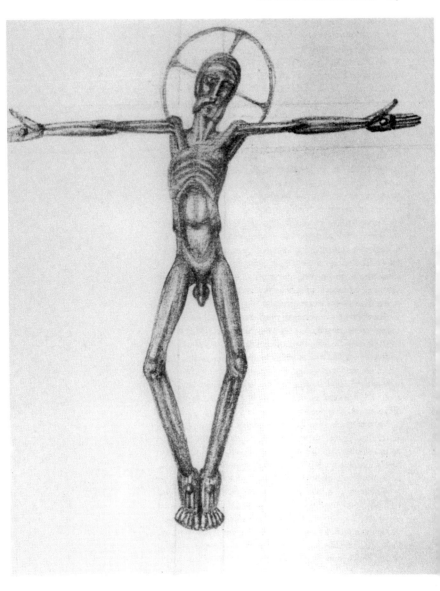

story in his biography of Reith adds, 'This with tetchy grace, the sculptor did.'[11] Gill was constantly surprised that other people did not see these things in the healthy frank way he did himself. Speaight tells that, 'Dr Flood once showed some examples of his *erotica* to a psychologist who said that Eric was more than a highly-sexed man; he must have had a particular phallic fixation.'[12] Speaight thought this did considerable damage to his work, for 'he was a very simple person and sex did not complicate him, it merely affected his judgement'. Part of Gill's simplicity is shown in his plea that if we see things aright then we are 'adorned with precious ornaments', and the genitals are just like the flowers of the field in their function, innocence, and loveliness: once believe this and all our pruderies will be overturned.

There may be something obsessive about Gill's curiosity which shows in his private drawings and there is a very direct jokey frankness in some of his recorded speech but there is never any sniggering, perversity or dirtiness about his attitude to sex. There is nothing, for example, to compare in his work with that of Egon Schiele whose curiosity is mixed with disgust, or with Hans Bellmer's where it is mixed with sadism. Gill's drawings rather invite comparison with the nudes of Modigliani as both generalize and depersonalize the body of the model, smoothing it out and sweetening the curves so they both move towards decoration rather than expressionism. In Kenneth Clark's terms they are 'nude' rather than 'naked', perfected rather than moving us to the disillusion and dismay of real bodies.[13]

In his art Gill's fastidious technique imposed a control over his subject matter fulfilling André Maurois' definition of the classical spirit as 'perfection of form imposed upon strength of feeling'. In his life he tried to make relationships and events as tidy and controlled as his work-bench by imposing the restraints of will-power and religion, but as we have seen he never achieved this total moral calm at any period of his life. Not that Gill was a wild Bohemian whose lapses affected his work – on the contrary. In this he was totally unlike Augustus John whose work was chaste enough, but whose life was a sapping and chaotic round of seductions; nor like another friend Stanley Spencer equally struggling in his muddled way to unite the lusts of his flesh with spiritual longings, but coming nowhere near Gill's worked out philosophy on this. The loose ways of his London-based art friends sometimes shocked the provincial Victorian prude in Gill even though he was producing more and better erotic work than any of them, except perhaps Spencer. He could still note in his diary (13 December 1913) that an exhibition of Epstein's showed him to be 'quite mad about sex'. The *Autobiography* records his early struggles to cast off the Victorian inhibitions he had been taught as a boy about masturbation, the opposite sex, 'the organs of drainage', and nakedness. In later adult life some of these ingrained prejudices occasionally re-appeared and he certainly never became permissive, or even tolerant, by modern standards, in his attitudes towards divorce, family planning, homosexuality, or even nudist colonies (they 'induced frigidity'). However, this powerful curiosity of which so many write, which could override most of his good intentions and take him into all sorts of places sacred and profane, can be seen at work in this snippet from Speaight's account of a brief visit Gill made to Paris in 1926.

'He saw Grock at the Palace and Josephine Baker's *danse de ventre* at the Folies Bergère. He called on Maritain at the Institut Catholique and looked in at "a strange place" – of which Gibbings had the address – where girls were lasciviously posturing in the nude. He drew from some models at the Académie Chaumière; visited Zadkine in his studio; heard Mass at Saint-Severin and Saint-Julien-le-Pauvre; made arrangements with the Galerie Briant-Robert to handle his affairs; and then lost his portfolio in a taxi.'[14]

We have seen that elsewhere Gill stresses that art is 'of the mind' and not just the free expression of personal emotions. Nevertheless, it must appeal to and embody both the matter and spirit which are in man. He tells us frankly that his first nude was carved because of his sexual frustration when Mary was pregnant in 1910.

He speculates that all men, whatever their work, feel

'the perpetual seethe of tumescence,' though for those in the factory or 'on the belt' at Cowley sex will have to wait for the times when they are not working. 'But for the architect, the draughtsman, the stone-carver, "the exuberance of nature" is a determining influence and the quality of the man is evident in his work. It either flows forward in a rich stream of enthusiasm or meanders in emasculated hesitancy. The urine of the stallion fertilizes the fields more than all the chemicals of science. So under Providence, the excess of amorous nature fertilizes the spiritual field.'[15]

Reclining nude (1926), pencil and crayon drawing, 25cm × 24cm

Gill, as we have seen, abhorred the photographic and the mere praise or criticism of nature which art has indulged in since it learned to 'hold the mirror up' at the Renaissance. True art is hieratic art. On the other hand, we have also learned that the senses are a route to God if we enjoy what we see, hear, taste, smell or touch to the full, without guilt, and then casting it upon the Rock, gives thanks. Now there might be a problem for the newcomer to Gill's private drawings, with no knowledge of this supporting theory and self-justification, seeing them as it were by an anonymous hand. Would such a person find them very different from any other skilfully-drawn, semi-realistic, detailed, but salacious drawings?

If we also recall Gill's eager wish to Kessler to illustrate the *Ananga-Ranga*[16] or 'Thirty-four ways of doing it,' and his remarks to the same patron (after asking Kessler where to buy erotic photos in Paris) that 'it is high time to create works of art to destroy the morality which is corrupting us all' and that 'all art is a rebellion against conventional morals,'[17] then might we not suspect that, like Lawrence with *Lady Chatterley's Lover*, Gill is seeking to *épater les bourgeois*? For the best possible motives of course, but would this be obvious in the drawings? Might they cross that delicate line from the erotic (a word meaning 'pertaining to the passion of love') into the obscene or pornographic, however we might define those difficult words to ourselves?

To answer these questions the reader really needs to have seen those drawings Gill obsessively accumulated in folders labelled 'Love Drawings' or 'Studies of Parts'.

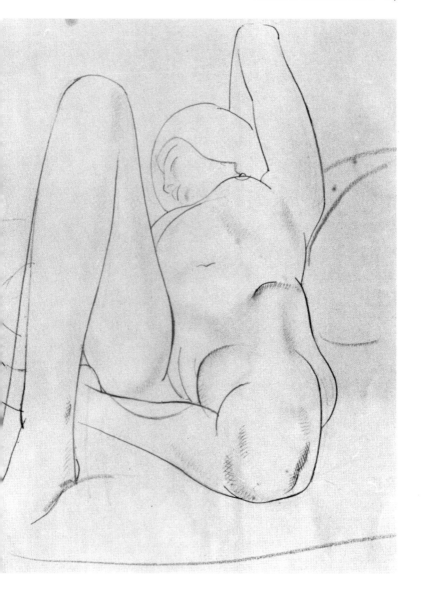

Earth receiving (1926) copper engraving, 12.4 × 8.8cm

The sheer numbers of these in both British and American collections indicate the time Gill spent upon them at all stages of his career, and the importance they had for him. They need then to be taken into account in any assessment of Gill's *oeuvre*. Unfortunately it is unlikely that they will be reproduced or exhibited within the next decade at least. I shall try, therefore, to give a brief account of them here.

In the British Museum Print Room lies a battered old book cover with 'Old England: A Museum of Popular Antiquities' tooled on the spine and Mary's father's name written inside. It contains three folders of uncatalogued and unstamped works, the first labelled 'Studies of Parts I', the second 'Studies of Parts II', and the third 'Love Drawings etc.' Clipped to the first is a note in Gill's dying hand: 'I desire that these sketches and studies should be given to my dear brother Cecil Ernest Gaspar. I suggest to him that it would be a good thing to give them to the museum of the Ryl. College of Surgeons. In my opinion anatomy books are not well illustrated in respect of the male organ. EG. 23 Oct '40.' Under this another note in pencil: 'Offered to R.C.S. Nov. 1948 but not accepted, not showing any pathological condition'.

Certainly the male organ dominates these folders with 68 sheets of studies, often with up to four drawings per page, of penises in all states of rigidity and flaccidity, both Gill's own and those of friends whose initials appear alongside. Another 9 sheets are of penises with detailed measurements recorded on their plans, side and front elevations. One sheet is a rubbing of a stone relief of an ithyphallic male ('stone destroyed'), two more show the organ being firmly grasped by female hands, and a further three show male and female genitals together. The vagina, on the other hand, is studied in meticulous close-up but on only four sheets, the latest in pencil and colour dated 26.2.38. Three sheets show women masturbating. Couples either copulating or in love-play appear thirty-two times, often in incredibly athletic postures taken from Indian or Persian works. Thrown in with all this carnality is a careful study of a kettle on a table and a landscape oddly entitled 'Jane.'!

In the Victoria and Albert Museum, London, in Safe E (for Erotic?) lies a slim folder whose chief treasure is the passionate white-line wood-engraving 'Lovers in a Tent' (1929), together with the privately circulated etchings for Powys Mathers' *Procreant Hymn* where sex and religion seem blended and God's hand appears to bless the earthy goings-on below, or to despatch a haloed and erect Christ towards the waiting Earth. The Texas University collection is essentially what used to be called the Samuels Collection when it was in private British hands. This includes six leather-bound books which when opened reveal the original wood blocks for such engravings as 'Leda', 'Lady C', and 'Lovers'. There is also a small watercolour of a woman fellating a man and the motto 'Suavium uxoris studium amoris habens' over the date

1911. In a similar delicate style is a tiny diptych of two
'Dancers' cavorting nude, except for the lady's scarlet
garters and shoes. In a bound volume called 'Love
Drawings' appear various athletic couplings, some of
them original Oriental works presented to Gill, or traced
for him, by Coomaraswamy. These are followed by
sixteen originals by Gill reworking the same themes,
sometimes from photographs. One of the best of these is
the delicate watercolour 'Lot's Daughter' where the
couple are seen from above with striped cushions spread
round them like the petals of an exotic flower. In another
American collection in Los Angeles appear several more
penis drawings, including a 'Self-Portrait' lacking only a
head. In the same place a sculpture of a loving couple also
omits the heads. A little bound volume of 39 erotic
drawings in ink, watercolour, gilding, and wood-
engraving covers the usual subjects, as well as 'The maid
servant in all humility prepared herself to be whipped'
('or she stoops to conquer'). Another tiny drawing is of a
supine female nude pointing to her genitals and captioned
'That's your Master', which could indeed serve as a
general title for many of these private drawings by Gill.
There is even a design for an erotic tombstone with 'In
memory of Lovers 1910' written upon it. The last works
are more genitals and couples in brown ink and wash
placed in an envelope dated by Gill February 1940.

The effect of seeing all these studies together is far from
erotic (at least to me), but the experience is not without its
humour – some of it deliberate on Gill's part, and some of
it unintentional, for he was apt to give his studies such
titles as 'Eric erect', 'The front yard', 'a bird in the hand',
'actual size approx', 'Man Root', or to record that certain
measurements were 'scribed on table'. On the back of a
masturbating male study he wrote 'Unus est artifex
Deus'. In other sketches he is not trying to record the
penis but to make fun with or of it. One phallus is given a
human head and arms with which to grasp itself, another
female figure on the back of a proof page of one of his
essays on Beauty has a skirt made of vivid red male
organs. A wash drawing of the Devil is captioned
'Suggestion for the Devil's Tail! Which, like other poor

Dancers (1929), pencil and gouache in folding diptych, 14.8cm × 14.5cm

devils, he carries between his legs.'

Other sketches show Gill's schoolboy level of naughtiness about sex, often nearer in spirit to Donald McGill's sea-side postcards than anything more sophisticated. One entangled couple have the corny old title, 'The Boy Scouts but the Girl Guides.' One is more inclined to groan

than laugh at his attempt at 'saucy' cartoons, though his illustrated limericks have more wit than most.

Sometimes the backs of drawings are also of interest. On the reverse of a tobacco packet for 'Churchman's Light Counter Shag: Support British Industries' is a raffish looking female, legs spread wide over the sides of a

Lot's daughter (1926), pencil and water-colour, 13.5cm × 11.6cm

Limerick drawing (c.1925), ink and
watercolour, 9cm × 11.5cm

peculiar tapering bed with the caption, '23.7.27 Lady X
de X in bed designed by E.G.' Another oddity, this time
of observation rather than fantasy, appears on the back of
an advertisement for a 280-page book on the making of
the locomotive Caerphilly Castle. It shows a dressed man
between the naked legs of a reclining woman together
with the note, 'seen in Hyde Park (abt. 20 yds from
pathway) 14.5.25 10.0 pm summertime i.e. not quite
dark. *Note well*: the couple were watched afterwards and
were discovered to be quite obviously an ordinary couple
of good middle class young people genuinely in love – he
about 25–30, she abt. 20–25. He looked like a student or
journalist – she like a girl in business. E.G'.

These pencil, ink or crayon studies, wood-cuts, wood
engravings, etchings and rubbings from stone appear
from all periods of Gill's adult life right up to the year of
his death. They also utilize all the varieties of technique
which we have seen in his better known works and use in
some works a heavy scribbled expressionistic pencil one,
which appears nowhere else. A large number of them are
on odd scraps of paper Gill must have had in his pockets
(some are even marked 'drawn on train'), others are

tracings of drawings now presumably in private hands, and others are marked 'from a photograph'. Obviously with many of them Gill is satisfying other needs than that of making a finished work of art, but others are squared up, perhaps in preparation for carving or engraving.* A good number are trivial and should have been thrown away by Gill, but some are very beautiful including the best of the genital drawings where the phallus is shown in the lurid colours of an orchid, or the female genitals are explored like a complex landscape. The moods and attitudes to sex revealed in the most interesting of these works cover the full spectrum from the true blend of religion and sex, through tenderness, via surgical detachment, to a full Rowlandson-like enjoyment of the buffoonery of all these odd organs and undignified posturings. England has always lacked an artist able to celebrate all the moods of love from the sublime to the ridiculous and perhaps if the best of these hitherto private drawings were more widely known Gill might emerge as the leading, perhaps only, contender for this honourable title.

An anecdote from Speaight illustrates that Gill was not unaware of the temptation to go beyond the erotic in his work and to plunge into the fetishistic or pornographic. David Jones accompanied him on a visit to Powys Mathers whose erotic poem *Procreant Hymn* Gill was then illustrating in two versions, the more explicit of which was for limited circulation only. The walls of Mathers' Lincoln's Inn Fields flat were 'plastered' with pornographic postcards, but 'these were too much even for Eric's indulgent attitude towards pornography. "If I were not a Catholic," he remarked to Jones, "I should be like this".'[18]

Gill recalled in his *Autobiography* the temptations which beset him when working in the architect's office amongst other young men in 'a turmoil of iconoclasms'. He thought he was always a physical and moral coward

---

* Goya wrote that his *Los Caprichos* etchings were works in which he could 'make observations for which commissioned works generally gave no room and in which fantasy and invention have no limit.' Gill's private works must have served a similar purpose.

(though nobody who knew him would have agreed with this), and part of his moral cowardice was always seeing several sides to every question (readers of his published works might demur on this point too). 'For example . . . even pornographic photographs are generally photo-graphs of things very good in themselves. I mean: what's wrong with a naked girl that you shouldn't look at the photograph of one? What's wrong with sexual intercourse that a picture of it should be considered damnable? You deceive yourself, I used to say to myself – you're just pretending; you only want such things to gloat on them. No, but honestly, I used to reply to myself, it's true, it's true, it's true – those things *are* good things and suppose I am gloating well, what's wrong with gloating if it comes to that? Can't I do a bit of gloating without going to the devil?'[19] It is evident from both the writings and the drawings that this debate continued throughout his life.

Whatever judgement we may come to individually over these private works, we must see them as sharply different from those published works that some of his con-temporaries also found erotic, such as his wood-engravings for the two versions of *The Song of Songs*. Gill himself made the distinction clearly. In his essay *Art and Love* (1927)[20] the depiction of the sex act in art is seen in a theological context, and with some rather sweeping art history to lend it perspective in time. Human love has always been seen in all Eastern and Western civilizations previous to this one as a type or analogue of Divine love, and human marriage as a type of the marriage of the soul with God. This accounts for the constant depiction of love scenes in the religious songs, paintings and sculpture of pre-commercial civilizations. Only in our modern industrial west have the intellectuals managed to strip human love of this divine significance and reduce it to 'unmixed lust or simply a secular arrangement for reproduction'. As this divine purpose and background is shed from art private judgement necessarily becomes the only taste of truth: 'Production is merely idiosyncratic; criticism is devoid of principles. The artist is the inventor of his own religion or merely a purveyor of lovable sweetmeats. The critic and the buyer, for the most part

Lovers (1924), intaglio wood-
engraving, second state, 7.8cm × 3.2cm
(N.B. There is also a large drawing of
this subject (91.8cm × 38.2cm) in the
William Andrews Clark Library
intended for a sculpture to be called
'Christ and his Church'.)

having no religion at all, are simply concerned with what takes their fancy. Such a condition of things is thoroughly abnormal and decadent.'[21] The arts then produce either the 'sentimental', which is everywhere applauded, or the sensual which is instantly a source of panic and calls down the wrath of those new secular guardians of the standards of ethics and aesthetics – the police. Not that Gill complains of 'police supervision of our public picture galleries' because what is to be found in there is 'provocative of disorder' insofar as it is photographic and therefore abnormal.

So for Gill the depiction of the sex act is not an evil, but rather when it is conventional, symbolic or hieratic it is the *major* theme. It is only when it is photographically depicted that it is intolerable and then 'the photographic representation of the intimacy of lovers is to be thought more indecent than such representations of landscape only because it is more provocative of disorder, for no other reason.'[22] However, as we have seen, he had no objection to collecting and looking at actual photographs of such acts.

As we know, medieval European art was Gill's first touchstone for what was sane and proper in art and society because it was Christian art, 'the art of man redeemed'. Under the influence of Coomaraswamy, however, he came to see that the Middle Ages in Europe were not 'the unique thing it had seemed to our fathers,' or at least to Carlyle, Ruskin, Morris and Lethaby. In India and China similar conditions had prevailed where 'religio-philosophical concepts of life have been widely accepted and acted upon'. Later he also swept in Byzantine, Pre-Periclean Greek, Mexican, Egyptian and the art of 'all primitive and savage people' as examples of hieratic, non-photographic art. In all these the artist works as nature works, rather than trying to produce criticism or praise of nature, or trying to 'hold up the mirror to nature' as the West has done since the Renaissance. One suspects he had little close contact with the works of all the cultures he uses as examples but was prepared to accept the interpretations of Coomaraswamy and rely on photographs. We know, however, that as early as 1911 he was taking a magazine *Wonders of the World* (7 pence per fortnight) because it contained photographs of Indian sculpture, and writing to William Rothenstein who actually went to India that he and Epstein agreed, 'the best route to Heaven is via Elephanta, and Elura and Ajanta'[23]. Rothenstein introduced Gill to Coomaraswamy and it was from him that Gill learned how Indian art, while sharing with European medieval art a hieratic canon, a negligence of anatomical verisimilitude, a lack of individual expression or idiosyncracy, and an art of public rather than private symbolism and significance, went further and combined all this with a guilt-free sensuality and open eroticism.* Here was what Gill had been looking for. He too believed Boga is Yoga: Delight is Religion. Even sexual intercourse was ritualized according to the *Manhanirvana Tantra* with the yogi saying a mantra for each action and each part of his partner's body. 'Eros' and 'Agape' came together in a way they rarely did in the Christian tradition with St Paul's stern reminder that, 'to be carnally minded is death'. Here were no virgin births, original sin, celibate Gods or a celibate priesthood. For the rest of his life Chartres and Ajanta represented the twin 'holy cities of art', as well as two forces within Gill himself. For one critic at least the fusion of the two never occurred, or even seemed likely. J.G. Fletcher repeated Gill's claim that works were not religious because of their subject matter but because they were concerned with absolute beauty – but if this were so, he pointed out, then 'The Splits' or 'Lovers' and the Rossall School War Memorial belonged to quite different religions: 'The one is ascetic, unworldly; the other is pagan to a degree in which not even the Greeks were pagan. Gill is a standing proof that the soul is not naturally Christian. For fundamentally he is interested in the human body and in its adventures of birth, love-making, begetting, toiling and death. And against these, the sombre ideas of self-sacrifice, atonement, ascetic denial, which his faith

* Coomaraswamy was himself a competent artist of the nude (c.f. *Twenty-eight Drawings*, published by Sunwise Turn Press, New York 1920), as well as an occasional poet on erotic themes (c.f. *Three Poems* (Ditchling, 1920) with wood engravings by Gill).

teaches, work like an irritant rather than an antidote. When he is pagan, in his engraving or his sculpture, he is free to express himself as Eric Gill; when he carves Stations of the Cross or attempts Madonnas, he is curiously hampered by the traditions of the past.'[24]

There is obviously something in this, but as criticism it hits very hard at Gill's own avowed intentions, for he saw it as no part of his task to express himself as Eric Gill, and in his religious work he thought the 'rails' of tradition gave him strength and freedom rather than hampered him. Finally, of course he *did* seek the asceticism his faith taught as an antidote to his inherent paganism, but with what intermittent success we have already seen, and Gill himself was painfully aware of every lapse.

Medieval European art was ruined, for Gill, by Renaissance commercialism and humanistic arrogance, and in the same way modern Indian art is doomed under British commercial and cultural colonialism to provide nothing but insipid copies of its past glories and to follow us down the road to decadence. In his introduction to a book on Indian Sculpture in 1922 Gill writes, taking his ideas directly from Coomaraswamy, 'We see the civilization which produced them long since decayed and replaced by the mechanical 'good government' of an alien and commercial people. We see this commercialism not as a thing in accordance with the will of God, but as a pestilent disease and disgrace, a thing inseparable from the servile conditions and spiritual slavery of vast masses of human beings, and a thing destructive not only of freedom, but of every kind of good quality in the work of men.'[25] In short, Indian art is now as dead as the Middle Ages, especially as puritanical Brahmin sects began to repudiate their own erotic heritage.

With his new inspiration in Hindu art Gill turned back refreshed to Christian art to see if it too found matter and spirit both good and managed to combine the two. In literature at least he could claim it had, though he has a lame excuse why Christian iconography offered such meagre signs of joy: 'From the Song of Songs to St Bernard and St John of the Cross, from St Teresa of Avila to St Thérèse of Lisieux, the theme of love has never been without vivid and unveiled expression. And if the paintings and sculptors of mediaeval Europe are less unclothed than those of India, the differences of climate and race are sufficient explanation.'[26]

Such hieratic art was not about personal feelings or fleeting moments of importance only to the individual, but about eternal and absolute values. As Coomaraswamy wrote: 'A secular and personal art can only appeal to cliques; but a hieratic art unites a whole race in one spiritual feudalism.' Such an art is rich in commonly accepted symbols and conventions, for as Gill admitted, 'choosing symbols is the only difficulty today, for in a strongly religious age all good things will be recognised as being types of divine things'.[27] One task Gill set himself was to renew some of the traditional Christian symbols and give them contemporary significance, even though he was no longer working in a 'unanimous society' and the odds were against him. So The Trinity, Madonna and Child, Christ and the Moneylenders, The Stations of the Cross appear time and time again. The Crucifixion too is constantly reworked, but never in a banal realistic way – it does not need to be to work in this simple iconic fashion, and neither do the other Christian themes. Similarly in his didactic engravings and sculptures the Devil has a tail, the Business Man a top-hat and money-bags, the Modern Woman a vanity bag and mirror, all rather in the oversimplified manner of church windows or Victorian children's books. I.M. Lippman claims that Gill came to see that the erect phallus could be made as much a unique heraldic symbol or sign against sexual degradation as the Cross had been against moral or spiritual degradation.[28] In illustrating the traditional 'love' poetry of the Christian canon such as *The Song of Songs* or *The Song of the Soul* Gill was underlining with his hard unambiguous engravings the books' message that the erotic and the spiritual are not opposites nor separable. Such poems in fact canonised sexual intercourse by making it the very symbol for Christ's love for His Church, His Bride. The various haloed lovers, or those blessed in their union by the hand of God, convey in direct pictorial terms the same message. Such elementary symbolism is easily followed

Crucifixion (1914), wood-engraving intended for use in *The Devil's Devices* by Hilary Pepler but not used, page size 17.3cm × 9.3cm

ET SICUT MOYSES EXALTAVIT SERPENTEM IN
DESERTO ITA EXALTARI OPORTET FILIUM
HOMINIS UT OMNIS QUI CREDIT IN IPSUM NON
PEREAT SED HABEAT VITAM ÆTERNAM - SIC
ENIM DEUS DILEXIT MUNDUM UT FILIUM SUUM
UNIGENITUM DARET UT OMNIS QUI CREDIT
IN EUM NON PEREAT SED HABEAT
VITAM ÆTERNAM

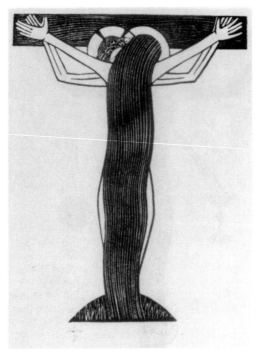

Nuptials of God (1922) used in *The Game* (1923) St Dominic's Press, wood-engraving, 6.5cm × 5cm

'by simple people not trained to philosophic thought living engrossed in the life and struggle of earth who should welcome such elementary symbols of love and the function of love as we find all over the world'.[29] So, his loving couples are meant to be read as symbols; icons pointing a way to holiness and wholeness just as crucifixes do. Human love is a participation in Divine Love, and modern society could begin to cleanse itself at this level of man-woman relationships. That would have to be within the family of course, for no matter what he actually did he never condoned promiscuity. One can detect the influence of Coomaraswamy in this theory, but also a strong dash of D.H. Lawrence, which is perhaps why the Church hierarchy did not always agree with this interpretation of Catholic iconography and the hieratic tradition.

Fr Vincent McNab reacted with angry shock to Gill's rather indifferent little wood-engraving *The Nuptials of God* (1923) which showed Christ on the Cross being sexually embraced by a female figure representing His Bride, the Roman Catholic Church.[30] Fr McNab thought this a metaphor which need not be taken as far as visual representation. We have seen, however, that the Crucifixion for Gill did mingle all aspects of love, for it was 'an image of the virility of God himself',[31] and 'the image of God spent utterly for love'. This explains too why so many of his Christs are naked on the Cross, and obviously virile in their endowments. This reworking of the central symbol of his faith obviously did not please everyone, and neither did his *Song of Songs*, whether in the English or the Latin editions.

Gill had already written an essay on *The Song of Songs*, in *The Game* in 1921, but after the controversy caused by the limited edition he illustrated for the Golden Cockerel Press in 1925 he revised this essay as 'Songs without Clothes' and included it in *Art Nonsense* in 1929. He returned to the poem with an edition in Latin, German and French for Count Kessler's Cranach Press in 1931. He argued again that the physical love depicted in the poem, and in his illustrations, was symbolic of God's love for man and His Church. Though there is no direct verbal evidence that the unknown Jewish author had meant it this way, it was a religious poem by virtue of its intrinsic quality ('all art properly so called is religious because it is an affirmation of absolute values'), and by interpretation because the Catholic Church had later chosen to see it this way and incorporate it into the tradition.[32] It is, he thought, a naked, but not naturalistic poem, heraldic in the clarity of its symbolism – and a good thing too in this hypocritical world where things do not get called by their proper names and 'any poet or artist who dares to see in human love a type of divine love, and yet refrains from dressing his view of the matter in the faded garment of modern ecclesiastical stained-glass is at once pounced upon as an erotomaniac, a danger to society, an immoral person, as though the Song of Songs were upon the Index and should be forbidden reading in seminaries and

suburbs.'³³ Anyway nakedness like this was not an occasion for sin but the half-hidden was, and 'irreligion generally wears the dress of politeness; those who love truth seldom love compromise'. So, 'In fact, when a man says: "I love the roundness of thighs" he may generally be understood to mean that he loves God, but when he says he adores "the hidden mysteries of his mistress's eyes – the gentleness of her gracious touch" he may generally be understood to mean that he loves lechery.'³⁴ All hard-hitting, if somewhat over-stated stuff, and still showing the smart he felt from the reaction to his *Song of Songs* engravings.

Gill had carefully chosen the text and had it edited by Fr O'Connor 'to disarm the criticism that I was doing something outside and apart from Catholic authority'.³⁵ But the engravings aroused priestly opposition and even

Inter ubera mea, from *The Song of Songs* (1925), wood-engraving, 6.6cm × 9.8cm

the Prior Provincial of the Dominican Order in England asked Gill to withdraw them. It seems odd, in retrospect, that an expensive limited edition of 750 copies had such a wide priestly circulation! Gill was surprised and disappointed by this reaction but in a letter to his closest friend Desmond Chute (himself a priest) he seems more concerned to discuss artistic matters such as balance of pictures to text; Chute's liking for 'At night on my bed' when Gill thought it the worst, Chute's failure to praise 'I sleep but my heart is wakeful' which Gill thought his best, and so on. He also admits that the Solomon and departing lovers in the background to 'The Dance' are coarse and uninteresting, and the dancer herself is good '. . . it's a pity about her belly – I tried hard to get a decent convention & spoilt it in the effort so had to leave it in that semi-naturalistic state'.[36]

These works obviously offended certain sensibilities by making too actual what was already a very potent poem.* His similar treatment of the Bride and Groom in *The Song of the Soul* (1927 translated by Fr John O'Connor) received much less attention, though they embrace just as discreetly and tenderly. Other published works which might be labelled erotic, but which had no Christian foundations, such as his volumes of life-drawings and the engravings for *Procreant Hymn* (badly timed to be issued within weeks of his devout *Passio Domini* in 1929 – though it was only the critics and not Gill who saw it this way), drew a curious but consistent reaction from contemporary commentators. They all seem slightly shocked that they should be erotic in the first place, but then they simultaneously condemn them for not being erotic enough in treatment! Kessler, for example, in comparing the drawings of love-making he had seen by Maillol and Gill said they were of necessity very similar in design, 'but those by Maillol have a far greater intensity and carnal atmosphere than is the case with Gill's somewhat cold-blooded eroticism'.[37] Kessler, it will be

---

* They also struck those other guardians of decency, American Customs officials, as 'unfit for showing in the U.S.A.' Gill was unsurprised and unperturbed. *Daily Mail* December 8th 1932.

remembered, had been outraged by the frankness of Gill's drawings from the model.

Speaight himself writes, 'Indeed he was not very interested in personality, and the reason why his eroticism – for all its careful definitions and theological warrant – was distasteful to many people was because it left the personal and psychological out of account. At least it did this in theory whatever it may have done in fact; and I think that the Jesuit priest who described it to me once as "baptized animality" was not far out in his judgement.'[38] On the contrary, this seems to me an absurd assessment. Attwater also echoes this charge of impersonality and coldness: 'Gill's engravings, drawings and carvings of naked men and women are characterized by a marked detachment, an objective vision sometimes almost amounting to coldness: even in the most circumstantial and unusual of them, the beholder is never moved to say this man is "kissing and telling".'[39] Garrett merely echoes all three.[40]

I think such critics have been misled by the sheer control of technique that Gill always exhibits whether in the painstaking engraving of wood or the swifter flow of a pencil or crayon on white paper. They assume one cannot have a warm heart and a cool hand simultaneously, or that a racing pulse will necessarily prevent the artist drawing a steady line. Gill's hand and eyes were strictly trained to render ideas directly with no fussing, no irrelevancies, no fudging: such training showed when he designed a letter, but it also showed when he drew the dead face of his son-in-law, when he did minute drawings of couples making acrobatic love, or when he drew from models he had just made love to, or was about to do so. It is true, of course, that the faces of figures are often omitted, or turned away, and it is to these that we usually turn first for signs of personality and psychology. But it does seem, to this beholder at least, that Gill is indeed 'kissing and telling' as he explores the bodies of his friends and models through the clear lens of his style. Many of the unpublished ones recall his question about erotic photographs – 'What's wrong with a bit of gloating if it comes to that? Can't I do a bit of gloating without going to the devil?'

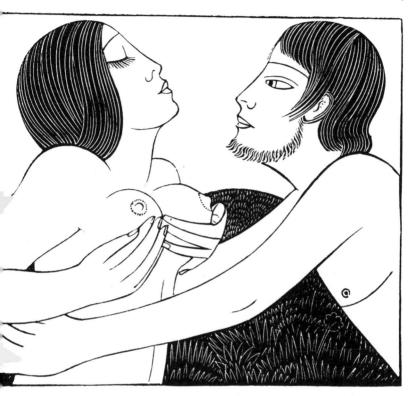

Ibi dabo tibi, from *The Song of Songs* (1925), wood-engraving, 7.2cm × 9.1cm

Gill certainly meant his works to be frank in subject and to cater directly to the senses, for, 'Art must be allowed to express the life of the senses as well as the life of the spirit, and to do so without evasion'. In his defence of *Song of Songs* he declared to ecclesiastical authority that he had no intention of taking 'the giggling Birmingham schoolgirl' as his standard of what was proper. He took a propagandist stand on this because, he wrote, 'I think the times are hard – the right and proper Naughtiness of life, as God made it, is classed by the police with mere filthiness. I think it well to go ahead doing what seems good – however naughty it be.'[41] But it was not the police who were his main targets in the campaign against prudery and hypocrisy, it was the priests themselves who were unable to see where their religious beliefs should lead them with regard to the body and sex. Two notable exceptions were Fr John O'Connor who saw Gill's nudes as works of piety and who backed him on *Song of Songs*, and the Rev Desmond Chute whose letter he quoted at the beginning of *Drawings from Life*: 'Nakedness is the only nobility left to the vast majority of contemporary men: their clothes, far from being for dignity and adornment, degrade them. Apart from their vulgarity when new, how often does not one see a godlike torso emerging from filthy nth-rate garments, almost radiant with the visible touch of the Creator! If naked bodies can arouse a hell-hunger of lust, they can and do kindle a hunger for heaven. May God bring us all thither. . . .'[42]

For the rest Gill found priests unwilling to contemplate any realistic acceptance of the flesh and only ask us to 'remember that life here below is like being in the W.C. (quite pleasant, not necessarily sinful, but only a dirty function). Such is the apparent attitude of our spiritual fathers!'[43] The act of love they see first as a means to fertility and secondly as a sanitary function – even if they can be got to speak of it at all outside the confessional. As a propagandist Gill wanted them to agree that the act is '*in se meritorious*' and only made wrong when fertility is prevented, or when the children resulting are born out of matrimony – 'and of the two the latter is probably the greater evil in the long run'. For too long sex had been made either a joke or filthy, sacred or sanitary.

Like D.H. Lawrence Gill connected bad sex with bad civilization, the oppressions of Puritanism with those of Industrialism and the essential failure of society to see work as an act of love. Go and read *A propos of Lady Chatterley* for the truly Catholic view of sex he instructed the priests. The priests however cannot talk about work either with any conviction, for 'they think that work is something like the Breviary, to be got through and never anything else'. For the most part they are wholehearted supporters of the 'uniquely evil civilization' Gill spent his life attacking and the material achievements of industrialization, of science, and the 'getting and spending' attitudes of their flocks they wholly approve. And as for art it is just so much nonsense, 'sauce for sermons,' mere 'museum stuff' and 'nothing to do with life except to titivate the drawing room or the Church (make the altar look pretty).' They fill their churches with tawdry repository rubbish which might indeed attract those whose sense of beauty has been stifled – but how many does it turn away? The fleshly appetites are indeed imperious and urgent and the priests are ready enough to praise the ascetic who mortifies his body, but what of mental self-indulgence? 'In nunneries and monasteries, where the utmost physical mortification is practised, the utmost aesthetic and sentimental licence is allowed. The intellectual depravity exhibited in most modern churches is appalling.'[44]

This is a savage reply to the critics of his work within the Church. He was prepared to concede the priests' authority on text-book theology and within the confessional but, as Gill admits: 'As they approve what I wholeheartedly condemn I do not find it surprising that they wholeheartedly condemn what I approve.'[45] These are old battles now and the extent to which the targets Gill so blasted with his paper pellets still exist is for the reader to judge. Given his belligerence it is certain that were Gill alive today he would still be sniping at the priesthood and the conduct of the Church whilst simultaneously believing, with all the passion of a lover, all of its central doctrines. He claimed to have invented his Catholicism and it obviously never matched at all points the one he found already in existence. David Kindersley recalls working with Gill on the scaffold and Gill talking out his problems as he carved:

'It was clear that he felt misunderstood, and in his turn he had misunderstood the contemporary Roman Catholic Church. Though his faith remained firm, he was tending more and more to relate his faith to the early Church. It remained a burning shock to him that so much of his belief was unsupported by the Church, and what was worse, the Church, almost without exception, sanctioned that which he most strongly argued against. His "fellow travelling" as the phrase goes, with the communist view of life gained much from his understanding of the early Christian communities, where material things were shared as between brothers. Undoubtedly, he was absolutely clear about the totally atheistic Communism in Russia, but he did not view the capitalist system of the west any more favourably. He thought both systems were out to achieve the same materialistic ends, and of the two evils he often appeared to favour Communism. This led him to frequent criticism and correction by the Roman Catholic hierarchy. However, Pope Pius XII has been quoted as saying, "This man has understood our Encyclicals".'[46]

Gill rightly saw that all freedoms are inter-connected, just as all abuses are, so sexual, political and artistic freedoms are inextricably linked.

The Kronhausens in defending their famous 1968 Exhibition of Erotic Art make some of the same points about the connections between freedoms. The strongest repression of sexuality and eroticism in art comes from reactionary or revolutionary societies. The reactionaries wish to preserve the political and economic *status quo*, and the revolutionary societies still feel insecure in their hard-won social and economic structures: either way freedom of expression in sexual activity or in erotic art will spread to freedom of expression in other areas and neither regime could tolerate that. It is not surprising, therefore, that the Kronhausens find, thirty or more years after Gill: 'Realizing this connection and inter-relation between sexual and political and even religious ideas, one need not be surprised that it finds expression in erotic art and literature as well . . . with regard to the Indian pieces, some of which express very definite religious and philosophical ideas in the interest of overtly erotic subject matter.'[47] They also note, as Gill did, that there may be an incompatibility between indulging one's sexuality and the regime's claims on one's time, loyalty and physical energy for economic ends. The Kronhausens' brand of sexual freedom and erotic exhibits would undoubtedly go too far for Gill and (after a good look round) he would recoil into his Victorian primness, but he would surely endorse their statement that: 'The more orthodox and doctrinaire one gets, the less room there is for anything else. And we don't think there is an inherent contradiction between sexual freedom and happiness and the essence of religion – all religions. Indeed it would be a sad state of affairs if you had to be anti-religious or irreligious to enjoy sexual happiness.'[48] Strange how the views of these trendy, liberal, psychologists come out so similar to those of Gill who was never trendy, hardly liberal in his social views, and despised psychologists!

As we have seen on the subject of sex in relation to art, faith, society, industry, and the individual, Gill wrote thousands and thousands of words. It was a topic he could not lay down. Much of this writing was abrasively opinionated, patently biased and often at odds with what we know of his life and some of the private aspects of his art. But, as usual, Gill is ahead of us in self-criticism and writes disarmingly: 'But, it must be added, let nothing I have written be taken to imply that I have not frequently failed, or that sheer sensuality has not often succeeded in hiding under a camouflage of intellectual purity.'[49]

Drawings

All artists draw. In fact this is usually how they begin to be artists. As a boy Gill drew pictures of locomotives because that was one way of exploring how they functioned and of recording those discoveries: 'I was very much concerned with the structure and movement and purposes of locomotives, because you can't make a good drawing of anything unless you know how it works and what it is for. This may be a "heresy" from the point of pure aesthetics but I wasn't interested in such things then and am only interested in them now in order to repudiate them.'[1] He was determined to master their shape because 'their character and meaning were manifest in their shape'. Later he realized that what he had really been after was their *form* rather than their shape. 'Form, though of course I didn't know it for many years later, is a much bigger word than shape. Shape is only the visible aspect of form . . . the thing I had really been concerned with during all those years of "engine" drawing.'[2]

Contact with a real engineer who was concerned with the physics and hydraulics of engines but not in the least interested in their 'form' put the young Gill off engineering as a career. Later, in his brief military conscription he was set to make a tracing of a motor-cycle engine, only to be told after two days' work on it that he had failed because he showed 'no mechanical knowledge' – clear illustration of the first quotation above. He was then set to drive lorries, presumably so he would learn 'how it works and what it is for'.

During his time at an architect's office Gill drew designs for other workmen to carry to completion. This architectural training, for all he despised it, stood him in good stead later when he came to draw designs which he himself then carried out. David Kindersley writes: 'Though he referred to his time in the architect's office as wasted, learning no more than to draw drains, this training – a facility with set-square and compass – made

Goldsmid (1896), pen and ink drawing, coloured, 17.8cm × 37.5cm

him considerably superior to most sculptors in the obtaining of work. Clear and, indeed, beautiful diagrammatic drawings for client and mason gave his work a greater chance with committees and clients, particularly when these were architects.'³ Landscapes are very rare in Gill's *oeuvre*, but drawings of (rather than for) architecture appear all the way through his career from his early Chichester days, from his winter in Salies de Béarn, Jerusalem, Chartres, and several other places he loved and wished to record. All show an architect's eye for detail, skilful perspective, flat light and a clarity which stayed with him no matter what he was drawing. These early watercolours, whilst still very nineteenth century in flavour, do show precocious skill and demonstrate that he could have become, had he wished and persisted, a competent academic watercolourist.

Gill believed in the practical application of skills and many of his surviving drawings, for example in the W.A. Clark Collection in Los Angeles, demonstrate his design work. Here are cap-badges for postmen or the Royal Flying Corps, roughs for the George VI stamps of 1937–40, seals, medals, glass, engravings on certificates,

S.John's, Bognor.

new coinage, display units, and even a design for a car. All
of these working drawings are instantly identifiable as
Gill's in their precision, clarity and practicality. His
friend Fr Vincent McNab called industrial design 'the
Devil's lipstick', because, like Gill, he loathed anything
which merely 'whitened the sepulchre'. In making these
designs, which other men would have to carry to

St John's Church, Bognor Regis
(1899), pen and ink drawing,
18cm × 19cm

Church interior, possibly Westminster
Abbey (1900), watercolour and ink,
39cm × 27cm (*right*)

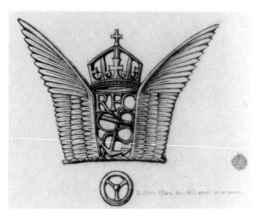

Design for shoulder insignia, Royal Flying Corps (1914), pen and watercolour, 12.7cm × 17.7cm

At Loustau's, Salies-de-Béarn (1928), pencil drawing, 19.5cm × 14.5cm (*right*)

completion, and in accepting the title of Designer to Industry which he did in 1937, Gill might appear to have muddied his principles, but at least he never compromised the purity of his line.

His portraits are very similar in technique to the designs for coins and medals insofar as they are usually in profile (even his famous self-portraits in wood engraving and pencil), very much concerned with the shape of the silhouette and the continuity of the line bounding it.

Designs for silver coins (1924), pencil drawing, 39.8cm × 18.5cm

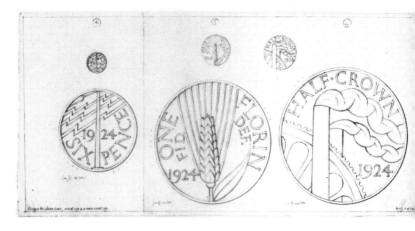

at Loustau's , Solis-de-Béam

These portraits are amongst the most appealing of his works, though if one is looking for Rembrandtesque revelations of the sitter's character (even his own or Mary's) there is little to be found. The sitter is looked at closely and each feature recorded with the same detail and clarity, whether an eye or a lock of hair, and the result is not photographic realism but a pleasing arrangement of lines – a thing in lines with no pretence at making an illusion of a living person.

Other drawings fulfil different purposes. Some were labours of love as when his daughter Elizabeth asked him to record the dead features of her husband as his body lay in their chapel. Others represent the crystallization of ideas for sculpture, engraving and inscriptions, but even here there is little evidence of muffled outlines or hesitations or second and third thoughts. The idea seems to be already clear in his head before it comes via a perfectly co-ordinated hand on to the paper. Most artists use paper as an external arena on which to shuffle and test half-formed ideas or even as a place in which to think, but drawings for Gill were ends, not means. Rothenstein comments, 'there was nothing of the sketcher in Gill'. This incredible sense of finish and sureness may be something of an illusion if we consider he may have destroyed drawings he thought failed to come up to his own high standards. One of his models, Leslie French, who posed for the Ariel studies recalls, 'Eric used to draw on a very large drawing block which stood on an easel; he drew many sketches all of which I thought were perfect, but nearly all of which were immediately destroyed. He never seemed to get what he wanted until he had done a great many "attempts". I could not bear to see these drawings being ripped from the great pad and being screwed up and thrown away for ever.'[4] We tend, I suspect, to think of Gill as something of a miniaturist, perhaps because wood-engravings have to be small and perhaps too because of the clarity and control of his lines and curves in the drawings, but it is interesting to note here the 'very large drawing block' and the size of some of the drawings reproduced in this book.

The young Gill never attended the Slade School of Art,

Portrait of Daisy Hawkins (1939), pencil drawing, 39.5cm × 26.1cm

from D. M. H.

6. 7. 39

then thought to be the most progressive in Europe, and so escaped the powerful influence of Henry Tonks (1862–1937). Tonks imposed a style of drawing and an attitude towards it on a whole generation of Gill's most distinguished contemporaries who had either to take it further or rebel against it. Tonks taught Augustus and Gwen John, William Orpen, Ambrose McEvoy, Paul Nash, Stanley and Gilbert Spencer, Mark Gertler, William Roberts, Edward Wadsworth, Charles Nevison, David Bomberg, Harold Gilman, Wyndham Lewis, Matthew Smith, Duncan Grant and Ben Nicholson amongst many, many others. The 'Slade style' differed from that taught in the Royal Academy Schools or any other London college in stressing constant daily drawing from the living model (in separate rooms for men and women students). It stressed speed, fluency, the ability to 'catch' in line the vital essence of a pose or movement, and the need to keep a drawing fluid and not to commit oneself to a defining contour too early. There was no necessity to go in for elaborate measurements and plumb-lines, or to produce painstaking 'finished' drawings working from the outline inwards. Outside the life-class the best teachers to be found were the masters of the Italian High Renaissance. Gill knew many of these ex-Slade artists, but his beliefs about drawing and his practice are opposed to theirs on virtually every point, except that he too worked with the sharp pencil point rather than trying to record tonal gradations by smudge or stipple. A comparison between a life drawing by Augustus John and Gill will bring out this enormous difference in approach instantly.

Unlike Tonks, Gill did not see the life-class as the basis of art, even though virtually all his work is concerned with the human figure. On the contrary it seemed to him a silly fetish of the art world since 'man is by nature a clothed animal and the insistence on studying him naked is about as reasonable as it would be to insist on the necessity of studying bare trees or shaved horses.'⁵ Of course Gill did draw from life, but he seems to have come to the practice incredibly late and with no teacher. Some writers say he was thirty-four,⁶ but his book *First Nudes* is dated Paris,

Nude with leg raised backwards (1927), pencil drawing, 50.7cm × 35.5cm

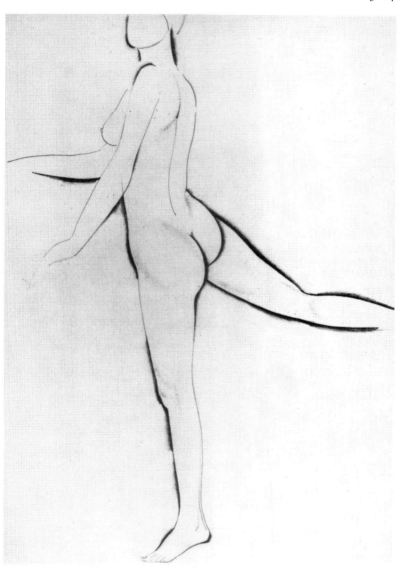

May 1926, and he says at the beginning, 'the first time I
did any life drawing,' which would make him about forty-
four years old. This late start is seen as a positive

Two girls (1928), pencil drawing,
30.7cm × 25.2cm

advantage by Gill and he recommends others delay too: 'If you are going to draw from the naked model at all the best time to do it is rather later in life, when the experience of living has fulfilled the mind and given a deeper, more sensual as well as a more spiritual meaning to material things.'[7]

Real naked female models, especially to a man of Gill's temperament, are too distracting as he found when he hired one for the day whilst still a young man. Of course he enjoyed looking at her, but 'The girl was too full of irrelevancies, too many charming and seductive accidents of fleshly by-play, dimples and what-nots. Such things tend to obliterate and overcharge the simple notion which is the *raison d'être* of the work to be done – at least the work I wanted to do.'[8]

Models are best used as a reference book or dictionary, rather than as a source of ideas for sculpture, for all too easily, 'the beauties of appearance seek to oust the beauties of thought'. Besides professional models 'as a result of art-school conventions, they think some attitudes are "nice" and some are not,' and that did not suit Gill! What are friends and relatives for if not to help in this way? So most of the female Gills and virtually all their female friends and acquaintances were pressed into service, and several of the men too, though he regrets perhaps not enough. 'Strange how one's natural male inclination to see and draw women, makes one, spurs one on to seize opportunities for drawing the girls of one's acquaintance & to neglect the boys – tho' I'm sure one's men friends wouldn't refuse. I really must put it to them, before it's too late. I really truly must.'[9] By then, however, he was in the last year of his life and it was too late.

Some of the weaker drawings verge on the pin-up and no doubt Gill used photographs for these. John Rothenstein recollects him appearing at Count Kessler's dinner table with a pile of nudist magazines, throwing them down, then, 'First look at the covers,' he said, insisting on showing Kessler the plump, comely young women posing nude among silver birches or on river banks, 'and then look *inside* them. Not a single proper nude. The whole

Nude with hands on hips (1928),
pencil drawing, 38.5cm × 29cm

thing is a swindle.'[10]

Life-drawing is not a necessity for the sculptor, thinks
Gill, but it obviously is for the engraver of surgical or
anatomical text-books, and the portrait painter or sculptor will have to 'at least see their sitters and study the
disposition of bones and flesh'. The only other justification for working from the model is if it is taken as an end
in itself, not as a means of producing 'sketches' or
'studies' or 'notes' for other works.* Taken like this, 'one
can imagine no more attractive trade than that of
supplying a willing public with good drawings of naked
men and women'.[11] Alas, the art-schools, at least in Gill's
time, only taught people 'to get somehow down on paper
or canvas smudgy or scribbly imitations of light and shade
observable on the model. That a pencil or chalk or brush
is a thing which of its nature makes a line if you pull it
along is somehow forgotten.' The students are too busy
being cameras to take life-drawing seriously, as an end in
itself. To draw from life you have to be a lover of life
otherwise you are just exercising empty skill. 'Art *is* skill,
skill is the very basis of art, the *sine qua non*. But it is the
skill of men – not of ants or bees or mere mirrorscopes. It
is the skill of men trained, disciplined by life, by the
intellectual and moral *regimen* imposed by conscious life
in society. Art is the skill of men employed in the making
of things which they and their customers need and deem
worth making. And life drawings are worth making and
are needed just as portraits of our friends or of public
persons are worth making and are needed.'[12] He asks,
should it not be possible in these enlightened days to sell
drawings of nudes in the same way we do picture-post-
cards of Oxford colleges or photographs of animals in the
Zoo? For some of Gill's franker studies the answer must
still, alas, be no.

Apart from this whole-hearted specialization in finished life-drawings there is very little necessity for life
drawings elsewhere in art. In making a crucifixion

* There is, however, a folder in the W.A. Clark Library containing 60
studies of hands and feet that are obviously notes for sculpture and not
just ends in themselves.

'anatomical exactitudes are obviously a frivolity,' and it is quite evident that the sculptors of the West Door of Chartres cathedral never had a life-drawing lesson in their lives.* 'It's what you've got in your head that matters, and what you've got in your head has got to get there from life – not from textbooks and academies,'[13] or from 'life' classes. Art schools stress the shape at the expense of the form. An 'image' after all 'means something imaginary, something seen in the imagination. It does not mean simply something seen in a mirror.' It is the really primitive mind which is merely a mirror and all the painstaking detailed realism of Victorian art was but an aberration in the history of art. In all the great periods of sculpture, 'not what they saw but what they loved, that

Lying nude (1938), pencil drawing, 28.5cm × 45.5cm. (N.B. This drawing was used in *Drawings from Life* (1940 but reversed).

Seated figure (1929), pencil and chalk drawing, 45.7cm × 30.5cm (*right*)

---

* There does seem to have been one recorded medieval incident however: when Abbot Hugh of Leven (1339–1340) ordered a new crucifix for his chapel the artist 'had a naked man before him that he might learn from his beautiful form and decorate the crucifix more accurately' [Chronicle of the Abbey of Meaux] from V.W. Egbert, *The Medieval Artist at Work* (Princeton, 1967) p. 76.

they carved. Truly they loved what they saw, but their seeing bent before their love as a sapling before the wind.'[14]

Not only must the draughtsman love the thing seen but he must love the thing made – the drawing itself. This at best should be 'heraldic', a favourite word of Gill's. 'Remember you are making a real thing and not merely a picture of a thing.' Of necessity we must grasp things by means of our senses, but then we digest, turn over, remake, re-form it in the imagination and only then do we create our work of art. 'It is not made out of nothing, but it is a new thing. It is the product of intelligence and will. It is the product of love. It is in this sense that we are made in God's image. For we are really creators.'[15] We collaborate with God in creating and improving on nature by making things which are the products of love, not mere obedience, or mere transcriptions of nature or our own emotions in front of nature. For this reason, in a secular age, a drawing of the nude might be seen as an 'ikon', a holy image which can 'kindle a hunger for Heaven'. In spite of the dangers of pornography we must believe that, 'the goodness of God is visible and tangible in all his works'.

Picasso said, 'I paint what I think, not what I see.' Gill wrote:

The child said: First I think,
    Then I draw my think.
The art student said: First I look,
    Then I draw my look.
The child is simply a young person;
The art student is a more or less inaccurate
    photographer.[16]

Speaight adds, that for all this theorising his own life-drawings suggest 'that he had said: "First I feel and then I draw my feel."'[17] It can be seen that Gill was saying the same kinds of things as the avant-garde were simultaneously saying on the Continent about the necessity of breaking away from the dominance of appearance,

Nude number 8 (1937), pencil drawing, 45cm × 28cm, reproduced in *Drawings from Life* (1940)

and in stressing that a draughtsman is one who 'by means of lines makes a sort of house to dwell in. Just as we dwell physically in houses of bricks and stones, so we dwell mentally in constructions of lead and chalk and flint.'[18] Today that revolution is won and the new orthodoxy is to neglect the discipline of drawing appearances, the drawing of 'looks' and to move straight to the making of 'constructions', but what are often omitted are Gill's other ingredients, of intelligence, will, and love.

As with all topics Gill writes challengingly and perceptively about drawing. When we come to look at his own works, however, do they match the high claims he makes for the art of drawing and the weight of theory he makes them carry? Put another way, if we had read nothing he had written would they still strike us as good drawings?

It needs to be frankly admitted that the earliest life drawings are inept. As John Rothenstein says in his preface to *First Nudes*: 'Regarded simply as drawings from life they are less accomplished than numbers produced each year in art schools: they are inferior to these, that is to say, as descriptions of their subjects.'[19]

Gill's stress on what was in his head rather than in the model meant his ideas stood between him and the subject so that in the worst of these 'nothing is observed, least of all the joints, wrists, elbows, shoulders nor knees exist,' though in the drawing Rothenstein particularly scorns one suspects Gill was experimenting timidly with cubism, or at least something nearer to Léger's 'tubism' version of it. Gill was not responding to a living body but seeing it through the spectacles of art, and for all his disclaimers it is often the idealized Renaissance and Victorian academic nude that is distorting his vision here. They are also unique, for a sculptor, in being hardly more than two-dimensional representations, with no feeling for volume. In a way this is not surprising for 'even as a sculptor Gill was singularly lacking in feeling for solid form'. In short, writes Rothenstein, 'both in outlook and by his want of early training, Gill was unfitted for the direct drawing of the naked model. Such drawings are the very last manifestation of the art by which his achieve-

Seated nude (1926) from *First Nudes* (1954), pencil drawing, page size 24.5cm × 17cm

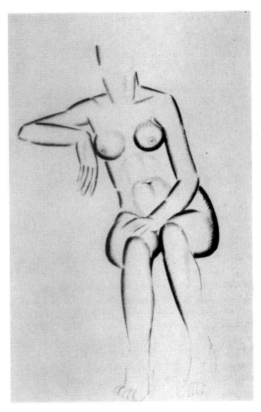

ment should be judged.' These are harsh words (especially in an introduction) but one must admit it would have been better if these *First Nudes* done in 1926 had not been·published posthumously in 1954. How much better for his reputation it would have been to publish the sketch book of nudes in the Victoria and Albert Museum. These were all done in 1927 and show Gill now coming to the height of his powers and experimenting with a range of styles from strong brutal volumes to the most delicate linear treatments. It is astonishing how far and quickly he has progressed since the 1926 studies, and how much life-

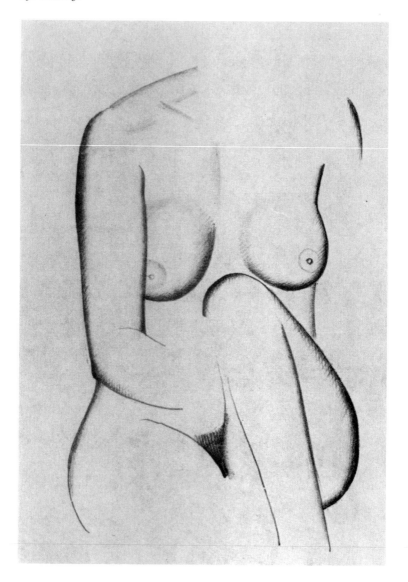

Torso (1926), pencil drawing,
16cm × 9.7cm

drawing he must have done to achieve this. *Drawings from Life* published in 1940 shows the sensitive shading and fastidious line Gill is best known by, but the small format of the book hardly does justice to the large originals from which the reproductions were taken.* These, and many others from the same period and model are now in the University of Texas and deserve a sympathetic reprint. These drawings also served as the bases for the wood-engravings of *Twenty-five nudes* published in 1938.

If we see many of these life drawings, and there are hundreds extant, then we find certain 'tricks' do recur too often. There is a use of a kind of chicken-wire cross hatching to represent the junction of two planes or the highest curve of a round limb. Also his trick of using a fringe of darker shading outside the form to emphasize the body contour, or to suggest shallow relief, becomes a kind of trade-mark for all its effectiveness in individual cases. There is also a weakness about the drawing of the hands and feet which makes them, at their worst, look like flippers. The faces too are generalized, depersonalized (as Speaight noticed) and often turned away or omitted – it seems that the further away parts of the body are from the all-too-fascinating pubic area then the less interest he had in them. The figures float with no sense of space or environment to give them weight. The models are invariably slim, beautiful young people or at least he makes them so, and this in spite of his condemnation of the general public's belief that beautiful art is the result of finding beautiful subjects and recording them faithfully. The Cubists' dismemberment of the body, and their demolition of the idea that art and the depiction of the beautiful are necessarily connected are sentiments he agreed with, but there is little sign in his drawings that he pushed his own practice into new directions in subject or technique.

I have stated the possible objections to his drawings as strongly as possible, but having said all this I must admit

* As a youth Gill tried the exercises in Ruskin's *The Elements of Drawing* and seems to have taken to heart Ruskin's saying that 'all great art is delicate' and that a sharp pencil should be used 'as if you were drawing the down on a butterfly's wing'.

The balcony (Moira Gibbings) (1933), pencil drawing, 51.2cm × 31.8cm

it was the drawings which first attracted me to Gill as an artist. I still believe that the best ones are, within their limits, some of the finest drawings produced this century. They come near to fulfilling the rule formulated by that other argumentative genius both Gill and Coomaraswamy admired so much – William Blake: 'The great and golden rule of art, as well as of life, is this: That the more distinct, sharp, and wiry the bounding line, the more perfect the work of art, and the less keen and sharp, the greater is the evidence of weak imitation, plagiarism, and bungling. Great inventors, in all ages knew this. . . . The want of this determinate and bounding form evidences the want of idea in the artist's mind. . . . Leave out this line, and you leave out life itself; all is chaos again, and the line of the almighty must be drawn upon it before man or beast can exist.'[20]

Gill traced and re-traced many of his favourite drawings, constantly simplifying the lines as he did so. The end result is a kind of sophisticated economy reminiscent of Indian Kalighat brush drawings, or the graphic works of Matisse and Modigliani. The line is sure, hard, continuous, delicate, decorative, with no tangles, no fudging anything, and with a panache and vitality all Gill's own. All the subjects, whether nudes, coins, churches or chimneys are all admirably disposed on the white of the page, as one might expect from a designer of typography whose first aim was always legibility. Gill writes in one of his notebooks when he is drafting an introduction to his engravings: 'It is not true that love is blind. Such then, O God are the things that I love: the round and the sharp, the firm and the flowing, and all things clear and clean.' This seems a fair summary of the qualities his drawings possess. That they are not the graphic equivalents to the complex, high-flown prose he uses to justify them is all to the good, and that they are, in spite of his theorising, frank recordings of an intense erotic curiosity and enjoyment of the human body is surely part of their strength. He did indeed draw the thing he loved, and it shows.

Wood-engravings

Gill began wood-engraving in 1906* as he tells us 'for the sake of lettering' rather than of image-making. However he was soon making Christmas cards and small illustrations for Hilary Pepler's Ditchling Press. Gill came to the medium at a very significant stage in its development and to appreciate fully Gill's contribution to this development it is necessary to recall, very briefly, some of wood-engraving's oddly ebbing and flowing history.[1]

Printing from carved wood blocks is the oldest form of printing known. It has been used in Europe for at least 500 years and in the East much longer than that. The oldest woodcut in the British Museum is the so-called 'Diamond Sutra' from China, dated at 868 A.D., but its sophistication indicates it was cut by an artist working in an already established tradition. Before Gutenberg's movable type came into use in Europe in the mid-fifteenth century the whole page of a book, letters and pictures alike, would be carved on one flat piece of wood, inked, and printed on paper in a press. After the invention of movable type only the pictures needed to be cut, but the blocks for these were made 'type-high' (i.e. the same thickness as the type letters) so they could be fitted into the press and be printed at the same time as the letters on the page.

These book illustrations, as well as playing cards, textile prints, broadsheets, calendars and popular or devotional prints, were all wood-*cuts*. An artist drew his design in pen or pencil or brush on to a plank of pearwood or cherry with the grain in it running side to side. These lines were then cut round with gouges and knives to leave them standing up above the cleared areas. The raised lines of the drawing would then be inked and printed in a press so that the print would appear looking very like the

Criseyde visits Troilus, from Chaucer's *Troilus and Criseyde* (1927), Golden Cockerel Press, wood-engraving, 17.8cm × 11.5cm

* Diary entry Nov 20th 1906: 'Tried wood-engraving a little in evening.'

Self-portrait, first state (1927). The third, final state of this wood-engraving was used as a frontispiece to *Engravings by Eric Gill*, Douglas Cleverdon, 1929, 17.8cm × 12.8cm

original drawing, but in reverse of course. Such prints depend for their quality upon the merit of the design rather than upon the actual cutting which is laborious and skilled but adds nothing in expression to the original. Artists known for the excellence of their woodcuts such as those of the 'Danube School', Albrecht Durer (1471–1528), Hans Baldung Grien (1484–1545), Albrecht Altdorfer (1480–1538) and Hans Holbein (1497–1543) probably never cut the blocks themselves but drew on the wood, then handed it over to a specialist cutter called a *formschneider* in their workshops. This man in turn would hand the cut block on to printers to multiply the facsimiles of the original design.

After this great period of German wood-cutting in the fifteenth and sixteenth centuries came something of a lowering of quality in the designs, although wood blocks were as widely used as ever, alongside copper engraving, to supply the European demand for cheap books and the flow of information. Then in the eighteenth century it was found that if a hard wood such as boxwood was sliced *across* the grain and the surface polished smooth, then much finer details could be cut. Newer, finer tools were designed to do this. This technical advance meant that designing could be in terms of the medium itself – the work of sharp tools in wood – rather than trying to imitate the effects of pencils, pens or copper engravings. With this shift to new techniques on end-grain blocks came a new term: wood-*engraving*. Artists began to cut their own designs in the wood directly rather than use a *formschneider* and probably the best known of these is Thomas Bewick (1753–1828). William Blake (1757–1827) and Edward Calvert (1797–1883) also left a few small works from this period which still serve as inspiration to today's wood-engravers.

These men brought a new way of seeing the block. If one regards the uncut block as a black rectangle (and most wood-engravers make it literally so by adding an ink-wash to the wood before cutting), then what the tools cut into it will be white lines – rather like drawing in chalk on a blackboard – and the design will naturally be built up of these white lines. The *formschneider* had assumed the block was like a white rectangle upon which appeared black lines, like a pencil or pen drawing. These fundamentally different ways of building up the design are still matters of debate in the twentieth century and, as will be seen, Gill used both.

End-grain boxwood blocks tend to be small, but they are very hard and can be pressed many times. Bewick estimated that one of his blocks had produced 900,000 prints without showing serious wear, which no copper engraving or lithograph could have done. Such durability and cheapness meant wood-engraving replaced woodcutting as the medium for disseminating visual material of all kinds (rather like photography today) and soon became an industry with its own apprenticeship system, not to produce artists but skilled tradesmen able to illustrate catalogues, visiting cards, newspapers, books, magazines, or even reproductions of popular paintings. Even Ruskin's pen and pencil demonstrations in his *The Elements of Drawing* (London, 1857) had to be reproduced in this painstaking way. Later the wheel turned again so that once more artists such as Rossetti, Frederick Leighton, Millais or Holman Hunt, or illustrators like Charles Keene or Frederick Sandys, drew with pen, pencil or wash directly on the blocks and left the skilled 'woodpeckers' to toil with their scorpers, gravers, spitstickers, and the new multiple-tint tools to interpret their scribbles, washes and cross-hatchings. Sometimes this collaboration worked, but often the artists, with no finger-tip knowledge of the wood-engraving medium drew designs totally inappropriate to it, and of course they usually had black-line pictures in mind rather than white because that is what 'drawing' meant to them.

Wood-engraving was now merely a reproductive medium, but it soon lost even that role with the development of cheaper and better photo-mechanical methods such as the line-block and half-tone processes. At best it lingered on in catalogues for machinery or optical equipment where clarity of line was paramount, but by the late nineteenth century it seemed that wood-engraving had lost both its utility and its earlier role as an artistic medium. However, William Morris, with his interest in all things medieval, decided to try the medium of black-line woodcut. But once the Kelmscott Press was established in 1890 and he wished to produce his great *Chaucer* edition of 1896 he had to call in an old reproductive engraver W.H. Hooper to cut his over-intricate borders for him and Burne-Jones's illustrations. Hooper in turn taught the next two significant wood-engravers Charles Ricketts (1866–1931) and Charles Shannon (1863–1937), life-long friends who designed and cut their own blocks and designed the type founts for the books they produced at the Vale Press. These illustrators were in the black-line tradition they had learned from Hooper and the fifteenth-century Italian book-makers they admired so much. The medium began to revive as an art form sufficiently for 'The First Exhibition of Original Wood Engravings' to be held in 1898 (the 'original' of the title was meant to stress they were not reproductive engravers). The pioneers of the revival represented here were Ricketts and Shannon, T.S. Moore, R. Savage, Lucien Pissarro and William Nicholson.

In 1899 Gill and Noel Rooke (1881–1953) met in Edward Johnston's lettering class. Gill also learned monumental masonry, which eventually led him to wood-engraving 'for the sake of lettering', whilst Rooke went straight from calligraphy to wood-engraving with such success that he in turn taught it at the Central School from 1912 to 1942. This meant that he taught the best of the next generation of wood-engravers who kept the revival going, such people as Robert Gibbings, John Farleigh, George Mackley and Clare Leighton. All these were encouraged by Rooke to return to the white-line technique of Bewick and Blake as being truer to the medium and capable of more subtle textural and tonal effects.

By the 1920s this revival was gaining momentum (even the Bloomsbury artists were dabbling in it), so much so that in 1920 The Society of Wood Engravers was formed to organise an annual exhibition. Gill was a founder member of this Society as were Rooke, Gwendolen Raverat (a close friend of his), Robert Gibbings (his collaborator and owner of the Golden Cockerel Press) and John Nash. Lucien Pissarro was the only member from the original pioneer generation who had exhibited in 1898 to survive and exhibit. Private presses flourished and gave work to wood-engravers and type-designers (and Gill was both), as well as private and public commissions coming in for covers, advertisements, book-plates and limited editions of fine prints. There were now several art schools teaching the subject, and producing enough engravers for there to be factions and for a splinter group to form the English Wood Engraving Society in 1926. Sadly, however, the 'Thirties saw the closing of many of the private presses, the re-merging of the two Societies in 1932 as work and funds dwindled, and then the war years saw the end of the careers of many of the finest practitioners, including Gill's. Since then, in spite of isolated engravers of the highest skill, wood-engraving seems to have gone through another of its down periods. Chamberlain says it is far from moribund, 'But the fact remains that the technique has been virtually ignored by painters and has been more neglected by print makers than at any time since Rooke and Gill. Most of the major engravers of the thirties have ceased to practise their art, and they have very few successors to equal them in skill, creativity and dedication.'[2]

It needs to be noted that wood-cutting has also undergone something of a revival this century in the hands of Gauguin, Munch and the German Expressionists, and then suffered a similar neglect by major artists. Gill himself did a few wood-cuts, notably a large 'Hound of the Lord' with a burning torch in its jaws, but wood-engraving was obviously more suited to Gill's reflective temperament and abilities. As George Mackley says, 'Wood engraving makes a particularly strong appeal to those who delight in what has, for some reason, been called "mere" skill, and to those who find satisfaction in the precise and clear-cut statement of a completely formed and pre-conceived idea, rather than a loose and suggestive vagueness.'[3]

In the slow, deliberate almost surgical, removal of all that is not needed of the block to 'free' the design, there is

Girl in bath (Petra) (1923), wood-engraving, 10.5cm × 10.8cm

something of the same satisfaction of sculpture, especially with white-line engraving. Black-line, on the other hand, is more calligraphic and seems painfully to build a design in much the same way Gill erected chains of reasoning in his essays. The limitations of the medium such as its small scale, the difficulties of using colour, the ever-present risk of a disastrous slip did not worry Gill, though Garrett claims he was worried by the degree of perfection expected of the result. 'Whilst in painting and sculpture it is not unusual for an indifferent performance to be excused on the plea of genius, with engraving, however brilliant the genius, the public and critic alike always demand a brilliant performance. Eric Gill would express concern about the aspect of perfection in engraving; because of his modesty this would have been an understandable worry for him.'[4] There are few 'happy accidents' in wood-engraving so the eye and hand can never relax.

Hilary Pepler recalls Gill at work in the early Ditchling days: 'The first thing which must have struck an observer of Gill at work was the sureness and steadiness of his hand at minute detail; the assurance and swiftness of a sweep of line is one thing (and in this he was a past master) but the hairs of an eyelash another – and he liked to play about with rays and hairs which can hardly be distinguished with a magnifying glass. He was always obliging. When I wanted a tailpiece to end a chapter or an initial letter with which to begin one, he would tumble to the point at once, improve upon my suggestion, supply the block ready for the press within an hour, and come in to see it being printed the same afternoon.'[5] Remember that the hand which carved the microscopic eye-lash also carved the $2\frac{1}{2}$ tons of 'Mankind' and the 196 square feet of stone in the Geneva panel. How many other artists had such a range, or such a hand?

Pepler and Gill saw his wood-engraving as a side-line or game at this stage with no pretentions about 'art'. Indeed the little magazine Gill, Pepler and Johnston were publishing was called *The Game*. Blocks were used several times over, even the Christmas card ones. To make the game a little more professional they hired the Alpine Club Gallery for a week in 1916 to show the Ditchling Press's wares. 'We drove up with our drawings, engravings, posters, etc., in the big waggon from our farm; at Charing Cross Gill and I disembarked, hung notice-boards over our shoulders and became sandwich men walking up and

Woman swimming (1936) used in *The Green Ship* by Patrick Miller, Golden Cockerel Press, wood-engraving, 7cm × 12.5cm

down Regent Street advertising the show nearby. Did anyone take the slightest notice of the men carrying boards? Not by the flicker of an eyelid – except for the professionals who tramped the same gutter to announce the latest play at the Savoy or Hippodrome; to them we were unknown intruders and suspect accordingly.'[6]

Soon, however, Gill had no need to peddle his engravings: the customers came to him. Eventually he illustrated 138 books with wood and metal engravings, and fifteen of these, possibly the best of all, were for the Golden Cockerel Press.[7] This was run from 1924 to 1933 by Robert Gibbings, himself one of the best and most prolific wood-engravers of the century.[8] He was a great adventurous, energetic extrovert of a man, and though Gill at first refused to work with him on the absurd grounds that he was not a Catholic, he persisted and eventually they became firm friends.[9] So much so that, as we have recounted, Gibbings became Gill's guide round the Paris underworld and Gill drew both the Gibbings in the nude.

Gill's professionalism was never questioned but it was never too serious or solemn as we can see in this incident

SERENADE.

SOLOMON : How beautiful thou art, my love,
How beautiful thou art!
Thine eyes are like dove's eyes behind thy veil.
Thy hair is like a flock of goats adown the slope of Gilead,

Serenade, from *The Song of Songs*
(1925), Golden Cockerel Press, wood-
engraving, 13cm × 10cm

Heppenstall recounts:

> Two consecutive illustrations, meant to be at the foot
> of the page, here, the sailor and, there, the maiden
> swimming through curly waves. Gill sat palming his
> graver between the edges of the boxwood grain and
> then inking the block and drawing off a print. He
> worked with a jeweller's magnifying glass in his eye.
> 'There,' he said, 'They'll do.'
> He patted and stroked the air over the damp and
> glistening block which showed the underwater lady.
> 'Dear little bottom she's got don't you think?'[10]

Soon commissions for private press productions came
pouring in as well as for all kinds of portraits, book-plates,
ordination cards and ephemera. Physick's Catalogue
records over 1,000 engravings in the Victoria and Albert
Museum Collection alone.[11] No one man could cope with
this flood of work, as well as keep up his writing,
sculpture, typography and stone-cutting so, as with his
other work, he had to rely on an assistant. In wood-
engraving this was Ralph John Beedham (1879–1975). He
joined Gill at Ditchling in the early 1920s and learned
lettering from him, but soon took over the chore of
clearing out the white areas of Gill's blocks – a skilled but
time-consuming job he also performed for Gibbings and
John Farleigh. It is noticeable how free these engravers
are with their white areas and perhaps it was Beedham's
assistance which enabled them to be so. In 1921 Beedham
wrote a book, *Wood Engraving*, which Gill introduced
and which they printed together at Ditchling. There are
no original engravings by Beedham himself because
despite his great skills he had no flair for draughtsman-
ship. He was, in fact, one of the last of the nineteenth-
century reproductive engravers to be trained, but before
he even finished his apprenticeship newer processes had
snatched his living from him. He passed on his skills to
newer engravers, such as Joan Hassall, and Garrett tells us
he engraved his last block at the age of eighty-three.

As one might expect Gill not only engraved wood, he
wrote about it. He began as usual by placing the medium

Autumn midnight, frontispiece to *Autumn Midnight* (1923) by Frances Cornford, The Poetry Bookshop, wood-engraving, 11.7cm × 8.2cm

in the modern industrial world where book production is merely a matter of profit in the hands of the business men. '. . . degradation is inevitable when one man draws, another touches up the drawing, another photographs, another touches up the negative, another prints it on the metal, another etches, another touches up the etching, another routs it, another mounts it, another proves it and another keeps the accounts and to crown all, another takes the profits. This excessive sub-division is inevitable where profit making is the motive power.'[12]

Wood engraving does not fit into such a set-up but rather into a small workshop system where quality, not quantity or profit is the test – indeed the would-be engraver should 'start with a clear understanding that there is no money in it'. However, as we have seen Gill did pass on some of the cutting to Beedham, and he himself did engrave other people's designs, notably some by David Jones, and Maillol's designs for Kessler's 1926 edition of Virgil's *Eclogues* and Christmas cards from his daughter's drawings. These were obviously labours of love, however, rather than a compromise of his principles.

Another attraction the medium had for Gill was that 'the graver and the wood both of them make their own demands and make mere imitation of nature almost impossible'.[13] The engraver must not 'strain after effects' but take for granted that 'a zig-zag pattern such as a child would engrave is better than the most expert imitation of a sunset'. In his Preface to the 1929 edition of his engravings he virtually apologizes for his early attempts to imitate light and shade and explains that his famous *Autumn Midnight* is a compromise between the 'senti-mental' imitation of light and shade and non-naturalistic engraving. For the rest: 'An apprenticeship to architecture followed by ten years exclusively devoted to lettering (in stone chiefly, but also in wood and paint) had weaned my mind from the common notion that art is primarily representation and that good art is simply representation of what is deemed good in nature.'[14]

Gill gives the totally impractical advice to the learner wood engraver that he make his own blocks from the trees in his own back garden and so become 'independent of the foreign merchant'. Otherwise his only practical advice, apart from learning the job by becoming an apprentice to an established engraver, is that 'the beginner should commence with patterns and pictures of white lines on black. The normal development of this first method is the silhouette with white lines upon it. Having attained skill with gravers and scaupers he may proceed to engrave patterns and pictures of black lines on white, first in plain outline, and then, last of all, he may attempt the modelling and elaboration of the general surface.'[15]

It can be seen here that Gill keeps his options open in the black line versus white line controversy which occupied the wood-engravers of the 1920s and 1930s. A wrinkle he did not pass on in print was his own habit of having the incised lines of his old blocks filled in with white gesso, the design sawn round and then mounted on a stand to be sold as a kind of miniature sculpture. This ensured both that no more prints would be taken, and a few shillings' extra income.

Gill was not a great technical innovator and seems to have deliberately shunned several of the possibilities opening up at this time. In an article about the Society of Wood Engravers which he wrote for *The Architect* in 1920 he made this clear: 'Membership of the Society is confined to those who use the European method of wood-engraving. This method distinguished from the Japanese or Eastern method by the fact that prints are obtained by means of the printing press, is more suitable to the tradition and temperament of European artists, and is of greater utility in connection with book production and decoration.'[16]

This turning away from the works of Hokusai, Hiroshige, Utamaro and the other eastern wood-cutters who were so influencing painters at the turn of the century seems rather perverse, especially as they too avoided the 'sentimentality' of imitative light and shade in much the same way as Gill himself. As well as rejecting the eastern influence, Gill also rejected the seductive technical possibilities of hand-burnishing pictures, transparent and hand-made papers, mixed inks, water-based inks, effects produced by the roller, chiaroscuro prints, tonal effects

Crucifixion (1922), wood-engraving,
20cm × 7.2cm

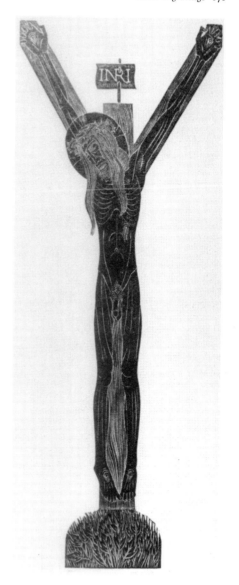

The sofa (1925), wood-engraving
printed *intaglio*, 10.8cm × 7cm

with a multiple-tool, or multiple blocks to produce
coloured prints. Like Braque who said he loved the rule
which curbed emotion Gill sought the simplest and
starkest methods because 'for me, art, and this art
especially, was always inextricably bound up with the
expression of ideas', and for this plain black and white are
sufficient.

There is one curious exception to this attitude of
technical puritanism however, and that is Gill's experiments with *intaglio* printing from 1924 onwards. He
found that the same block could be used for both relief
and *intaglio* printing. To do this he cut a block in which
the surface printed black and the incised lines white, as
usual. Then he took the block, over-inked it so that incised
lines were flooded with ink, wiped the raised areas of the
block clean of ink and printed damp paper under extra
pressure so that the lines now printed black and the raised
surface white – in short an *intaglio* print just like a copper
etching. In terms of art this is a kind of interesting party
trick, but it leads nowhere. It also breaks his own rule of
being true to the demands of the medium.

The next logical step from these experiments was to do
real *intaglio* printing with copper and zinc plates, and Gill
approached this with the same boyish zest he had shown
for wood-engraving. He wrote to Desmond Chute from
Capel-y-ffin in 1925: 'I've sold a good many prints since I
left Ditchling – every now and then there's a bit of a spurt
and its quite a business. Doing my own printing is great
sport and I've got a large and a small printing press here
and a copper plate press too. Copper engraving is a great
game. I hope to do something in that line.'[17]

What he did was more of the same subject-matter,
sacred and profane, that he had dealt with in wood-
engraving. Engraving on metal demands much the same
methodical working through of a preconceived idea we
have seen Gill follow in other media, and it also permits
the same clear, unshaded linear effects he sought in all his
graphic work. Again Gill was no great technical innovator
but worked supremely well within the limits he set
himself. He illustrated his own works, such as *Id Quod
Visum Placet* (1926), the best-known plate for which was

'Flying Buttresses' which showed part of Chartres and an aeroplane flying over, presumably to suggest that both are beautiful in being perfectly adapted to their function. His *Art and Love* (1927) includes the plate oddly entitled 'Adam and Eve in Heaven, or The Public House in Paradise'. Gill's son-in-law, Denis Tegetmeier, was also a talented and more specialised metal engraver and the two collaborated, for example on Gill's book *Trousers* (1937) where Tegetmeier provided the frontispiece. Sadly, it fell to Tegetmeier to engrave the five drawings Gill was working on during the last weeks of his life to illustrate *Glue and Lacquer*[18]. The translator's note explains the title: '"like glue and lacquer" is a common Chinese metaphor for the closest of human intimacies'. One can see from the engravings that the subject still had the power to arouse the visual inventiveness of the dying Gill, and that his line is as controlled and witty as ever.

Gill began wood-engraving in a small way on Pepler's press and soon graduated from letters and end pieces to illustrating Pepler's book *The Devil's Devices* (1915), and their three-man magazine *The Game* which ran from 1916 to 1923 (though Johnston resigned his part editorship as Gill and Pepler pushed it heavily into Catholicism). They also home-produced a series of ten 'Welfare Handbooks' on a variety of burning social topics such as Birth Control, Dress, Riches, and Health. These early works rely heavily on black silhouettes and a style of unsubtle, didactic caricature which kept cropping up in later works where Gill was dealing with social topics such as *Clothes* (1930), *The Lord's Song* (1934) and the picture 'Safety First' which first appeared in *Labour Woman*. Early book illustrations like those to Frances Cornforth's *Autumn Midnight* (1923) and to his sister Enid Clay's *Sonnets and Verses* (1925) also show a dominant black with pure 'white-line' technique – all works he eventually came to see as too heavy for the texts. Other single works such as the famous 'Thorn in the Flesh' (1921) demonstrate this style at its witty best. Then, in *Song of Songs* (1925), he switched to a black-line approach which complements the text better in its weight, and also to a stylization of the nude and of drapery which makes all his future work so

Rachel Rothenstein (1926), copper engraving, 25cm × 17.8cm

Hortus conclusus, fro
Canticorum (1931), Ci
wood-engraving, 14.4(

Meeting of Troilus and Criseyde, from
Chaucer's *Troilus and Criseyde* (1927),
wood-engraving, 17.8cm × 11.3cm (*right*

Girl and Cupid, Girl with knee raised
and Cupid: border decorations from
Troilus and Criseyde (1927), wood-
engravings, both 17.7cm × 9cm
(*overleaf*)

recognizable. We have already commented at some length on the outrage some of these illustrations caused. This black-line approach was abandoned, however, for the Cranach Press Latin version of *Canticum Canticorum* (1931),[19] possibly to avoid repeating himself after *Song of Songs*. Now he uses dense black plates with the forms picked out in delicate stipples and the contours of the figures are given the characteristic Gill relief-shading, only in wood-engraving this of course appears as white, like a nimbus round the limbs. So fine was the tooling in these blocks that a first blank tint block had to be used to take up some of the porosity of the heavy paper and so prevent the fine ticking Gill had done with the lozenge tool being lost or filled in. These are amongst his finest works in my opinion.

When he came to illustrate Chaucer for the Golden Cockerel Press one might expect the earthy humorous side of the poetry to appeal directly to similar strains in Gill, as indeed they did. The full-page illustrations to *Troilus and Criseyde* (1927) are richly sensuous and mix in a most satisfying way areas of black-line and white-line work, though his marginal decorations did not please everybody. John Rothenstein in reviewing it objected to its 'misplaced naturalism' whereby a wholly flesh and blood woman reclines on a heraldic plant, and to the way Gill had mixed archaic and modern conventions, often in the same decoration. 'Nor do the decorations share in the homely geniality of the poem. There is about them a quality infinitely remote from the spirit of Chaucer,' though indeed some are 'lovely and grand' and pure in form.[20] Many of the conventions he had invented for the *Troilus* (or derived partly from medieval illuminated manuscripts) Gill carried forward into his next related work *The Canterbury Tales* of 1928–1931, such as the sinuous upward fronds in the borders. Speaight thought that by this time he was working under too much pressure so that 'a good deal of the illustration is pretty mechanical; those etiolated borders do not quite match the richness and the occasional earthiness of the text. There is even a hint of decadence which is the very reverse of Chaucerian.'[21]

Other purely literary works he tackled were *Hamlet* (1933) and *Henry VIII* (though Speaight tells us he had little knowledge of Shakespeare and not much liking for him) and his sister Enid's second volume of verse *The Constant Mistress* (1934). He devised yet another new style for the wood-cuts of *The Holy Sonnets of John Donne* (1938). His last splendidly full-blooded book was *25 Nudes* (1938) in which the plates are totally black except for the wiry white outlines to the nudes themselves and an occasional scrap of cross-hatching. Here he had no print to balance and could indulge both his love of the subject and the logic of the material to the full.

From the beginning Gill used his engraving to illustrate and propagate his religious views, and it is amongst these works that the finest of all are to be found (also, it must be confessed, some of the weakest in terms of their over-sweetness). In 1917 he made his Westminster Stations of the Cross designs into a series of wood-cuts, and in 1919 he had made a single block of 'Christ and the Money Changers' which is very similar in design to the later Leeds War Memorial of 1923. The *Passio Domini Nostri Jesu Christi* of 1926 is pure black-line engraving with a very medieval feel about it. One critic thought of the plates in this work that 'Such prints as the "Agony in the Garden" and "The Crucifixion" are unsurpassed among any work today in emotional strength and originality of treatment.'[22] And Speaight, never one to praise lightly or unironically, thought of the 'Agony in the Garden' that it had an 'extraordinary beauty' and 'Eric never did anything better in wood-engraving. Here, and elsewhere, the figures have the formal impassivity of an ikon – diagrammatic rather than descriptive.'[23]

Nevertheless, it is *The Four Gospels* of 1931 done for Gibbings at the Golden Cockerel Press that most people seem to think is the best thing Gill ever did. Here is black-line engraving at its peak with text and decoration balanced to perfection. Garrett calls it a work of importance and rare achievement, showing the most inspired work of Eric Gill. 'This masterpiece of book production and design can be grouped alongside the Kelmscott *Chaucer* and the Doves *Bible*. *The Four Gospels* is a superb

Death be not proud, from *The Holy Sonnets of John Donne* (1938), printed by Hague and Gill, wood-engraving, 11.5cm × 8.5cm

example of collaboration between the artist and the typographer. . . . The book is set in Gill's Golden Cockerel type and is decorated with forty-one of his engravings; Gibbings considered the Gill engravings for this book to be the finest he had ever published.'[24] Indeed it is difficult to conceive how the figures could have been played off against the angularities of large capitals or single words in a more satisfying way. The Crucifixion takes place over the word 'Then', the Deposition over 'And', whilst The Burial of Christ takes place, perhaps less successfully, through a foliated 'And'. These are moving works, but even here there are unexpected touches of humour, as the negro beheader of John the

The agony in the garden, from *Passio Domini Nostri Jesu Christi* (1926), Golden Cockerel Press, wood-engraving, 15.6cm × 11.3cm, with 18pt Caslon Old Face type

Baptist handles his sword as if Gill still had in his mind's eye Ranjitsinghi's cover-drives in his childhood Brighton, and there is also a naughty little glimpse up Salome's skirt.

Other religious works are *The Passion of Our Lord* (1934) and the Aldine editions of the Bible (1936) where yet another style appears where the blacks are never dense nor the whites extensive but there is an over-all silvery quality achieved by finely cut hatchings on the rhythmic drapery and figures. Towards the end of his life he published *The Travels and Sufferings of Father Jean de Brébeuf* (1938) where the naïveté of the illustrations appears too forced to move the reader very much and the backgrounds too fussily cut to satisfy the purist.

Gill had a habit of working on a theme in several media at once, as we have already seen with the engraved and sculpted versions of 'Christ and the Moneylenders' and

ET HYMNO DICTO, EXIERUNT IN montem Oliveti. Tunc dicit illis Jesus: ✠ Omnes vos scandalum patiemini in me in ista nocte. Scriptum est enim: Percutiam pastorem, et dispergentur oves gregis. Postquam autem resurrexero, præcedam vos in Galilæam. Respondens autem Petrus, ait illi: Et si omnes scandalizati fuerint in te, ego nunquam scandalizabor. Ait illi Jesus: ✠ Amen dico tibi quia in hac nocte, antequam gallus cantet, ter me negabis. Ait illi Petrus: Etiam si oportuerit me mori tecum, non te negabo. Similiter et omnes discipuli dixerunt. Tunc venit Jesus cum illis in villam quæ dicitur Gethsemani, et dixit discipulis suis: ✠ Sedete hic, donec vadam illuc et orem. Et assumpto Petro et duobus filiis Zebedæi, cœpit contristari et mœstus esse. Tunc ait illis: ✠ Tristis est anima mea usque ad mortem; sustinete hic, et vigilate mecum. Et progressus pusillum, procidit in faciem suam, orans et dicens: ✠ Pater mi, si possibile est, transeat a me calix iste; verumtamen non sicut ego volo, sed sicut tu. Et venit ad discipulos suos, et invenit eos dormientes: et dicit Petro: ✠ Sic non potuistis una hora vigilare mecum? Vigilate et orate, ut non intretis in tentationem. Spiritus quidem promptus est, caro autem infirma. Iterum secundo abiit, et oravit, dicens: ✠ Pater mi, si non potest hic calix transire nisi bibam illum, fiat voluntas tua. Et venit iterum, et invenit eos dor-

M ANE AUTEM FACTO, CONSILIUM
inierunt omnes principes sacerdotum et se-
niores populi adversus Jesum, ut eum morti
traderent. Et vinctum adduxerunt eum, et
tradiderunt Pontio Pilato præsidi. Tunc videns Judas, qui
eum tradidit, quod damnatus esset, pœnitentia ductus,
retulit triginta argenteos principibus sacerdotum et senio·

9

'The Stations of the Cross'. Other subjects to get this
treatment are 'Belle Sauvage' which appears in at least
three wood-engraved versions and one sculpture. One of
his rather pompous stone reliefs of Odysseus and
Nausicaa done for a hotel in Morecambe (1935) reappears
as a wood-engraving printed in vile green ink above the

The carrying of the cross, from *Passio
Domini Nostri Jesu Christi* (1926),
wood-engraving, 11.4cm × 11.1cm,
page size 25.5cm × 15.3cm

that when Jesus had finished these parables, he departed thence. And when he was come into his own country, he taught them in their synagogue, insomuch that they were astonished, and said, Whence hath this man this wisdom, and these mighty works? Is not this the carpenter's son? is not his mother called Mary? and his brethren, James, and Joses, and Simon, and Judas? And his sisters, are they not all with us? Whence then hath this man all these things? And they were offended in him. But Jesus said unto them, A prophet is not without honour, save in his own country, and in his own house. And he did not many mighty works there because of their unbelief.

T THAT TIME HEROD THE TETRARCH HEARD OF THE FAME OF JESUS, AND SAID UNTO HIS SERVANTS, THIS IS JOHN THE BAPTIST; HE IS RISEN FROM THE DEAD; & THEREFORE MIGHTY works do shew forth themselves in him. For Herod had laid hold on John, and bound him, and put him in prison for Herodias' sake, his brother Philip's wife. For John said unto him, It is not lawful for thee to have her. And when he would have put him to death, he feared the multitude, because they counted him as a prophet. But when Herod's

37

Page 37 from *The Four Gospels* (1931), Golden Cockerel Press, wood-engraving with 18pt Golden Cockerel typeface, page size 34.4cm × 23cm

London, Midland and Southern Railway's breakfast menu with the title, 'There is Good Hope that Thou Mayest See Thy Friends'. Other practical applications for his engravings are an advertisement for The National Institute for the Blind, a Hog and Wheatsheaf design for the paper bags of a bakery, and several certificates and

THE SOLDIERS OF THE GOVERNOR

Page 74 from *The Four Gospels* (1931),
wood-engraving, page size
34.4cm × 23cm

NOW WHEN THE EVEN WAS COME

Page 125 from *The Four Gospels* (1931)

St Mark, from *The Aldine Bible*, Volume 1 (1934), wood-engraving, 15.5cm × 9cm

diplomas for institutions. Other single plates are portraits of friends, sometimes in flat black profile like brass-rubbings, or more fully worked like his own famous 'Self-Portrait', also in profile, commissioned by Douglas Cleverdon for the 1929 edition of his engravings. As might be expected other works are nudes and erotic works in a variety of styles.

Gill was also an acknowledged master in the small specialised field of book-plate engraving, and in the opinion of this craft's historian, B.N. Lee, 'Gill can truly be said to have created the modern engraved label, and

Title-page illustration to *The Travels and Sufferings of Father Jean de Brébeuf* (1938), Golden Cockerel Press, wood-engraving, 12.7cm × 9.7cm

Reynolds Stone has been his more than worthy successor'. Gill's fifty or more *Ex Libris* labels engraved on wood or copper made him 'perhaps the most influential and important bookplate artist of the century'.[25]

Gill's reputation as a wood-engraver has remained high all this century and all the books on the subject from about 1919 onwards pay lavish tribute to his skill in marrying illustration and print in the books he was involved with. The latest authoritative work on British wood-engraving has more references in it to Gill than to any other engraver and sees him as being as unique to Britain as Marangoni is to Italy, Favorsky to Russia, Escher to Holland and Lepère to France.[26] Praise indeed.

However, many of the writers whilst freely acknowledging Gill's strengths do express reservations. One of the

great popularisers of the wood-engraving during its renaissance in the 'Twenties was Herbert Furst, and early in 1921 he was already complaining that Gill was not 'woody' enough in his cutting and that most of his works 'grate on one a little by reason of a persistent affectation of ascetic Byzantine mannerisms'.[27] By 1924 Furst's opinion has further hardened:

Belle sauvage IV, title page of the ordinary edition of *Art Nonsense* (1929), wood-engraving, 6 × 5cm

> We find . . . in Gill's design, an ineradicable self-consciousness, a sense of personal value and importance which were objectionable but for the fact that the artist never spares himself; the slightest thing he does is executed with meticulous care and with an intellectual nicety that divides his art by a world-width from Brangwyn's. Whatever emotions he may possess they have passed as it were through a narrow purging flame

Belle sauvage V, title page of the large paper edition of *Art Nonsense* (1929), wood-engraving, 6cm × 5cm

of intellectual white-heat before they reach the material in which he happens to be working. I say narrow flame, because his intellectual capacity seems keen rather than broad. As a xylographer he shows no sign of sympathy with the material; his engraving is done with perfect precision and control on hard wood with a sharp tool and might with equal aesthetic result be done in metal; indeed some of his prints, such as the 'Christ driving out the money changers' look almost like a rubbing from a Church brass. The style of his design outwardly associated, now with Byzantine rigour, anon with sensuous freedom and cut in the simplest and nakedest of white lines with extraordinary skill and Euclidian precision, is aesthetically unimpeachable. Gill's conception of the function of his art is that it should furnish the intellectual substructure for the emotional or religious requirements of the spectator.[28]

There is obviously some justice in this judgement, though a testy little footnote saying Gill will not allow his work to be reproduced in the book because it is in photographic line-block hints at a cool distance between the two men. In a letter to Furst written in 1939 Gill replies to Furst's charge that his black-line work might as well be in pen by saying it is perfectly appropriate with print and that 'I think, like many people, you take rather a prim line – a sort of artistic-moral-theology line'[29] – which is rather ironic, coming from Gill.

Even Albert Garrett for all his admiration of Gill writes of his style as 'erudite and puritanical', or 'tight and austere', and of, 'a certain coldness in the perfection of Gill's craftsmanship and there is a flawlessness in his skill which gives his work a certain God-like character which some people cannot recognize.'[30] This is the same charge of coldness and objectivity we have already discussed at some length in connection with his drawings and erotic works.

These and other criticisms seem to point to what Gill did not do, rather than to faults in what he did. He broke away from the Bewick tradition and was never concerned with the realistic rendering of grass, water, leaves, clouds, shadows, space, perspective, flesh, or fur as many other contemporary engravers were, or in bravura demonstrations of the wide variety of tool marks that can be produced on a few square inches of boxwood. Others do these things far better and in so doing perhaps express themselves more openly and warmly. What Gill was concerned with basically was expressing ideas over a limited range of subject matter, and technically he chose to do this through clear edges, long sinuous curves, flat decorative silhouettes and the balanced patterning of black and white so that his illustration formed a unit with the whole page spread on which it appeared.

Before we leave these recurring charges of impassivity we should consider Gill's replies to them. In his Introduction to the 1928–1933 *Engravings* he wrote: 'As to my lack of emotional display I think that the business of wood-engraving is very much like the business of typography. I think tenderness and warmth in such things are not to be looked for except in the workmanship. You do not want the designer of printing types to wear his heart on his sleeve – my engravings are, I admit, only a kind of printer's flowers.'[31] Since printer's flowers are stylized floral borders used round the edges of a title page this last modest touch is obviously absurd, but the claim to be doing just a job of work with no more emotional (as opposed to intellectual) involvement than a plumber, is one he repeatedly makes. In this letter, for example: 'I, on the other hand, and in my Olympian wisdom, view all

St Luke, from *The Passion of Our Lord* (1934), printed by Hague and Gill, wood-engraving, 12.3cm × 5cm

"art work" as I do house building or knitting. The psycho stuff fits in but is subordinated. I ask: what is it? (the artist), what's it for? (the percipient), what's it made of? (the art work), how's it done? (the technique). . . . And emotions are *post hoc* & not *propter hoc* – i.e. consequences not causes.'[32]

One wonders if he meant this argument to apply equally to his markedly erotic work too. However, on those illustrations for which Gill is best, and deservedly, known Mackley puts the choice before us succinctly: 'Gill's work does not please those who are interested in a variety of texture, in spontaneous expression or in subtle relationships of tone. It appeals to those whose delight is in reading a beautiful page.'[33]

Girl in leaves, device used in *Uncle Dottery* by T.F. Powys (1931), wood-engraving, 2.5cm × 5cm

Sculpture and architecture

Until about 1909 Gill's work was primarily with lettering, on stone, shop-fronts, and books, whilst anything to do with the human figure he thought of as another trade. He called in a sculptor friend to carve the cherubs or angels if the customer demanded these on a tombstone. He was drawing such things as flowers, but with no straining after realism, only trying to render them heraldically and for this one needed to understand the subject and then communicate this understanding by drawing the thing as it *is*, not as it appears to be. Finally, what broke through his irrational prejudice that sculpture of the figure was somehow different and needed to be naturalistic was the fact that Mary became pregnant. The 'comparative continence' so imposed meant that he tried hard to be a modern Pygmalion, 'as I couldn't have all I wanted in one way I determined to see what I could do about it in another – I fashioned a woman of *stone*. Up to that time, I had never made what is called an "erotic" drawing of any sort and least of all in so laborious a medium as stone. And so, just as on the first occasion when with immense planning and scheming, I touched my lover's lovely body, I insisted on seeing her completely naked (no peeping between the uncut pages, so to say), so my first erotic drawing was not on the back of an envelope but a week or so's work on a decent piece of hard stone.'[1]

He remembered only then that the medieval artists had a continuity of approach in both their drawings and their figure sculpture – neither being slavishly realistic. This first carving, called pretentiously enough, 'Estin Thalassa',* is a dwarfish little figure 'with no waist to speak of' cramped in a triangle and holding up the Greek words of her title. However, it impressed Count Kessler, Roger Fry and William Rothenstein so, 'I went home very much

---

* The full quotation used might be translated as: There is the sea; and who will dry her up; i.e. the undying sea.

bucked and determined to do it again as often as possible'.
His next effort was a Madonna and Child and then, Mary
having given birth, a series of Mother and Child figures in
all of which the full-breasted mother suckles her child.
His lack of art-school training in life-drawing and
technique is turned into a positive asset in these charming
little works and he realized for himself, 'Stone carving
properly speaking isn't just doing things in stone or
turning things into stone, a sort of petrifying process;
stone carving is *conceiving* things in stone and conceiving
them as made by *carving*. They are not only born but
conceived in stone; they are stone in their innermost
being as well as their outermost existence.'[2]

There were no other artists thinking like this in the

Mother and Child (1912?), brass,
16.5cm × 5.4cm × 4.2cm

London art world at this time so he found himself taken up by the fashionable trend setters. Rothenstein noted in a letter of March 5th 1910 that 'Fry in a rash moment praised him [Gill] to Lady Ottoline [Morrell], who immediately found his things too inexpressively beautiful and is now universally eloquent on the subject to all and sundry.'[3] Other critics were less kind and assumed he was deliberately being naïve or archaic or Byzantine, 'whereas the real and complete truth was that I was completely ignorant of all their art stuff and was deliberately doing my utmost to copy accurately in stone what I saw in my head'.[4] When that vision failed he or his friends could always strip off to refresh his memory of what was joined to what. From this start his work increased in volume so much he could have a one-man show in January 1911 and he could be invited to show eight pieces in Fry's second Post-Impressionist Show at the Grafton Gallery in 1912. In the opinions of Mark Gertler and Rupert Brooke Gill more than held his own alongside the Post-Impressionists, Cubists and Fauves on show. As we shall see Gill too felt fairly superior to his Continental rivals, feeling by then that he was his own man with a personal vision and style to develop.

This determination to think things out for himself appeared in another incident when his patron Count Kessler arranged for Gill to meet and assist Maillol (1861–1944), a sculptor whom he knew Gill admired. Some sculptors are primarily carvers (Moore, Hepworth, Modigliani, Brancusi), and others modellers (Rodin, Epstein, Giacometti, Degas), and Maillol was definitely a modeller. From his clay or plaster models assistants would work up his finished stone statues by use of a 'pointing' machine, a simple mechanical measuring device which enabled them to reproduce the clay shape in stone. This machine had been in extensive use since the eighteenth century, but Wittkower suggests the Greeks might have already had such a device by the first century B.C.[5] Kessler hired a house for the Gill family near Marly-le-Roi and took Gill over and put him up at the Grand Hotel in Paris. Gill became steadily more depressed by the pomp of the hotel, and the prospect of exchanging

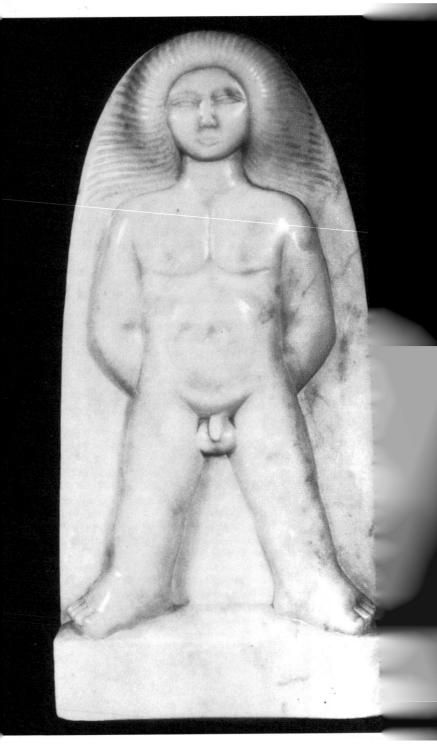

Cupid (1910), Portland stone,
28cm × 13.5cm × 9.5cm

Ditchling for a French suburban villa, so in the end he jumped on the next boat home and ran away. Gill was right, for though he admitted, 'in his own line of business . . . Aristide Maillol is the greatest man in the world,' he knew he would learn nothing about the technicalities of carving from Maillol and would be better off to apprentice himself to an ordinary monumental mason. Gill already knew he was totally in the carver's camp. Artistically too he was in danger of being swamped by the older man's vision, which in many ways was very like his own, for 'one *must* be in opposition and achieve whatever is possible through my own struggles, in my own battle with life'. Gill's integrity got him through a difficult episode and he still retained the friendship of both Kessler and Maillol. Oddly enough Henry Moore later received an introduction to Maillol from William Rothenstein, and he too was overcome by shyness and doubts on the threshold and turned away.[6]

Gill was not opposed to modelling as a means of making sculpture, and was very sharp with William Rothenstein for suggesting he was. 'I have never said or thought that modelling was sinful or even silly. On the contrary, I have frequently said and written that carving and modelling are two arts, each having its own proper and good qualities – as is obvious.'[7] Indeed he did a few small clay and plaster works himself but he obviously did not hold modelling in very high regard as we can see in the essay 'Stone Carving' (1921).

What Gill objected to was the translation of clay maquettes into stone sculptures by artisans with mechanical aids. This process made the artist a mere designer and perpetuator of the division of labour which pervaded the whole of industrial society. What Gill was asking for was that the unity of a work should be achieved by one responsible man working from inspiration to execution in one medium. Drawings had to be provided for clients, naturally, and if trial versions were necessary then a smaller version, say of one inch to one foot, could be cut in a softer stone. Indeed some of Gill's freshest works are these smaller trials where the inspiration is still new and the finish need not be so smooth (e.g. 'Prospero and Ariel'

Lovers (date unknown), bas-relief
38.5cm × 19.5cm × 7.5cm

Adam and Eve (date unknown),
42cm × 28cm × 7.6cm (*right*)

and 'The East Wind', both in the Tate Gallery). This
return to direct carving, as it is called, is to return to the
methods used from the earliest times up to the eighteenth
century and comes back to the Latin root *sculpere* to carve.
Several writers make claims like the following: 'At the
time when the late Eric Gill began the revival of direct
carving, no 'artist' had carved in stone for a period of
nearly two hundred years. In the year 1909 he became the
first man in modern times to carve a figure directly in
stone.'[8] Whether this is literally true is difficult to
establish, though his advocacy of it was very influential in
England. Ruskin had preached the doctrine as early as the
1880s and Hildebrand (1847–1921) and Barlach
(1870–1938) had practised it on the Continent. Of the
next generation Brancusi and Modigliani both worked
direct into the block and Arp followed them. In England
Epstein, Gaudier-Brzeska and Dobson also were strong
propagandists for it, and the younger sculptors such as
Moore, Hepworth and Skeaping took it up with fanatical
zeal. Most of these sculptors, however, adopted it because
they admired primitive Mexican, African, Pacific or
European works all of which were directly carved with no
preliminary drawings or maquettes, and often in wood
rather than stone. In 1952 Barbara Hepworth still
believed 'carving is to me a necessary approach – one facet
of the whole idea which will remain valid for all time. It is
in fact a biological necessity as it is concerned with aspects
of living from which we cannot afford to be deprived.'[9]
On a less elevated level carving is very hard work and
perhaps the satisfaction a sculptor gets from it is
proportional to the sweat he sheds.

This revival of a neglected way of working was timely,
but in retrospect Henry Moore thought: 'gradually you
find that these simple-minded crusades always leave
something out. So now I don't believe that direct carving
in itself produces good sculpture; it doesn't. What
produces good sculpture is a good mind. You don't make
a good sculpture just by using a certain process, although
it could help.'[10] Moore himself moved on to hand-sized
plaster maquettes which could be built up or carved away
at will so the whole process was in three-dimensions from

Prospero and Ariel (1931), Caen stone,
127cm × 46cm × 36cm (N.B. the
stigmata on Ariel.)

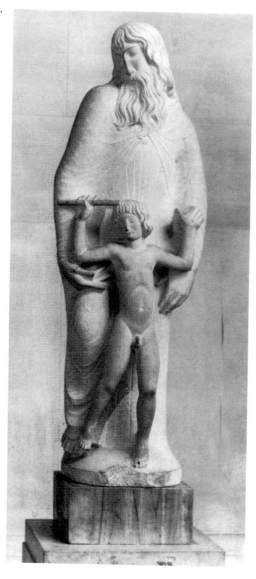

the start, with not even a preliminary drawing.

Stone imposes its own limitations on the sculptor, so few of Gill's works are pierced or have freely moving limbs or centres of gravity outside the base – all things better achieved with clay on an armature, or with light hollow bronze. The sculptor had to collaborate with his material rather than impose ideas upon it which were inappropriate to its strength, texture, or surface. The mind says what to make, but the stone says how. Anthony Foster, a former apprentice tells us Gill 'took stone as it came. No piece was a bad piece for him – difficult maybe, but with its own divinely ordained qualities which made each carving a work of discovering the idea in that particular material.'[12] This is the 'truth to materials' belief which also occupied the minds of sculptors early this century, and is obviously related to the belief in direct carving. Stone does not look like hair or flesh or fur or leaves – though in looking at a Bernini one might be fooled into thinking it did. Gill said stone should look like stone, but then he seemed to contradict himself by painting many of his works. There is of course a long tradition from the earliest Greeks to the Renaissance of painting statues, all over, or with touches of gold or colour. Gill revived this practice by touching up lips, eyes, nipples, hair, bangles, necklaces and lettering, often to the detriment of the work. This, however, was a fashion the other major sculptors did not follow.

As we have seen Gill's reputation as a sculptor was quickly established. When he became a Roman Catholic in 1913 his new Church was not slow to find him work. He was commissioned to carve the fourteen 'Stations of the Cross' to be placed on the pillars of the newly completed Westminster Cathedral. The building was designed by J.F. Bentley in a semi-Byzantine style and was in use before the interior was decorated, indeed he left the detail of this vague with the idea that it would be completed as funds allowed. He died before much could be done leaving the interior of plain brick and the roof domes in concrete. Gill's attitude to this building seems equivocal. On the one hand he wrote: 'I hold that Westminster Cathedral is as disgraceful a piece of sham stylistic

Headless female torso on base
(c.1920?), high relief from single block
of Portland stone, painted nipples,
45.7cm × 17cm × 13cm

Station IV of the Stations of the Cross, Westminster Cathedral (1914–18), Hoptonwood stone, 170cm × 170cm

building as any Pugin Gothic. It is endurable because brick and concrete construction happens to be a suitable method for industrial building. The outside of the building is absurd. The inside will soon be equally so. As to Brompton Oratory the same applies. It is a fine spacious and well-proportioned church but architecturally it is a sheer nonsense. The virtue of medieval building was that it represents the builders as much as those who paid for it. Both Brompton Oratory and Westminster represent the snobbery of those who paid.'[12]

On the other hand in an essay 'Westminster Cathedral'[13] he concedes Bentley's 'noble plan', 'great interior space' and 'great Building' in spite of its dead ornament, the absurdity of the plan to cover the interior walls with marble and mosaic, and, of course, the evil of using a servile and irresponsible workforce degraded by industrial society. In 1935 when the authorities were rattled by the opposition to the mosaics Gill's opinion was sought. He supported Lethaby's plan that the whole interior should be whitewashed – a suggestion too drastic for the authorities to follow. In spite of these reservations the young Gill was delighted by his commission. 'But I really was the boy for the job, because I not only had a proper Christian enthusiasm but I had sufficient, if only just sufficient, technical ability combined with a complete and genuine ignorance of art-school anatomy and traditional academic style. Of course they didn't know this. They thought I was carving in the Byzantine style on purpose! Certainly I was carving in what might be called an archaic manner; but I wasn't doing it on purpose, but only because I couldn't carve in any other way.'[14] He was also cheaper than the 'posh' sculptors. Gill carved the Stations in a random order starting with the tenth until the whole fourteen were in place by March 1918. The four years' work meant Gill had virtually missed the war, both physically and mentally. The Stations are 5′ 8″ square, of Hoptonwood stone and are fixed well above eye-level on the massive brick piers of the Cathedral nave. Each has a differently designed border and each has a Latin inscription amongst the figures and an English title at the base. They are in very shallow relief. Gill tried heraldic colours on them at first, blues and reds and greens, though he later erased these. After his death the authorities filled in the lettering with red and added gilding and black, but even so they still look remarkably restrained against the rest of the church furniture.

Relief sculpture suited both the building and Gill's own developing strengths as a sculptor. As Farr comments, 'Gill's hard linear style is well suited to the conventions of bas-relief carving, for even in his free-standing pieces there is often a flattening of the frontal planes, a conscious underemphasis of plasticity, that seems to keep the figures still imprisoned in the slab from which it was carved. This predilection for limited three-dimensional volumes was carried over from Gill's early training as a monumental mason and letterer.'[15] Reliefs need clear and definite edges to catch the light (and Gill complained constantly about the light in the Westminster Cathedral nave) and the lateral movement of the figures and their recession in the shallow space have to be almost diagrammatically indicated. Eric Gill's drawings of this period are virtually diagrams and are particularly

VIDEBUNT IN QVEM TRANS-
FIXERUNT

XI JESUS IS NAILED TO THE CROSS

suited in their style to the task in hand.

First reactions to the works were about equally for and against, many taking the view of the lady who interrupted Gill at work to say she did not like them, 'I don't think they're nice.' Gill replied, 'Madam, I don't think the subject is nice.' McGreevy took up the charge of 'Byzantinism' and pointed out that real Byzantine works are characterized by their immobility, whereas the incidents along the Via Dolorosa demand a variety of expression and movement. 'Gill compromised. He represented the figures in attitudes that imply movement, but he made the draperies fall in folds that do give weight and dignity to the design, but concede too little to the lines of the figure beneath. And similarly in the matter of expression he

Station XI of Stations of the Cross, Westminster Cathedral (1914–18), Hoptonwood stone, 170cm × 170cm

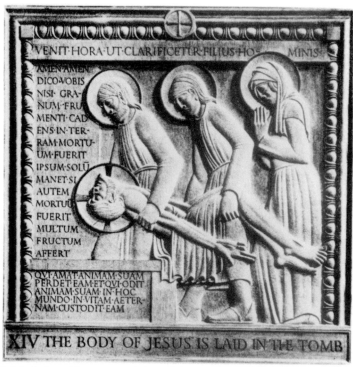

VENIT·HORA·UT·CLARIFICETUR·FILIUS·HO   MINIS·

AMEN·AMEN·
DICO·VOBIS
NISI· GRA-
NUM·FRU
MENTI·CAD
ENS·IN·TER-
RAM·MORTU-
UM·FUERIT
IPSUM·SOLU
MANET·SI
AUTEM
MORTUU
FUERIT
MULTUM·
FRUCTUM
AFFERT

QVI·AMAT·ANIMAM·SUAM
PERDET·EAM·ET·QVI·ODIT
ANIMAM·SUAM· IN·HOC
MUNDO·IN·VITAM·AETER-
NAM·CUSTODIT·EAM

XIV THE BODY OF JESUS IS LAID IN THE TOMB

Station XIV of the Stations of the Cross, Westminster Cathedral (1914–18), Hoptonwood stone, 170cm × 170cm

conceded a minimum only to the human drama, yet conceding so much brings his conception somewhere below the level of the "sublime". This is, of course, to judge the then youthful artist by the very highest standards, and if we take into account the fact that in 1913, when the Stations were begun, sculpture in England as a whole was still to all intents and purposes Victorian and academic, Gill's fourteen reliefs in the great church constitute a unique and outstanding achievement.'[16] This seems a fair judgement on the Stations as works of art. For Gill though, such a judgement would miss the point. Writing under the pseudonym of E. Rowton he explained his intentions in the *Westminster Cathedral Chronicle* (March 1918 pages 50–53). The works are a necessary part of the furniture of the church, a means to inspire devotion, not an occasion for idle sightseeing or aesthetic judgements. They are there to promote the Church's ideas, not the artist's, who is totally subject in these to religious authority and had checked their orthodoxy at each stage. As he never tired of repeating, 'The Catholic artist is only free in the sense that he is free to run on rails'.[17] Deliberately he left aside 'all personal fancies as to physiognomy, costume or emotional expression', for 'they are meant to be in stone what in words we call "plain language".' The spectator is put in the position of the crowd on the Calvary road and as a worshipper he has to bring his own feelings to the Stations. 'They are like the beads of a Rosary; he must say his own Aves and make his own meditation.' Gill writes it is no business of his to provide emotions for people – that is just another aspect of the modern tendency to pay others to do everything for us, whether to play games, or entertain us, or to allow the state to feed our children. In this way the music, images, decorations and architecture of the modern Church have become more and more over-rhetorical, emotional and sentimental (hence the demand for a vernacular mass) in an attempt to spoon-feed people. Given these views the sheer cool restraint of Gill's Stations is explicable on other than aesthetic grounds.

This Giottesque dignity and unfussy technique characterizes Gill's work for all denominations of churches. Gregory I's pronouncement that pictures in churches were there not for worship but to instruct the minds of the illiterate applies to all Gill's ecclesiastical work, whether grave-stones or crucifixes. Gill echoed Gregory in saying that all art is religious because it *is* worship, not *for* worship. Religious art is rhetorical, propaganda art and a 'better crucifix nourishes the soul better than an inferior one'.[18] This direct teaching function is nowhere better illustrated than in his open letter to the parishioners of St Andrew's Church Croydon[19] explaining detail by detail what his work for them *means*, and how to read it.

The Westminster Stations brought a request in 1919 from his friend Fr O'Connor to provide some for his

Crucifix (1925), Portland stone with
painted hair and wounds, made in two
pieces: lower 120cm × 24cm × 6.3cm,
upper, 95cm × 95cm × 6.3cm

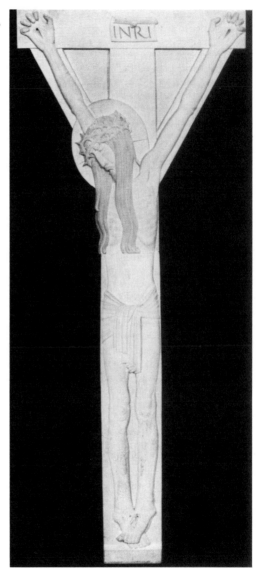

church St Cuthbert's in Bradford. These are in Beer Stone, 30″ by 30″ and are based on designs by Desmond Chute. These are less complicated, less moulded, with less fussy borders, and the lettering does not get between the figures so much as in the Westminster works. The experience gained has led to increased simplification – though how the Greek script used can be reconciled with the 'propaganda' function is not obvious!

Other ecclesiastical commissions include a large Calvary group on the outside of St Thomas' Hanwell Middlesex, a font at Pickering Yorkshire, a St Dominic for the Dominican study-centre in Oxford, a splendid St John for the gateway of St John's College, Oxford, and another for the Anglican cathedral at Guildford. Further designs for Guildford had to be completed after his death by his assistant Anthony Foster.

Gill's later connections with Westminster Cathedral were not so happy. He was commissioned to carve St John Fisher and St Thomas More for the altar of the Chapel of English Martyrs. Gill depicted More's pet monkey clinging to his robe to indicate the humane character of the saint. At his death the sculpture was not quite finished so Laurie Cribb perfected it and it lay about at Pigotts until its installation at the end of the war. It was then noticed that the monkey had been carved off at the orders of some tactless but nameless cleric. This shocked his friends, but would probably have not disturbed Gill too much: 'Speaking as a sculptor (artist) I maintain that if a man buys from me a statue and does not like the shape of any part of it he is quite at liberty to remove that part or alter it or do anything he jolly well pleases. All this talk about the sanctity of the work of artists, as though it could be claimed that artists were directly inspired by the Holy Ghost, is, I think, flat nonsense.'[20] This applies equally to Michelangelo's Sistine paintings or the 'throttle valves' in our motor cars. Just as well, since his central altar for Blundells School, Tiverton which the pupils helped him build in their chapel was subsequently taken away and is now, according to Speaight, in a home for unmarried mothers. A Madonna and Child over the west door of St Mary's, Glastonbury, was found not conventional enough and ended up as a headstone in a Cambridge cemetery.

While these large ecclesiastical works were under way Gill still maintained a steady trickle of smaller works, usually for his own pleasure rather than for clients in the first instance, though of course he subsequently exhibited and sold them privately or in galleries. Augustus John acting as a kind of advisor and agent to the American collector John Quinn did not share Fry's enthusiasm for them.

'Personally I don't admire the things and feel pretty certain that you wouldn't either. I admit that Gill is an enterprising young man and not without ability. He has been a carver of inscriptions until quite recently when he started doing figures. His knowledge of human form is, you may be sure, of the slightest and I feel strongly that his experience of human beings is anything but profound. I know him personally. He carves well and succeeds in expressing one or two cut-and-dried philosophical ideas. He is much impressed by the importance of copulation possibly because he has had so little to do with that subject in practice, and apparently considers himself obliged to announce the gospel of the flesh, to a world that doesn't need it. Innes calls him 'the naughty schoolmaster,' Gore calls him 'the precious Cockney' and I call him 'the artist of the Urinal' . . . I'll let you know when I see a thing of Gill's which I can really respect and admire. His present things are taking at first glance as they look so simple and unsophisticated – but, to me at least, only at first glance.'[21]

Three years later in January 1914 Gill's work had so gained in assurance that John could write to Quinn, 'I also ordered you one of Gill's things, a dancing figure in stone . . . Gill has made good progress and his things are admirable now, both in workmanship and idea.' The 'Dancer' John bought is a rhythmic little piece already displaying the stylized hair and drapery which are marks of Gill's mature style. Figures in movement or in strained positions pre-occupy him at this early period such as 'The

Contortionist' (1910), 'The Tumbler' (1913), and
'Boxers' (1913). This interest persisted so that his
headless, legless, crouching 'Adam and Eve' (1920)
grapple each other as if for the best of three falls, but still
make a satisfying interplay of shapes. 'The Splits
(Seated)'* and 'The Splits (Standing)' both of 1923 are
nowhere near as satisfying, being rather lumpy maidens
in painted Beer Stone doing quite unlikely things in order
to display their pudenda to best advantage.

Throughout his career Gill carved female nudes such
as 'Torso and Head' (1913), 'Torso' (1920), and 'The
Head-dress' (1928) which may be in humbler stones than
the Victorian Academician's marble confectioneries, but
which differ little from them in subject, treatment, and
sweetness. Gaudier-Brzeska reviewing a sculpture exhibition in 1914, which may well have contained some of
Gill's nudes, wrote scornfully that apart from his own and
Zadkine's work, 'The rest of the sculpture is an agglomer-
ation of Rodin–Maillol mixture and valueless academism
– with here and there some one trying to be naughty:
curled nubilities and discreet slits.'[22] As Ezra Pound
points out, 'We all of us like the caressable, but we most of
us in the long run prefer the woman to the statue'[23] – so of
course, did Gill, but here he is surely trying too hard to
make his Galatea speak. The female heads also suffer
from this prettiness and Gill's habit of painting bits of
their anatomies only adds to the feeling of tartiness they
have, at least for me. Perhaps we should exempt from
these strictures the 'Girl in Capel-y-ffin stone' (1925)
where the contrast between the rougher stylized hair and
the rhythms of the smoother body work very well indeed.
The Bath Stone 'Anadyomene' (a real Academy title) of
1920 barely emerges from the rough block and avoids a
too easy 'caressability'. 'Tobias and Sara' (1926) succeeds
in parts but narrowly avoids absurdity in having two
identical profiles and Sara's painted nipples exactly echo
the painted eye-balls so one seems to be seeing double, or

---

* According to his first notes and drawings this was originally destined
for the 'top of handsome marble clock'. Instead it is now on a shelf in
Texas University with a broken foot. The companion piece was even
more badly damaged in transport and awaits restoration.

Splits no. 2 (1923), Beer stone,
awaiting restoration

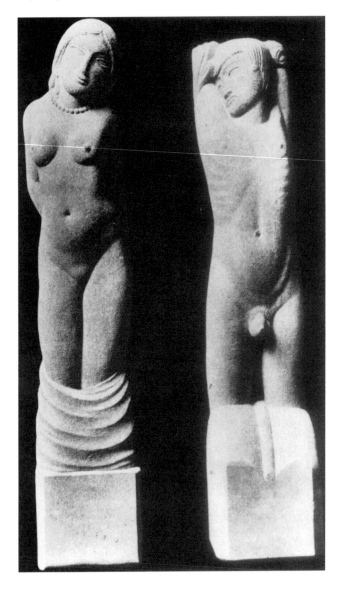

Adam and Eve (1928), Bath stone.
Eve: 64cm × 15cm × 15cm; Adam:
79cm × 16cm × 14.5cm (*left*)

St Sebastian (1919–20), Portland stone,
100.3cm × 20.3cm × 25.4cm

even triple. In all these, however, Gill seems to have forgotten his own invective against the belief that beautiful works come from beautiful subjects, or that art should be related to use rather than merely destined for the museum or the 'little home museum of the mantel shelf.'

The male nudes are more robust. I consider the 'Adam' (1928), now in Texas, to be superior to the companion piece 'Eve' (1928) in the Tate. Both are set up to their knees in the block, but Eve is noticeable for the over-use of the drill to create shadows in the pubic area. 'St Sebastian' (1919–20) has a similar pose to the Adam with hands clasped behind the head and the nude body following a graceful curve towards the spectator. Gill modelled this figure on himself, as he wrote to its purchaser André Raffalovich.[24] In spite of its title there is not a scrap of religious feeling about the work. In this Gill has followed the Renaissance tradition of showing him as a graceful nude young man (but here minus the arrows) rather than the medieval tradition in which he appeared as older, bearded and clothed. The original saint was a captain of the Praetorian Guard under the third-century emperor Diocletian condemned to be shot for his Christian faith. When this failed to kill him he was bludgeoned to death and thrown in the main sewer of Rome. The medieval artists did not shirk the full cycle of his sufferings nor put him in such a camp pose as Gill has done.[25]

A similarly languidly curving nude is the black marble 'Deposition' of 1924. This Gill considered his best work – 'about the only carving of mine I'm not sorry about. It's now at the King's School Canterbury and that seems a decent home for it. This carving, very appropriately, was done in the coal cellar because I had, at that time, nowhere else to work.'[26] The Christ is young, untroubled by his ordeal, and seems to be sleeping, though in an upright pose cut off at knees and right elbow. The figure is two feet high in shallow relief carved at both sides and highly polished.

The 'Sleeping Christ' of 1924 is a head and hand only with sensual lips, stylized hair and the serenest of

Torso Deposition (1924), black Hoptonwood stone, 76cm × 30cm × 10cm (*left*)

expressions. Perhaps this is the one referred to in the following incident. 'He had been carving a head of Christ and came into the living room for tea looking, as he often did, extremely tired. After explaining his difficulties, he broke into a smile. "Never mind," he said shyly, "He assured me it was alright".'[27] Another work which must have given him pleasure was 'The Foster-Father' (1923) carved to celebrate the adoption of Gordian. It is simple, direct, and moving.

Many of these works, especially the early ones, are very small, some only six inches high. All are presented frontally with no great complexity in the inter-relationships of the planes, or movement about an axis. They are simply conceived, unfussily executed, and sometimes doll-like in their seeming naïveté. Many are missing limbs or hands or heads – a trick learned from Rodin. At best they look as if they had just been dug up or fallen off a medieval cathedral roof and lost a limb

The sleeping Christ (1925), Caen stone, 30.6cm × 43.3cm × 9.2cm

through the accidents of time – the extremity is implied rather than present. In other instances it looks awkwardly as if inspiration, or the block, did not stretch that far.

Other minor works include a fifteen by seven foot frieze for the Morecambe Hotel on the unlikely theme of 'Odysseus and Nausicaa'. It does not look as if Gill's heart was in it. Another is a rather Disney-like crocodile on the walls of what is now the Department of Aerial Photography in Cambridge. Gill had little feeling for animals and usually left these to assistants such as Laurie Cribb. An early (1912) attempt at 'The Golden Calf' in gilded stone looks for all the world like a fancy milk-jug.

Gill's work is largely in stone, usually Portland, Beer, Bath or Hoptonwood but he also did small works in plaster, ivory and brass. His works in wood, a medium sometimes more difficult to handle than stone since it is neither inert nor homogeneous, are few but they are impressive. The haloed hugging figures of 'The Divine Lovers' (1922) in boxwood are a very satisfactory relief composition. The 'Caryatid' (1927) now in California is carved from a massive eight-foot-high log of Wellingtonia pine.* This approaches in its monumentality and simplification the work of Henry Moore and makes one regret that Gill did not work more often in this manner and this medium. Other more 'applied' works include a painted grandfather clock last exhibited in the Hayward Gallery in 1979, and a carved oak bed-head for his American friend Graham Carey in 1929. This has three relief panels showing 'child-bed', 'marriage-bed' and 'death-bed' scenes with appropriate Latin inscriptions. Insofar as one can judge from photographs[28] it is a superb piece of craftsmanship, in spite of Gill's own modest disclaimer to Carey that, 'it will be evident to you that I am a very inexpert wood carver'.[29] Another major work is the Rossall School War Memorial, seven feet wide by three feet high in oak. This is a triptych in six sections with the fifteen figures skilfully disposed across the panels in poses of great variety and contrast. It is a masterpiece of its kind.

* Or, as the Americans insist, Redwood.

Caryatid (1927), Wellingtonia pine, 214cm × 35.7cm × 30.6cm

Clock designed and painted by Gill
(1930), 168cm × 44.6cm × 10.2cm

HIC·NATITUR·DOLORE SAD·CAPIENDVS·PER
HIC·RENOVATVR·IN·AMORE SPONSALI·GENVS·HOMINVM
HIC·TANDEM·OBRIG SCIMVS·MORTE·PŒN

PARTVM·VIRGINEVGV PLVSNENNA·RVBILIA
MORTALE·PER·SPONSALIA· CHRISTI·PER·ECCLESIA·MIRIFIC ·ECCELCOLAMVS·IMMORTALE
PECCATI·PER·ADESCVL PAVPERES·VRRECTIC XI·PORTA·SOLAVITI·E

Three panels representing Birth, Marriage and Death carved on a bedhead (1929–30), oak. The two outside panels are 30.6cm × 26.7cm and the centre one 31.8cm × 36.9cm. These were carved by Gill, but the carpentry and letter cutting was carried out by Romney Green

After the carnage of the First World War virtually every village and institution in England wished to commemorate its dead with a memorial. These were invariably commissioned by a committee seeking a safe academic rendering and few have much merit as works of art, or move us by their poignancy. Gill and his assistants provided numerous crosses, memorials, plaques and monuments across the whole of southern England each marked by an undemonstrative honesty and clarity which raise them well above the average of such works. Examples can be seen at Chirk near Wrexham, Bisham near Marlow,* South Harting near Petersfield, Trumpington near Cambridge, and a Cross at Bryantspuddle Dorset, all dating from the 1917–1920 period.

In 1916 Gill submitted a design for a colossal bronze memorial for the dead employees of the London County Council. This design came to him 'quite of its own accord, apparently' whilst having his portrait drawn by William Rothenstein when he had determined to think about women ('in some detail') instead.[30] The subject was Christ expelling the Money-changers from the Temple. This was rejected; 'p'raps they took fright,' speculated Gill, 'or were insulted at the awful suggestion that London were a commercial city or that England were a Temple from which a money-changer or two might not be missed.'[31] However, Michael Sadler, the Vice-Chancellor of Leeds University liked the idea and asked Gill to carry the idea through in stone for his university, and at a fee of £1,000. Here at last was the chance to make a public statement in stone of his religious and political beliefs – and how often does such a chance come a sculptor's way?

Sadler was a knowledgeable patron of the arts having already bought works by the young Henry Moore who described him as 'a man who had bought Cézanne and Gauguin before 1914, and translated Kandinsky, and really knew what was going on in modern art'.[32] He was also an adept organizer and able to get his ideas through university committees. He was to need all his diplomacy before the memorial was finally unveiled.

Gill's ideas seem to have centred on this incident in Christ's life. He had already done a wood-engraving (1919) of this one 'occasion upon which God, in the form of Christ, used violence to enforce his will. Thus for all time the use of violence in a just cause is made lawful.'[33] He had also used it as an image in a savage letter to Raffalovitch after hearing of the destruction of Rheims and Louvain, places we had turned from Temples into museums full of 'priceless treasures'. 'I have often said we had need to construct a whip of thongs wherewith to drive the money-changers out of the Temple of England. God has found a whip of German guns wherewith to deprive the money changers of the temples of France. Why should Paris be indignant? What was Rheims to it? A blooming museum – a kind of provincial branch of the Louvre. I do not care. The sculptures of Rheims are gone. Good. If we cannot construct a Christian Europe in this age, we are certainly not fit to be the guardians of the evidences of the Christian Europe of the past. The whole thing should be wiped out. It would be completely just. When we want an altar we can build one. And when God has finished with this whip He will discard it. May we deserve to be His instruments.'[34] Given the opportunity

by Sadler he saw 'here is the sermon given into my hands so to say'. He wrote that 'I'm thinking of making it a pretty straight thing – modern dress as much as poss., Leeds manufacturers, their wives & servants, don't you see', and confessed with glee that 'as "citizen of this great country" and member of Christ's Bride, I rather like the job of, the revolutionary job of turning out the money changers'.[35] When Sadler steered the design through the university committee Gill commented to Fr O'Connor, 'By Jove! Will they stick that cornice inscription? What price James, V.1. If they stick that they'll stick anything.' The inscription Gill hoped to goad the rich Yorkshire merchants with was, 'Go to now, you rich men, weep and howl in your miseries which shall come upon you. Your riches are putrid,' but he took care to keep it (and John II.15) in Latin. He no doubt saw himself as the dog with the burning torch in its mouth which he carved following the indignant Christ in the frieze – the dog of the Lord (*domini canes*) from which the Dominicans take their name. This chases and burns the heels of the retreating Fashionable Woman, Pawnbroker, Pawnbroker's Clerk, Politician and two 'nondescript Financiers'.

The local Conservative press, predictably enough, did not like the modern dress (spats, vanity bag, feathery hat,

Rossall School War Memorial (1927), oak, 101.6cm × 22.1cm × 5.1cm

Christ's boots), the pawnbroker's sign, the cash-book with LSD on it, and the moral pointed at the local rich manufacturers who had after all benefited the university, lost their sons in the war, and paid for the memorial. Few could take Gill's vastly over-simplified view that the war was a simple struggle between Justice and Cupidity. Sadler continued to negotiate and placate, only to have Gill publish an explanatory pamphlet which was both flippant and patronizing in tone,[36] and which inflamed further those who thought a war memorial dedicated to the memory of dead patriots an inappropriate place for an 'illustration' (as Gill called it). However, the memorial was eventually unveiled on June 1st 1923 on a site near the university library.

In retrospect Gill thought, 'Yes, Leeds was an amusing business. How they did take on! It's "all quiet" now, apparently. The carving was really good in parts – but I found it difficult to be very enthusiastic about it myself. It seemed a failure – lacking much beauty as a whole – how much better if the figures had filled the panel to the top thereof.'[37] When Gill died Sadler wrote in his private diary: 'Eric Gill is dead. A fine draughtsman, a vain poseur, a tiresome writer. . . . He departed egregiously (without telling me until it was too late) from the earlier design he had chosen. And he broke his word by publishing at the worst moment of acute controversy, and sending down to Leeds, a contentious political interpretation of the Memorial's significance. He behaved like a

Leeds University War Memorial (1922–3), Portland stone, 168.3cm × 459cm

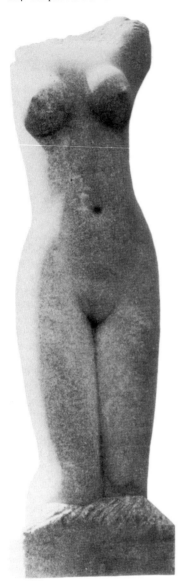

Mankind (1927–8), Hoptonwood stone,
241.5cm × 61cm × 48cm

vain, wilful child. The Memorial is a fine piece of work,
but not nearly as good as it might have been. The mood is
too obviously underlined.'[38] This may seem harsh to
many of Gill's surviving friends, but there is no doubt
that Gill did not come out of the incident altogether well.

This sermon in stone survived a subsequent Vice-
Chancellor's attempt to choke it with ivy and its later
move indoors. It is now approached down a broad shallow
flight of steps into the dim foyer of the Arts Building. The
work is set on the ground, and being only 5′6″ high it
seems to me to be on the wrong scale making the figures
dwarfish and enacting their little drama below eye-level.
Several of the details and handling of perspective are very
awkward and in close up the surface is now chipped and
scaly. Still, there is a rhythm and haste to the money
changers' retreat before the vigorous swing of Christ's
whip. One suspects it attracts few glances and no
controversy today.

One work which now attracts no glances at all is the one
single work for which Gill earned most critical acclaim in
his life time. This is 'Mankind' (1927) which I tracked
down to the Tate Gallery's store on an industrial estate in
North Acton. This is a female nude eight feet high lacking
head, arms, or feet. Unfortunately, it is now turned to the
warehouse wall, immovable, forgotten, and has not been
displayed, or even unwrapped, for many years. In its day
its massive classical calm excited much admiration and it
was seen as evidence that Gill could, if he wished, carve a
figure which was truly in the round. Critics were not slow
to compare it to the best of Maillol, and indeed the pose
does resemble his bronze torso 'Ile de France' of 1921.
Even Gill seemed overwhelmed by the enthusiastic
response when it was shown at the Goupil Gallery in
1928. '. . . the blooming show is an absurd success –
monstrous. Approbation galore and you know what
absurd things critics say when they try and in the
mundane sphere: well, we look like clearing a thousand
pounds – fancy that! a lot of things have sold. For the big
figure I carved in that big lump of Hoptonwood which I
had and never used at Ditchling I'm getting £800 . . .
Eric Kennington is buying it (Rotten bad photos of it in

Illust London News & in *Sphere*. Notice in *Times* really very decent, also *M'chester Guardian* little to complain of.'³⁹

He was able to pay off debts of £375 and to put down a £500 deposit towards the £1750 Pigotts cost in 1928 – that is for two large barns, stables, a farm house, two cottages, a chapel, an orchard and sixteen acres of grass. As he said of the 'Mankind' sale, 'If this isn't providential – what, oh, what is.' Providential, but also deserved, as this work simplifies the body without losing its sensuous quality, and is massive in conception as well as scale. It seems a pity that such a major work is not on public display, especially as its only precursor, the stiffly columnar and frontal 'Mulier' of 1914, which is over seven feet tall, is now set so superbly over a reflecting pool in the Sculpture Garden of The University of California in Los Angeles. The two works hardly deserve their respective fates.

On the other hand 'The Crucifixion' of 1910, which is also in the same Acton warehouse, is best left where it is. It is badly cracked, a dull concrete colour, and seems to me to be totally inept. It is all very well for Gill to claim 'A crucifixion is not a versimilitude of the crucifixion. And even in a picture of the crucifixion the anatomical exactitudes are obviously a frivolity,' but here the tubular, tapering legs and microscopic genitals seem to distract from any reverence it is meant to evoke. However, the very peculiar choice of supporting texts, Psalm 147.10 and Matthew XIX.12 might go some way towards explaining these distortions.

As we have seen Gill made free-standing 'gallery' sculptures, open air memorials and works to go inside churches. Another possible source of income was work meant to combine with modern secular architecture. Gill's early training in an architect's office and his rather late vocation as a sculptor meant he had much to say about both, separately and in combination.⁴⁰ His thoughts here are strongly worded but repetitious so what follows is an attempt to summarize many thousands of words. As one might predict his arguments rest upon an abhorrence of sham and a need for truth to material.

Mulier (1914) approx. 215cm high

Architecture is the type and mother of all the arts in combining to the highest degree what is useful and what is delightful. It is above all a social art in both its making and its setting (unlike music or painting which can be made and enjoyed privately), and therefore must reflect the modern society in which it is set rather than any past, dead society. The architect's job is to do the best he can with his resources including the human resources which are now 'hands', 'factory coolies', a 'crowd of unintelligent and unwilling wage earners', rather than being both the architect and builder and the leader of a gang of good responsible workmen, as he was before the Renaissance. His materials are also products of factory methods and he must take this into account too. 'In a word – we live in an industrial world and, therefore, all ideas which derive from a time before Industrialization must be ruthlessly scrapped.' It is a loathsome situation to both moralist and aesthete and offers very unpromising ground from which delight can spring. The temptation for the architect is to resort to 'veneering', borrowing earlier styles, or making 'stage scenery' to impress us. The architect of Tower Bridge, for example, tried to pretend that metal engineering had not replaced stone engineering and disguised his work as an ornamental Gothic building. Fortunately this phase has already passed, claims Gill, and rising costs and the demands for 'conveniences' are such that 'the modern architect, if only to save himself from complete unemployment, is forced to be intelligent', and that means 'honesty and attention to business'.

In a machine age it is dishonest to indulge in ornaments, hand-made or sculptured mouldings of any kind. If your stone-workers are near machines themselves you cannot design their exuberance or inventiveness in an office. Such frivolities add nothing to a building's function or utility and are thus unnecessary. This applies most severely, of course, to sculpture, which today would be both 'irrelevant and ridiculous'. Should the architect be so misguided as to use a sculptor to decorate his building it would be 'as though he placed a real plum in the middle of a concrete pudding'. At most the sculptor should emerge from his studio to provide small heraldic designs, should the customers require them, to distinguish one building from the next, so on the 'Prudential Insurance Company a statue of Prudence might be appropriate'. Otherwise, the only honest way a modern building can achieve any grandeur (and he instances the B.S.A. building at Smallheath, the Lots Road Power Station and Guildford Cathedral) is by the strongly directed use of mechanized labour, machine-made materials, (steel, concrete and glass) and by attention to function and design from the inside out. Plainness is a negative virtue perhaps but it is all the future can honestly offer, unless there is a new heaven and a new earth and the masses rise up to demand work with responsibility.

What then might one predict would be Gill's response to offers to make decorative sculpture for plain modern buildings? Wrong. He grasped the chance with both hands. London Transport had always been an enlightened patron of the arts under the leadership of Frank Pick, noticeably in the posters it commissioned and in the use of Edward Johnston to design its lettering. In 1928 the architect of its St James Headquarters building, Charles Holden, was able to ask the then controversial sculptor Epstein to carve two figures representing 'Day' and 'Night' over the doors of the entrance. These turned out to be so provocative that it was twenty years before Epstein received another large public commission. Gill was asked to lead a team of five other sculptors to carve relief figures representing the 'Winds' for high up on the walls of the seventh floor. The symbolic relevance of any of these figures to the London Underground is not obvious. To accept this work Gill must have had a struggle with his principles, but by now he had a family. He was not alone in this dilemma for Henry Moore records the reluctance with which he, like Gill, did his own part of the work. 'In 1928 I agreed to carve a relief for the Underground Building at St. James', although I had never felt any desire to make relief sculptures. Even when I was a student I was totally pre-occupied by sculpture in its full spatial values . . . I was extremely reluctant to accept an architectural commission, and relief sculpture symbolized for me the humiliating subservience of the sculptor to the architect, for in ninety-nine cases out of a hundred, the architect only thought of sculpture as a surface decoration and ordered a relief as a matter of course.'[41] The difference here is that Gill's most natural medium *is* the sculpture in relief and this usually needs a surface to support it. Moore lived on to see and benefit from later architects' conversion to the idea that sculpture could be placed outside a building and in a formal relation to it, rather than just stuck on as an afterthought. In spite of his reluctance Moore produced a heavy, deeply cut, and simplified figure representing the West Wind on the north side of the east wing. Farr thinks 'Gill's three squarely-shaped figures are each set against horizontal or near-horizontal folds of stylized drapery which detach them from their background without any gain in dynamic effect.'[42] I feel the smaller works cut by Gill to try out his designs, particularly the East Wind in the Tate, do work well when isolated from this looming and elephantine building. The whole enterprise seems, in retrospect, to have been misguided and Farr's judgement is probably a fair one: 'The siting of all the four pairs of reliefs at such a height above street-level makes it difficult to view them properly: one of them can hardly be seen, and another is completely invisible from the street because of the restricted site upon which the building stands. The relationship of the sculptural enrichment to the building is not entirely happy for the reliefs look a little lost against the mass of this ten-storey structure surmounted by a

The east wind (1928), Portland stone, 25.5cm × 30.5cm × 10cm. This is the model for the larger version on the north side of the west wing of St James's Park Underground Station, London

seventy-five foot high central tower. It was a brave attempt, given the circumstances of the time, but it showed up the divorce that had occurred between sculpture and architecture in which the old tradition and scale of proportion no longer obtained and no new *modus vivendi* had yet been achieved.'[43] Gill could probably have made the same judgement himself before he began the work.[44]

Similarly he could have predicted his problems with his next architectural sculpture for the BBC's Broadcasting House, but as he wrote to Desmond Chute, 'This job will occupy all of 1931 and as it is well paid we are in luck.'[45] The sentence before reads 'the building is commendably plain and machine made in appearance as in fact'. On to this he had to put three six-foot by four-foot panels representing Ariel, supported by angels, learning celestial music, Ariel between Wisdom and Gaiety,* and Ariel piping to the children. Over the doorway he was to provide a ten-foot high group of Prospero and Ariel and for the foyer a figure called 'The Sower'. Naturally, once committed, Gill had some fun at the expense of this pretentious symbolism both in private letters and a public article in *The Listener* (March 15th 1933). This latter purported to explain the carvings' meaning but only demonstrated his ignorance of *The Tempest* and his lack of belief in the ideas he was supposed to embody. In the *Autobiography* he wrote that these works, 'from my point of view are a failure. I mean simply that I don't much like looking at them. The idea was grand but I was incapable of carrying it out adequately. Prospero and Ariel! Well, you think. *The Tempest* and romance and Shakespeare and all that stuff. Very clever of the BBC to hit on the idea, Ariel and aerial. Ha! Ha! And the BBC kidding itself, in the approved manner of all big organizations (British or foreign, public or private), that it represents all that is good and noble and disinterested – like the British Empire or Selfridges (and the U.S. Constitution and the Comité des Forges, not to mention

Gill at work on Prospero and Ariel over the porch of Broadcasting House (1931), Caen stone

* Gill had his own fun with this topic as a sketch in one of the erotic notebooks in Los Angeles shows Ariel and Gaiety doing things to each other which seem to surprise even Wisdom.

The Broadcaster or Sower, showing the full size figure and the half-size trial version (1931), Corsham stone, the smaller version is 144cm high.

our superb and all-powerful and all-pure Nordic race).'[46]

His dislike of broadcasting was deeply felt, though one cannot help feeling he would have made a good broadcaster himself with his quiet voice reaching a wider audience than he ever would through his torrent of published works or his public lectures. His frustration with this BBC work must have been compounded by the trouble over the size of Ariel's penis already recounted, and with, 'Bad weather, bad stone and bad health' – though it was his own choice to work on inadequate and exposed scaffolding. From this perch he was heard to shout to a passing friend, 'You know, this is all balls'.

'The Sower' was also done with some cynicism as he wrote to his brother Cecil; 'I am about to begin the statue, representing a man "Broadcasting", to stand in the entrance hall. Comic thought, when you consider the quality of BBC semination, to compare it with the efforts of a simply countryman sowing corn! However, it's their idea, not mine. Mine not to reason why . . . mine simply, to carve a good image of a broadcaster.'[47] This figure, incidentally is now known to the BBC security staff as the 'Overtime King' symbolically handing out the overtime hours on extra pay.

Gill is dismissive of these works which took a year of his time, but we need not agree with him and his cynicism certainly does not mean he skimped on craftsmanship. True the panels are rather sweet, come very near to looking like framed pictures in stone and are awkwardly placed for viewing. The Caen stone figures of Prospero and Ariel do still have a presence and dignity in spite of their stained and weathered state. This probably reflects Gill's determination to see them 'as much God the Father and God the Son as they are Shakespeare's characters'. The smaller trial version in the Tate is in a more sympathetic stone and obviously in better condition, never having been out of doors. It is on a much smaller scale ($50'' \times 18'' \times 14''$) and still shows the claw-marks whereas the full-scale version is smoothed down, perhaps too much. 'The Sower' also exists in a smaller version in Manchester, but both versions have built-in awkwardnesses. It is not clear why the full-scale one needed to be

proposed Church of St Peter Apostle, Gorleston-on-sea
View from South West

made as a relief (about 12″ deep) but most of its oddities such as the left hand and arm and ugly left foot stem from this self-imposed restriction.

Towards the end of his life Gill was given the chance to put into practice the architectural ideas he had preached for so long but had had to compromise so often. He could also incorporate his views, expressed in *Mass for the Masses*, that the altar should be at the centre of a church in the midst of the congregation and away from 'the mystery mongering of obscure sanctuaries separated from the people'. He was commissioned to provide a 300-seat Catholic Church for Gorleston-on-Sea near Yarmouth, and he was given a free hand to use a central altar and to provide sculpture as he thought fit. Gill was determined it was to be a plain building built by local workmen and carpenters, and if the Rector insisted on electric light and heating (and he did) then Gill would accept the customer's wishes too. His drawings of the proposed exterior show a plain building with a traditional cruciform plan, steeply pitched roofs, plain pointed windows, with arches springing from the floor, and only the figure of St Peter near the door to break the surface of the brick walls. Gill sensibly co-opted a local High Wycombe architect to help, but together they kept it as free from 'architectooralooralism' and unnecessary industrial products as they could. The whole was designed from the altar outwards for as Gill wrote in 'Plain Architecture' a church is there 'first and chiefly as a canopy over an altar'.[48] The interior had white walls and a red floor with the 'furniture' made at Pigotts, including paintings by Denis Tegetmeier, Gill's son-in-law. The whole cost £6,700. From his account of the opening in 1939 in a letter to Chute Gill was evidently justifiably cock-a-hoop over its reception by the congregation, clergy and Bishop.[49] Since those times Gill's too small confessional has been converted into a cupboard, the pulpit taken away and the open porch glassed in. These and other minor adjustments to facilitate the modern liturgy Gill would no doubt have approved. Today it seems less remarkable, but this is probably a tribute to Gill whose ideas on liturgy and plain architecture have come into their own.

Proposed church at Gorleston-on-Sea, Norfolk (1938), pencil and watercolour, 40.2cm × 26cm (*above left*)

Two views of the interior of Gill's church of St Peter's at Gorleston-on-Sea (*left*)

Persia, panel from the John D. Rockefeller Archaeological Museum in Jerusalem (1934), Hoptonwood stone

One other architectural sculpture commission which deserves brief mention is the carving in Hoptonwood stone of ten panels for the New Archaeological Museum at Jerusalem. These are perhaps minor works in Gill's *oeuvre*, and involve decorative designs representing the ten nations who had a cultural influence on Palestine (Egypt, Phoenicia, Persia etc.). There was much research and consultation with learned men before Gill and Laurie Cribb finally installed them. The results, as far as one can judge from photographs, are a good workmanlike job.

More important than the sculptures for Gill was the experience of working in the Holy Land for four months in 1934, and again in 1937. The experience changed him. He felt he grasped something of the essential values which still survived there even as the society underwent both the evils and benefits of rapid modernization. 'I only want to, somehow, make it clear that since going to Palestine my mind is pervaded by a different order of living – an order previously only guessed at, but now experienced – an order not only human but essentially holy.'[50] There was bad there, but the good was not yet dead. He saw there 'as it were eye to eye, the sweating face of Christ,' and preferred the noisy half-ruined holy places and their squabbling sects to all the grandeurs of Rome. David Jones who visited Gill there happened to see Gill, unaware of being observed, kiss the diseased stump of a beggar woman's hand. From this period he was even more of a dedicated pacifist and antagonistic to the whole foundation of European capitalist-industrial society, and, unless the Church was prepared to see and say the same things, then he would inevitably appear to be antagonistic to the Church too. Sculpture then took second place to the urgency of spreading his message as Europe slipped into Fascism, and Gill approached his final years.

One last major public commission appeared to give him an opportunity to say some of these things in stone to a world-wide audience. In 1935 Gill had what he called 'the amazing honour' to be asked to sculpt the British Government's gift to the League of Nations building in Geneva. Ironically, by the time the politicians had argued over his designs, and he had carried out the three huge panels in seventeen sections and transported them from Pigotts for installation, it was late 1938 and all that the sculpture and the League of Nations stood for was about to be destroyed by war. Gill's first thoughts on receiving the commission were to turn yet again to his 'Christ Driving the Money Changers from the Temple' because, as he naïvely explained to the Secretary General (a former French Minister of Finance) the League should be primarily concerned with 'the ridding of Europe and the World of the stranglehold of finance, both national and international'. To his surprise the idea was received quite coldly and the Americans perceptively pointed out that to install such a sculpture would be 'the last and greatest hypocrisy of the British Empire'. Gill gave in to this argument, and the one that it was too specifically Christian for such an international body. Instead, as he proposed to Anthony Eden: 'Imagine the centre panel 28ft. long and 7ft. high, practically entirely filled with a naked figure of a man reclining (rather as in the picture of the 'Creation of

Adam' by Michael Angelo) a vast and grand figure of Man with hand outstretched and the tip of his finger touching the tip of the finger of God which is coming down from above, and in fine letters on the background, in Latin because it is a universal statement and not specially an English one, the words, 'AD IMAGINEM DEI CREAVIT ILLUM'. Because *that* is the point, Man was created in the image of God and it is *that* image which is being defaced and befouled.'[51]

In English, because it was an English gift, would be words from Gerard Manley Hopkins' *Wreck of the Deutschland* beginning 'God mastering me,' and the two side panels would depict, on the left, animals, electricity, trees, machines to show God's gifts to Man, and on the right Man's gift to God: ourselves. As usual each detail was worked out in terms of its symbolic meaning, so for example, 'I particularly wish the head of the MAN to go out of the top of the centre panel; for I don't want the panel to be simply a picture frame into which the figure of a man is neatly fitted, but I want it to be the universe itself into which man does not really completely fit.'

Speaight writes: 'This was the last considerable work Eric carved for a public building, and much the best. Even now, when the League of Nations has taken its place among the failures of the past, it is at once an eloquent explanation of its failure and a reminder of the only secure basis on which any such associations can be built. Comparisons were naturally made with Michelangelo's painting in the Sistine Chapel; but then Michelangelo was not called upon to spare the feelings of those who did not profess the Christian religion, or who did not profess any religion at all. Eric had been remarkably successful in conceiving and carrying out a work of art in harmony with modern aesthetics and not too deliberately offensive to modern agnosticism. It was all that could be expected of him in an age of disbelief. 'They think I'm a prophet and seer,' he wrote to his brother Cecil, 'but they don't believe in my prophecies'.[52] At least the work made him solvent for the first time in eleven years.

How important was Gill as a sculptor? First we have to see him in the context of his time. It was a very exciting

Gill with the League of Nation's Creation panel in the workshop at Pigotts (1937). The panel was installed in Geneva in March 1938

one for European sculpture. Up to the seventeenth century sculpture had been the dominant form in the visual arts, but from then, apart from isolated figures such as Bernini, it had taken second place to painting. Then came Rodin (1840–1917), who almost single-handed overthrew the vapid academicism of nineteenth-century sculpture. This meant that any younger sculptor born when Gill was had first to encounter the colossus of Rodin and either build upon it or react against it. Gill knew his work and perceptively called him 'the great navvying faun', but then spoilt his insight by writing in the year of Rodin's death, 'Of the Academy sculptors I suppose Auguste Rodin is the boss, but then academy sculpture is a rum old game and, like George Robey, I should say to it "buzz off",'³³ which is to miss the pioneering importance of Rodin's greatest works. Gill's friend William Rothenstein persuaded Rodin to exhibit in London in 1899 and from then onwards he exhibited and was lionized as much in London as he was in France. There would have been many opportunities for the two men to meet, but there is no record of their having done so. A pity, as they would have had much in common. Rodin was a sensualist, even in his ostensibly religious works, was obsessed by the nude, an enthusiast for Indian sculpture, loved Isadora Duncan's dancing, knew Kessler, and was reported to have said, 'People say I think too much about women. Yet after all, what is there more important to think about?' There, however, the two men's affinities ended. Rodin was a modeller moulding clay for bronze-casting, and when he did produce marbles it was via a clay model and a pointing machine. His works are turbulent, swirling, multi-facial, moving the spectator round their intricate forms in ways which Gill never attempted. Their sheer passion makes Gill's look merely pretty. Rodin had no interest in architecture as a setting for his sculptures (though he wrote a book on French cathedrals, which Gill must have known), whereas Gill believed, against all the contemporary evidence 'there cannot be a great school of sculpture again until we get a great school of builders again', and of course that could not happen again until 'we throw away our pride in our own judgement and admit that the Church is the Bride of Christ'. Again sentiments Rodin would have been impatient with.

Rodin's younger contemporaries, the great sculptor-painters Daumier, Degas, Renoir and Modigliani, Gill seems to have known little about, at least their sculptural works. Of Matisse's work in the 1910 Post-Impressionists Show he had this to say, after explaining the critical infighting going on amongst the pros and cons, the old guard and the new: 'If, on the other hand, you are like me and John and McEvoy and Epstein, then, feeling yourself beyond the reaction and beyond the transition, you have a right to feel superior to Mr Henri-Matisse (who is typical of the show – though Gauguin makes the biggest splash and Van Gogh the maddest) and can say you don't like it.

But have you seen Mr. Matisse's sculpture. . .?'[54]

This smug dismissal by the young Gill seems absurd today when we can no longer feel the shock waves this show caused in the London art world, even though some of the works on show were already over 25 years old. By the second show in 1912 Gill himself was exhibiting eight pieces alongside the Cubists and Fauves so he was well

Gravestone (1928), Portland stone, 22.4cm × 50cm (*below left*)

Mater amabilis (1928), Portland stone, 8.9cm high (*below right*)

aware of the latest work in Europe. One exhibitor, Picasso, Gill referred to occasionally in his writings as a type of the modern studio artist isolated in his eccentricity and lost in experiments in abstract form – 'as if they were typical – as if *they* cut any ice – as if they made any difference to the manufacturers of Birmingham or Brad-ford'. Picasso's assemblages of 1914 would have meant nothing to Gill, busy on his Westminster Stations. Apart from a visit to Zadkine's Paris studio after the war and a reference to him as 'a considerable genius', there is no sign that he knew of or learned from the works of such sculptors as Archipenko, Duchamp-Villon, Lipchitz or Henri Laurens who pushed Cubism in new directions; nor of Boccioni whose 1912 'Development of a Bottle in Space' suggested that there might be other subjects the sculptor could tackle besides the tedious old human figure. As late as 1930 Gill seems to be attacking nineteenth-century Academicism and dismissing modern experiments in terms which show he has firmly closed his mind against the latter: 'If you knew precisely what a statue is you wouldn't attempt to sit on two stools at once – one of which is the photographer's tripod and the other the high horse; you would be content with the stool of repentance. For in this business of statue-making it is not today at all clear whether a statue should be a petrified photograph or an exhibition of its maker's mysticism – and "false mysticism" at that'.[55] It reads very amusingly, but just *who* was he talking about of any importance who was either producing 'photographic' or 'mystical' sculptures in 1930?

In his visits to Kessler's home in Weimar (which was designed by Van de Velde) Gill must have seen his patron's collection of Munchs and German Expression-ists. Though his reactions are not recorded one could surmise that he would not have found them congenial in their lack of finish and for 'going off the top in psychological miasmas'.[56] Weimar was the home of the Bauhaus, and later when it was disbanded by the Nazis many of its leaders such as Gabo, Mondrian, Gropius, Moholy Nagy and Brueur spent some of the 1930s in London. Gill continued, right up to his posthumously published *Autobiography* to belabour over-decorated buildings and to call for a clear rational modern style appropriate to the machine age without seeming to know, or care, that people like Le Corbusier, Saarinen, Mies van der Rohe and Frank Lloyd Wright had long achieved what he called for, at least abroad if not in England.

Other groups who were so good at self-publicity he could hardly have missed them, he must have found temperamentally repellent, such as the Futurists with their worship of machines, speed, and noise; and the Dada and Surreal groups with the slogan 'All art is meaningless'. Other European sculptors who stood outside all this clamour of 'isms' and, like Gill, stayed close to a traditional figurative style, such as Minne, Barlach or Lehmbruck he seems not to have known – though if he had he would probably have felt impelled, as he was with Maillol, to assert his own independence from them. Carvers such as Brancusi and Arp receive no mention. As he wrote with some complacency in his *Autobiography*, 'I don't consider that I have come much under the influence of foreign parts or foreign people,'[57] excepting of course Jerusalem but then that was not art influence.

Nearer home he knew Epstein well, indeed they planned a new sculptured Stonehenge together. Here was a cosmopolitan man who knew personally most of the great Europeans already mentioned, and who in addition was one of the first in England to collect the 'primitive' arts of Africa and Oceania. In 1913 he produced Rock Drill perhaps the first piece of twentieth-century sculpture in England. None of this rubbed off on Gill – indeed the influence seems to have been the other way round as the carving methods he learned from Gill are distinctly visible on his 'Rima' statue. Later relationships cooled, and after quoting Gill's criticism of his Hudson statue as 'dull, mechanical, lifeless – making the sculpture look as if Epstein had gnawed it with his teeth', Epstein dismissed all of Gill's writing as 'doggerel'.[58] Epstein's connections with Gaudier-Brzeska and the noisy Vorticists or with the art-theorist T.E. Hulme do not seem to have appealed to Gill either. These were the 'abominable art world', his alienation from which he gratefully lists amongst his 'escapes'.

If there is a determined insularity in Gill's relationships with modern art he was equally narrow and
intractable in his views on earlier periods. We know
already of his devotion to medieval European and Indian
work, but when it came to the Greeks he dismissed
Phidias' work as 'specious' and wanted to shift all the
labels round. 'It is indeed desirable that what is at present
called Classic should be called Decadent, and that which
is now called Primitive should be called Classic. For, if by
"Classic period" we wish to denote the highest or best
period, it is obvious that our current nomenclature is all
wrong.'[59] Eventually the Oxford Reader in Classical
Archaeology, Stanley Casson, wrote a book on this period
Gill had so highly praised, and recounted in it how Gill
had learned from his researches the technique of using
the 'point' vertically on the stone to 'stun' it and so make
it easier to clear off the block.[60] Gill was not abashed by
the author's expertise and curtly dismissed the book in a
review. Casson's letter to Gill began, 'I have just read
your review !!xx!!xx It is bloody rude and no mistake. But
almost every point you make is wrong.'[61]

The First World War put a temporary stop to the
'isms' and after the war yet new groupings and names
emerged. In England Moore and Hepworth began to
overshadow the 'moderately modern' sculptors such as
Frank Dobson, Leon Underwood, Mestrovic, and of
course Gill himself. Gill remained a non-joiner, an
English isolate in a time of international styles. Moore he
admired unstintingly, even owning a statuette by him,
and their published pronouncements on art and society
often overlap to an astonishing degree – but starting from
similar premisses see how widely they diverge in practice.
Gill joined no school and founded none: in sculpture at
least he could not say he was easily led, nor say look how
good my leaders are. Temperamentally he is nearest the
anonymous medieval carver-masons of France and
England and at his best he achieves a kind of timeless
dignity and repose. At his worst he seems a throw-back
only as far as the nineteenth-century Victorian sculptor
with his mildly sexy nymphs. Either extreme avoids
contemporary reference, modern materials, or major

technical innovation. His nearest contemporary equivalents are other eccentric solitaries such as Stanley Spencer, David Jones or Gwen John, though no equivalent sculptor comes to mind.

Obviously then we must conclude that Gill the sculptor is not a major European or world figure, though this is not to say he did not produce pieces which were magnificent in their own terms. However, he is demonstrably less important in the history of sculpture than he is in those of type-design or wood-engraving.

His close friend David Jones published a clear-eyed appreciation of his work after Gill's death in which his major shortcomings are swiftly sketched in. 'His carvings could be irritatingly mannered, and like all of us, he often copied himself. Sometimes there was a feeling of toyishness and lack of weight and volume. I think he conceived in relief rather than in the round even when the work was technically "in the round". That is to say, the four sides of a block of stone were each worked rather as separate faces and so contrived as to "join up" satisfactorily – rather than growing organically from the centre of the block, as seems to happen in true "in the round" sculpture. Both approaches have, historically, produced works of wonder'.[62] Also, Jones wrote, 'Linear grace he always had, but not always foiled enough, so that too often an elegance and sometimes a positive slickness harmed his work – the workman again! His accomplishments as a workman and the speed at which he worked partly accounted for this. Prudence can be a great hustler. His work never profits by those technical incompetences and fumbling which, one must admit, sometimes add to the interest of less accomplished artists. He sometimes spoiled works by "completing" them in some technical sense – again the workman – and the man.'[63]

It is true that Paul Valéry's dictum that 'a work of art is never finished only abandoned' does not apply to Gill's work in any medium. Moore too has pointed out that craftsmanship of this high order can, in itself become a snare. 'I don't want to put too much stress on the actual act of carving, or on the craftsmanship involved. Craftsmanship in sculpture is just common sense –

anyone can learn it. It's certainly easier than painting I'd say. The mental grasp is difficult, and the three dimensional conception, but the workmanship, which people like Eric Gill thought so important, can degenerate into a most awful mental laziness, like knitting or polishing the silver.'[64]

Perhaps the difference between the artist and the workman-craftsman is that the artist takes risks and innovates in subject matter, materials or techniques or any combination of these, whilst the craftsman is content to say much the same things in the same language no matter how superbly.

Gill insisted that, 'A work of sculpture may resemble other things or it may not, but such resemblance is accidental not substantive', and 'in our work we have to use our materials as things of which to *make* things and not as things by which to represent things'. We must look again as children. The photographic approach is a 'degradation'. Modern academic art is 'for the most part, as soft as slime, sentimental as cocoa, and as illogical as angry women', and as a corrective the modern artist must tackle *abstract* ideas, and 'oh that the T square were as much part of the equipment of a studio as a milk sop model'. All these are unimpeachably modern, even avant-garde, ideas for the time they were written, but the disappointment for the modern reader, with a full knowledge of how twentieth-century sculpture developed, is to go from these words to the actual works.

A work of art which was not a work of propaganda, that is did not embody *meaning*, was for Gill merely and solely about aesthetics. Shape only becomes the first criterion of judgement in times like these when the sculptor has no common culture to draw upon and works in his studio isolated from the everyday life of his fellow men. 'From the point of view of human beings meaning is a more primary and more important criterion; and that is as inevitable as it is right and proper that the ordinary person should dislike works of art whose meanings revolt him.'[65] Here we get, perhaps, to the essential difference between Gill and his contemporaries. His best work is done in the service of an idea which has nothing to do with a programme of aesthetics, but which is passionately held – his religious belief. For this commitment he was distrusted by 'progressive' artists and critics who felt, David Jones tells us: 'Poor Gill, he was a superb stone-cutter – had great possibilities – pity about this Roman Catholic thing.'[66] As Jones said 'he sought to work as though a culture of some sort existed or, at all events, he worked as though one should, and could *make* a culture exist'. If he adds nothing to the arcane language of modern sculpture he did do his best to re-establish a tradition of ecclesiastical sculpture and sculpture for use, and in this where are his rivals let alone his equals?

And Venus passed straightway to the house of Jupiter to beg from the the service of Mercury, the god of speech. And Jupiter refused not her prayer. And Venus and Mercury descended from heaven together: and as they went, the former said to the latter "Thou knowest, my brother of Arcady, that never at any time have I done anything without thy help; for how long time, moreover, I have sought a certain maiden in vain. And now nought remains but that, by thy heraldry, I proclaim a reward for whomsoever shall find her. Do thou my bidding quickly." And therewith she conveyed to him a little scrip, in which was writ—

'Absolutely legible-to-the-last-
Degree letters' in stone and ink

Lettering is the most wide-spread and applied of all the arts, but at the same time the most transparent: if it calls undue attention to itself then, with the exception of display lettering, it has failed. This self-effacing ideal is particularly true in typography where all the reader wants is a page which is pleasant to look at and easy to read. It is only when we look back over the history of printing that we realise such seemingly modest aims are not so easily achieved. That history is a complex one and it needs specialists to explain (and disagree over) the nuances which make one typeface superior to another. As a non-specialist I can only record my own impressions as a reader that Gill Sans seems to me the essence of clarity for public notices, and that Joanna and Perpetua are a balm to the eyes for extended prose. In spite of being designed half a century ago now they still appear perfectly 'modern'. It is unfortunate that the methods and economics of modern printing mean that they are now rarely used.

Perhaps it is wrong to leave lettering until the last chapter in this book as it was an interest which Gill had from his earliest days and one which earned him his bread and butter all his adult life. However, it should now be apparent that the characteristics of his lettering are also much in evidence in those arts discussed in previous chapters. Readability is the basis of all lettering – clear, unfussy, initial impact in black and white. A page depends on the balanced distribution of lights and darks, of thicks and thins, and the irrigation of the whole flat surface by white blank paper. These are the formal virtues which distinguish Gill's drawings, wood-engravings, and by extension his relief sculptures. Readability is the basis of all his art.

The child Gill had taken as much care over the name-plates on his locomotive drawings as he had over the pistons and wheels. Later at Chichester Art School study-

Calligraphic exercise (*c*.1903), pen and ink, page size 22cm × 14.5cm and text size 15cm × 10cm

THE Ancients held there to be a fate which would have its fill, though women wept and men died, and none could tell whose was the guilt nor who fell innocent. Thus did they blindly wrong God's providence ∴∴ Yet, save that we are taught to believe that all is ruled, we are as blind as they, & are still left wondering why all that is true & generous & love's own fruit must turn so often to woe and shame, exacting tears and blood

Calligraphy (*c.*1907–8), pen and ink, 56.1cm × 46cm

ing with George Herbert Catt he had tried his hand at 'the most monstrous perversions and eccentricities' of the art nouveau lettering then in fashion. When he was seventeen he was one of the seven students who attended Edward Johnston's first lettering class on September 21st 1899: it was Johnston's first real job at the age of twenty-seven. He had been directed by the Principal, W.R. Lethaby, to revive the all-but moribund art of calligraphy, and to do this Johnston had turned back first to Morris and then further to the medieval scribes for inspiration and models. He admired these men for doing something socially useful with their skills, and then realised that if you were to lecture on lettering you must begin with a survey 'which related the subject to its position in heaven and earth'.[1] Artists must not 'pose as geniuses at play' working to fancy aesthetic theories, but aspire to be workmen. He also taught 'the forms of written letters would somehow properly depend upon the pen which wrote them' – a kind of truth-to-materials theory. Gill later acknowledged that 'art nonsense' and 'thought nonsense' could not stand against him, and 'he profoundly altered the whole course of my life and all my ways of thinking'.[2] He also affected Gill's emotions, for when he began to write with a pen, 'and I saw the writing that came as he wrote, I had that thrill and tremble of the heart which otherwise I can only remember having had when first I touched her body or saw her hair down for the first time'.[3] Gill tells us he fell in love with Johnston, as he might have with Socrates, because he revealed the truth and made it desirable. Until Johnston's marriage Gill shared his lodgings in Lincoln's Inn Fields, and later when Gill himself married they were neighbours first at Hammersmith and later at Ditchling where Johnston eventually died and was buried. The two men were the closest friends for sixteen years but drifted apart after Gill's conversion to Catholicism and his departure for Wales. What the two men had in common was their love for God and for craftsmanship, and their concomitant hatred of industrialisation. In terms of character though they could not have been more different as Johnston was 'born tired' and was totally disorganised and untidy all his days. What he did produce was of superb quality, but it came with none of Gill's ease and dash. In his lack of aggression and his asceticism he was approaching the saintly. The young Gill, as he later admitted, 'was hasty and careless and ready to jump to conclusions and make rash generalisations', so Johnston's extreme deliberations of thought and speech acted as a useful brake.

Gill became a skilled calligrapher under Johnston's tuition and a life-long believer in his tenet that 'Letters are to be *read*'. In 1904 Kessler, who had already employed Johnston, recruited Gill to design calligraphic title pages for Insel Verlag in Leipzig. Gill continued this work from 1905 to 1909 using a light, sharply serifed style. From 1907 Gill also wood-engraved letters in his work for Kessler, usually titles and initial letters for chapters. One interesting collaboration took place in 1925 when Gill was asked to engrave chapter initials for an edition of Virgil in white on black, and then Maillol painted figures on the block behind and around the letters which Gill then engraved.[4] However, calligraphy alone did not offer enough scope to a man with the energy, curiosity and drive of Gill, not to mention the financial pressures of a growing family. Anyway calligraphy tended to lead in the Arts and Crafts direction, and as we have seen, Gill soon became disillusioned with that. Johnston, on the other hand, had a small private income, fewer talents, and a stronger sense of loyalty to Morris's ideals and all the Arts and Crafts Movement stood for. Lethaby encouraged all his students to learn a trade so Gill went part-time to the Westminster Technical Institute to learn stone-masonry – a discipline which ideally combined lettering and doing something socially useful. Gill's first commission was a tombstone which took him three months of evening work after his frustrating days in the architect's office. After several small jobs like this he was offered the chance to carve the inscriptional work on the new Medical Schools at Cambridge. With only the slightest hesitation Gill threw up the opportunity to be a gentleman architect in favour of getting his hands dirty, and as he wrote at the end of his life, 'from that day to this I have never been out of a job'.

As one might expect by now, Gill no sooner mastered masonry than he was telling everybody how it ought to be done. In 1905 he began to teach, part-time, monumental masonry at the Paddington Institute. Then in 1906 came Johnston's great book *Writing & Illuminating & Lettering*,[5] with a Preface by Lethaby and wood-engravings by Noel Rooke. Gill supplied the final chapter on 'Inscriptions in Stone' which is the most practical, straightforward writing he ever did. In it the craftsman's decisions about what stones to use, whether incised or raised letters, Roman capitals, Roman small letters or Italics, gilding or colour, whether to set out in a 'massed' or symmetrical way, and whether to work from the top or the bottom of a panel, are all clearly discussed. So are the choice, use, and care of the tools – so chisels, for example should be kept sharp enough to cut paper. Beauty of form will come from the right use of these tools and diligent study of the Trajan

GOETHES
DRAMATISCHE
DICHTUNGEN
BAND I

LEIPZIG
MDCCCCIX
IM INSELVERLAG

Decorative lettering for title page for Insel Verlag, 16.8cm × 10cm

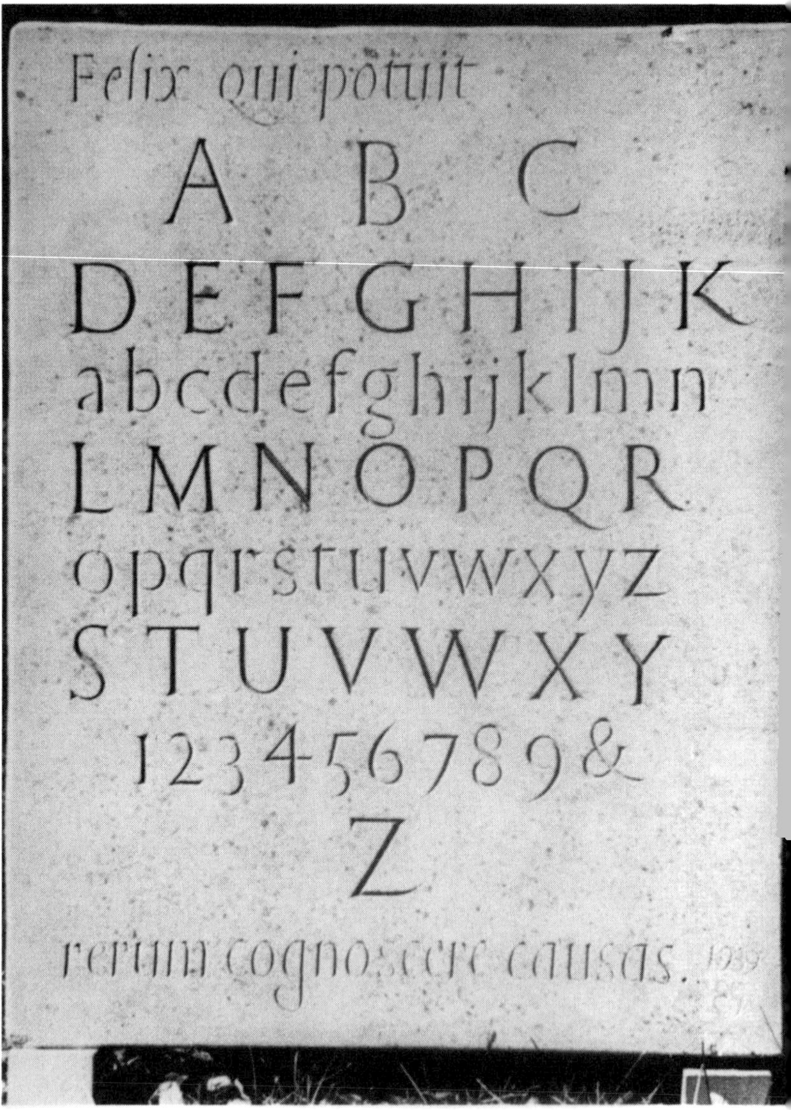

Felix qui potuit

A B C
D E F G H I J K
a b c d e f g h i j k l m n
L M N O P Q R
o p q r s t u v w x y z
S T U V W X Y
1 2 3 4 5 6 7 8 9 &
Z

rerum cognoscere causas. 1939

Alphabet cut for Graham Carey (1939), Hoptonwood stone incised and painted. Present whereabouts unknown. A rubbing of the alphabet measures 56cm × 44.6cm

Column for Capitals, and of sixteenth- and seventeenth-century tombstones for small and Italic letters. In a letter written in 1934, however, he denies any strict adherence to these classic models because, 'we have to take the lettering of our own time and, if necessary, improve it by rationality and good workmanship. My inscriptions are no more like the Trajan than Caslon's type is.'[6]

The demand for lettering in stone grew so that by 1906 Gill had to employ his first assistant, fifteen years old Joseph Cribb, the first of the twenty-seven apprentices, pupils or assistants he took on over the next thirty-four years. A necessary book for any study of this aspect of Gill's work is *The Inscriptional Work of Eric Gill: An Inventory* (1964), by his brother Evan Gill. The author admits it is no longer possible to say which pieces are wholly by Gill himself. He quotes Desmond Chute, himself an assistant from 1918 to 1922, on this problem: 'Everything made there [Gill's various workshops] was wholly inspired and entirely due to him. This does not necessarily mean that all works came wholly from his hand. For if in a period when sculptors' use of the pointing machine was taken for granted, he was adamant against this or other devices that rob men of responsibility, on the other hand he made ample use of the collaboration of fellow stone-cutters, esteeming this a mutual benefit. Nor did he hesitate to set his name to work thus produced – metaphorically in most cases, for he did not hold with signed work.'[7]

In short, Gill's hand may not even have touched a piece from his workshop, but it would bear the strong imprint of his mind and teaching. His working procedure was to submit a rough sketch to the client, and then if it was approved he made a full-scale working drawing which was transferred to the stone. He preferred to carve *in situ* so he could see the effect of the light falling on the letters. A rubbing was then taken of the finished work. Many of these drawings and rubbings still exist, but there must be many more works we have no exact records of. Nevertheless Evan Gill managed to account for 762 works in 328 different towns, including works in Australia, France, India, America, Israel and South Africa. These vary in scope from a few words to whole war memorials involving over 5,000 letters. There can be few people in Britain who are more than a short journey from one of these pieces. Several of them must have had an additional poignancy for Gill who was called upon to carve tombstones or memorials for people he had known, such as Ottoline Morrell, Rupert Brooke, Ambrose McEvoy and G.K. Chesterton, and some he admired such as Beardsley. No matter who the client though, the line and the lettering are always sharp, clean-cut, functional and perfectly adapted to the job in hand.

Gill enlarged his scope to include painted shop front lettering and in 1903 travelled to Paris to work on W.H. Smith's frontage there. Another side-line was to market at six shillings each plaster casts of his cut stone lettering to serve as models for masons and sculptors. He also began to draw alphabets adapting and varying typefaces then in current use. This he seems to have done for his own amusement long before any invitation to design a real typeface came his way, but it is obvious that these experiments are already more related to his experience

Memorial to Aubrey Beardsley on a house in Brighton (1927), Portland stone, 55.5cm × 47.8cm

with a chisel than they are to earlier work with a pen. It was to be a unique qualification when the invitation did arrive.

When the Ditchling Press was set up Gill left the actual printing to Pepler and confined himself to engraving initial letters and illustrations. Pepler had only an early Stanhope and a folio Albion press, and two founts of Caslon Old Face type. Pepler may not have been the best introduction to printing for Gill as his methods were somewhat sloppy – he was not above drawing in a missing letter with a pen or by applying type held in his fingers to save re-setting a whole page.[8] Gibbings at the Golden Cockerel Press set a better example and he soon had Gill designing decorative initials and headings, followed in 1929 by the Golden Cockerel type for the exclusive use of his press. However, we have already discussed much of Gill's work for the small private press in earlier pages and we must move on, as Gill did, to his work for large commercial machine presses.

Gill designed eleven printing types in all, but the only one which bears his name is Gill Sans. This was developed in response to a request from Stanley Morison of The Monotype Corporation.* This type was not entirely without precedents in the nineteenth century, and in 1916 Johnston himself had already designed a sans-serif lettering for exclusive use on London Underground Railway name-boards and publicity. Johnston's initiative inspired several attempts in Europe to design a letter that could be drawn by anyone with a ruler, compass, and the ability to follow instructions – notably Paul Renner's 'Futura' and Joseph Erbar's 'Erbar'. These developments probably spurred Morison to look around for a suitably qualified English designer.

Gill had been in on the early discussions over Johnston's Sans Serif, but had been too busy with the Westminster 'Stations' to become an active collaborator. Later at Capel-y-ffin he and Cribb had painted signs to

* Originally the Lanston Monotype Corporation, but after 1931 called simply Monotype Corporation Ltd. It no longer exists as a separate company and the best of its Gill materials are now in St Bride Printing Library, London.

direct visitors, and MEN and WOMEN signs for the chapel ('Eric thought it indecent that husband and wife should kneel together'⁹) using similarly plain letters. In writing up Douglas Cleverdon's name on the fascia of his Bristol bookshop in 1926 he again used plain monotone lines. In a letter to Chute in May 1925 he wrote of working on a set of alphabets for the Army and Navy Stores which needed '1, good letters, 2, absolutely legible-to-the-last-degree letters, 3, letters which any fool can copy accurately and easily. So I'm doing them simple block letters. It's rather fun cutting out great big letters out of white paper & sticking them on big black sheets – they don't half stare at you – fine test for astigmatism.'¹⁰ Gill had acquired the qualifications Morison was looking for.

Gill Sans was greeted with disapproval and cries of 'typographical bolshevism' when it was shown to a trade conference in 1928, but when it was used in public the next year it created no stir amongst non-specialists. Gill freely acknowledged his debt to Johnston but added, 'I do think the alterations I made might be said to be an improvement from the point of view of modern methods of production'. Gill's version was designed from the start for type and machine punch-cutting and, 'therefore [it] seemed desirable to me that the forms of the letters should be as much as possible mathematically measurable and that as little reliance as possible should be placed upon the sensibility of the draughtsmen and others concerned in its machine facture'.¹¹ In short, he was back almost to drawing both sides of a wrought-iron gate as he had done in Caroë's office. Yet he did owe a very considerable debt to the technicians at Monotype who helped him with this and subsequent typefaces, which makes all the more tactless his constant writings about the moron machine-minders in commercial printing. Harling thinks Gill's the most readable and legible (not always synonymous qualities) of the post-war sans-serifs, 'yet even his design has severe limitations as a text type, limitations which are unfortunately not always regarded, and were not always so regarded by Gill in his own printing-shop'.¹² But then it began life as an alphabet of capitals only, and was never intended for extended prose, as in a novel or text-book,

Gill Sans capitals (1927), brush and ink, 24cm × 33cm. Gill Sans lower ca (1928)

ABCDEFGH
IJKLMNQRS
TUWXYZ

abcdefghijk
lmnopqrst
uvwxyz

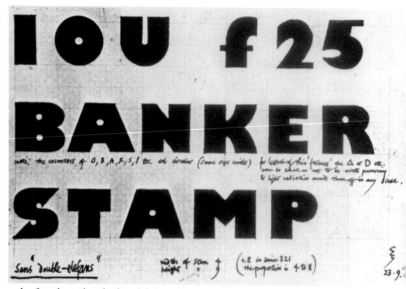

Gill Sans 'Double Elefans' (1932), brush and ink, 12.6cm × 18.7cm.

only for those hundreds of jobs where clear direct instructions or information are to be conveyed. In his book *Typography* Gill is scathing about modern display (i.e. advertising) faces which are developed from every basic successful new typeface, but confesses on the last page of that book, 'There are now about as many different varieties of letters as there are different kinds of fools. I myself am responsible for designing five different sorts of sans-serif letters – each one thicker and fatter than the last because every advertisement has to try and shout down its neighbours'.[13] Harding has hard words to say about this seeming double standard, especially 'the designs for "Gill Extra Bold", the most horrendous and blackguardly of these display exploitations' which Gill on his design sheet called, perhaps self-deprecatingly, 'Double-elefans'.[14]

By 1937 the London and North Eastern Railway had adopted Gill Sans in its various sizes and forms for all its signs, time-tables and publicity and Gill himself was asked to paint the name-plate of the famous Flying Scotsman. This the eternal schoolboy did, and was

A page from *The Monotype Recorder* (1933) showing the use of Gill Sans in the lettering and type standardization of the London and North Eastern Railway, one of the first examples of a commercial house-style (*right*)

ve: MR. **ERIC GILL** PAINTED, AND AFFIXED
TH HIS OWN HANDS, THE NAME-PLATE OF
E MOST RENOWNED TRAIN OF OUR DAY, THE
YING SCOTSMAN". HE IS SEEN HERE (AT THE
T OF GROUP) AFTER THIS CEREMONY AT
IG'S CROSS HAD MARKED THE COMPLETION
THE GIGANTIC LETTER-STANDARDIZATION
SCRIBED IN THIS NUMBER. AT THE RIGHT OF
E GROUP IS MR. **C. G. G. DANDRIDGE**, ADVER-
NG MANAGER OF THE LONDON AND NORTH
STERN RAILWAY, WHO INITIATED THE REFORM.

right: REDUCED PHOTOGRAPH OF A TWO-COLOUR
MANENT SIGN IN THE CABINS OF THE L.N.E.R.
AMERS SAILING FROM HARWICH.

IMPORTANT.

Passengers travelling to England are reminded that the Custor
Examination of Registered Baggage—whether accompanied or sent in advan
and irrespective of Destination—takes place at Parkeston Quay (Harwich) ai
the Passenger must be present ; **otherwise the Baggage will be detaine**
there.

WICHTIGE MITTEILUNG!

Reisende nach England werden höflichst daran erinnert, dass d
zollamtliche Untersuchung des über Harwich nach London und sämtlich
anderen Bestimmungsorten eingeschriebenen Gepacks—gleichviel ob vo
Eigentumer begleitet oder nicht—stets in Harwich (Parkeston Qua
stattfindet. Reisende mussen der Zollrevision personlich beiwohne
widrigenfalls bleibt das Gepäck **in Harwich zuruck.**

IMPORTANT.

Il est rappelé aux Voyageurs se rendant en Angleterre que I
Bagages Enregistrés, accompagnés ou expédiés d'avance, pour n'impor
quelle Destination, sont visités par la douane à Parkeston Quay (Harwic
et que le Voyageur est tenu d'assister à la Visite : **autrement les Bagag
seront retenus à Parkeston Quay.**

rewarded by a trip on the footplate.

After the success of Gill Sans Morison asked Gill to design a typeface for use in books. Stanley Morison (1889–1967) was not exactly one of Gill's 'leaders', but he was certainly an influential and powerful personality able to push new challenges towards Gill, and then to supply the money and technology to back him. Morison was like Gill in being a self-taught, self-made man, with a similar reputation for dogmatism, rationality, and perfectionism. He too was a Catholic convert and inclined to bend his theoretical studies of typographical history to suit his theological beliefs. Like Gill he was sometimes in conflict with orthodoxy, and in particular seemed to resent the 'Roman' part of Catholicism ('a bunch of macaroni merchants'). He was a life-long Socialist and Republican, and unlike Gill was jailed as a conscientious objector in the First World War, and strongly supported Britain's entry into the Second. He was not only a scholarly historian of typography and newspapers, but a practical editor, publisher, lay-out expert, publicist and entrepreneur, who saw it as his task as typographical adviser to the Monotype Corporation to change the 'stiff, thin, regi-mental and savourless' commercial types then in use for something modern and better. To do this he re-introduced several old classical typefaces (Bembo, Fournier, Poliphilus) to educate the reading public, and the printing trade itself who bought their typefaces from Monotype. Then, he thought, they would be ready for a truly modern face designed by a living artist.[15] Morison chose Gill for this task because by now Gill had moved away from calligraphy to cutting letters in wood, metal, and stone and Morison was looking for a design which was not calligraphically derived. By the 1920s punches were invariably cut by machine, but Morison chose to take Gill's drawings to one of the last of the skilled cutters of punches by hand, Charles Marin of Paris, who began laboriously to cut and file away at the 14 point size, then the 12 point, and finally the 22 point capitals[16]. Trials were made with these candle-smoked proofs, and after further modifications by Gill and the Monotype engineers the whole complete alphabet emerged in August 1928. It had

Page from *The Passion of Perpetua and Felicity*, translated by Walter Shewring. The blood in the wood-engraving is printed in red. Perpetua type

he was a novice), herself set it upon her own neck. Perchance so great a woman could not else have been slain (being feared of the unclean spirit), had she not herself so willed it.

O most valiant and blessed martyrs! O truly called and elected unto the glory of Our Lord Jesus Christ! Which glory he that magnifies, honours, and adores, ought to read these witnesses likewise, as being no less than the old, unto the Church's edification; that these new wonders also may testify that one and the same Holy Spirit works ever until now, and with Him God the Father Almighty, and His Son Jesus Christ Our Lord, to Whom is glory and power unending for ever and ever

AMEN

its first appearance in the final issue of *The Fleuron*, a magazine of fine typography edited by Morison, in which it was used to set Walter Shewring's translation of *The Passion of Perpetua and Felicity*. From this the type acquired the name Perpetua for the roman and Felicity for the italic forms. Gill's own *Art Nonsense* (1929) was its first commercial use, though the italics were not ready by then so his emphases had to be underlined instead.

Gill later wrote about Perpetua that, 'the drawings were not made as being specially suitable for printing type but simply as letters – letters as normal as might be according to my experience as a letter-cutter in stone and a painter of signs. To Mr Morison and the Monotype Corporation belongs the credit for making useful and presentable typefaces from them. Perpetua is a typographical version of an inscription letter'.[17] Beatrice Warde thought the laborious process by which it was made paid dividends as, 'the intervening hand of the punch-cutter, working in technical sympathy with the hand of the stone cutter, has left a vitality and honesty in the form of the letters which could never be found in the pantographic reproductions of a calligrapher's design'.[18] Morison too was pleased and exploited its 'noble monumental appearance' in the Order of Service books he designed for both the 1937 and 1953 coronations. The popular capital sizes became widely used for title-pages, and in a kind of full-circle, architects and town planners adopted the larger sizes for war-memorials and other public lettering where clarity and dignity were needed.

Gill consolidated his success as a designer of typefaces with 'Joanna', cut by the Caslon Type company in 1930 for use on Gill's own machine presses. With his son-in-law René Hague Gill set up as a commercial printer, not as a private press producing arty books for a specialised public, but as ordinary jobbing printers responsive to public demand. The fourth book they produced was Gill's own *Typography* (1931) which was set in 12pt Joanna. This type, Gill pronounced, 'was not designed to facilitate machine punch-cutting. Not at all. Machines can do practically anything. The question isn't what they *can* do but what they *should*. It is clear that machine products are best when they are plain. Machine-made ornament is nauseating. Assuming that the serif is not an ornamental but a useful addition to letters (especially) in book faces, the Joanna is an attempt to design a book face free from all fancy business. . . . I only claim that it is on the right lines for machine production'.[19] The italic too was designed as a book face in its own right, and not just for emphasis or footnotes. The publishers J.M. Dent later acquired the use of it until 1958, when it was released for general use by the trade.

This is no place to consider in detail Gill's other typefaces, but mention at least must be made of 'Solus' of 1929 which never got beyond four sizes of roman, and the lovely 'Golden Cockerel' designed for Gibbings and seen at its best in *The Four Gospels*. Others were 'Aries' (1932), 'Jubilee' (1934), and 'Bunyan' (1934). He also experimen-

An example of Bunyan typeface

A Sentimental Journey

¶ The type from which this edition of 'A Sentimental Journey' will be printed is a new 14-pt Roman designed by Eric Gill and cut by H. W. Caslon and Co. Ltd. ¶ The paper has been made by hand by J. Barcham Green and Son, Hayle Mill, Maidstone. ¶ The 8 Illustrations are etched in copper by Denis Tegetmeier. ¶ The size of the book is Demy 4to, about 150 pages. ¶ The binding will be in full linen with gilt top. ¶ The printers are Hague and Gill, High Wycombe, England.

Greek lettering (early 1920s), brush drawn

ted with Hebrew and Arabic letter forms as well as the signs of shorthand. Perhaps the most interesting and radical experiment was to try and rationalise Greek so that it would harmonise with the Latin alphabet. Accents were eliminated and the traditional italic form abandoned in favour of one basic graeco-roman fount with special characters for the Greek letters where necessary, but otherwise with a continuity of style across the two alphabets. This seems a good idea whose time has yet to come at least for the academics, though the Greeks themselves have had it cut for newspaper use in Cyprus.

We must now consider the question that several writers have posed – given Gill's views on industrialisation, what was he doing designing commercial typefaces for machine production and machine printing? Does this represent a change of view, or a sell-out by Gill?

As early as 1924 Morison had asked Gill to write an article on lettering for *The Fleuron*, but Gill had refused, saying, 'Typography is not my line of country'. He certainly would not have been converted by Morison's specious argument that the monk in his scriptoria would have loved a printing machine to multiply and spread the Gospel faster than he could have done it by hand. Gill knew enough history to know that once printing was invented then the demand for law books soon outstripped those for theology, and that the break up of that unified medieval world he so admired was accelerated beyond control. He had no illusions about the sanctity of printing or the motives of printers, for had it not been for the insubordination of men of business and the proletarianization of the peasantry, 'it is certain that the "power" press would never have been invented or developed, and the consequent plethora of cheap books and magazines and newspapers and advertisements would never have brought the art and craft of printing and the business or profession of publishing into the disgrace they now so abundantly deserve'.[20] Printing today 'is to produce profits for those who sell it, and to the majority of those to whom it is sold its primary use is dope'. He was also extremely rude to an audience of Master Printers over their concern for profit, and their ignorance of actual printing which they left to machines and their moron minders. Like the architects and priests they hypocritically pretended they lived in a pre-industrial world, 'carrying on as though James Watt & Co. had never existed and are even proud when their 20th century books are mistaken for books of the 18th'.[21] Let us have a little intellectual honesty in printing and throw out old notions about 'justification', resuscitated old types, fake hand-made papers, and all that ornamentation. The intelligentsia are already converted to the idea that plain is best, but, 'as to the morons: we shall have to rely on the B.B.C. to tell them so'.

There can be no doubt, I think, that Gill did see designing type as 'working for the enemy', at least at first. Yet he ended by designing eleven types, one of which was specifically meant to be mechanistic, fool-proof, and to give the local sign-painter copying it no scope for personal responsibility whatsoever. He also wrote an influential book on typography, and printed it on his own commercial presses. It is a paradox Beatrice Warde set herself to explain.[22] As a colleague, fellow convert to Catholicism, intimate of Morison, and a model for Gill, she was well placed to do so, especially as she tells us she nagged Gill about it for a year. Morison's personality was one powerful factor, she believed, as here was 'a man of equal mental stature, similar intellectual integrity, and the same faith – which, in this case, meant the same concern for the dignity and dilemma of humanity'. Morison was concerned that Monotype's powerful position in the typeface market did not tempt it into slacking on standards in the interest of profits. He seems to have inveigled Gill into helping him in this by interesting Gill in the actual physical processes of manufacturing type; so Gill wrote after a visit to their works at Horley, 'I enjoyed it very much indeed. I want to go again and spend longer in the pattern shop – i.e. where they photograph and enlarge and draw and trace and cut wax. It would certainly be an admirable thing if I had an "experimental station" there.'[23] He also found the Corporation good people to do business with, and admitted, 'few associations can have been either more honourable or more pleasant – or, from my point of view, more helpful.'[24] It must have brought home to him that all business men were not devils with top hats and money bags, as he liked to caricature them, nor all machine operators irresponsible morons.

To Beatrice Warde's direct challenge as to whether Gill saw any chance for the handcraftsman against 'the massed battalions of modern industry', he replied, 'Let us distinguish. They are not necessarily armed camps drawn up for battle. They are different ways of life, but given honesty and consistency on each side, they can respect and even help each other.'[25] This message is reiterated on the first page of *Typography*, where he admits that by now (1931) industrialism has won an almost complete victory over handicraft methods, though these will not die 'because they meet an inherent, indestructible, permanent need in human nature'. This being so, 'The two worlds can see each other distinctly and without recrimination, both recognising what is good in the other – the power of industrialism, the humanity of craftsmanship. No longer is there any excuse for confusion of aim, inconsistency of methods or hybridism of production; each world can leave the other free in its own sphere.' Let

A page from *The Four Gospels* (1931), Golden Cockerel Press, wood-engraving with Golden Cockerel typeface, page size 34.4cm × 23cm

IT CAME TO PASS IN
THOSE DAYS, THAT
THERE WENT OUT A DECREE
FROM CÆSAR AUGUSTUS, THAT ALL THE WORLD
SHOULD BE TAXED. (AND THIS TAXING WAS FIRST
made when Cyrenius was governor of Syria.) And all went to
be taxed, every one into his own city. And Joseph also went
up from Galilee, out of the city of Nazareth, into Judæa,
unto the city of David, which is called Bethlehem; (because
he was of the house and lineage of David:) To be taxed with
Mary his espoused wife, being great with child. And so it
was, that, while they were there, the days were accomplished
that she should be delivered. And she brought forth her

137

there be no more faking and merging at either extreme, or the kind of hypocrisy whereby men-of-business-with-taste turn out 'period' work with resuscitated eighteenth-century types, and private presses run by men-of-taste-who-are-also-business-men turn out books at high speed by machine-setting and corrupting their workers. This is dishonest to the potential of each world to produce its own kind of beauty, for, 'the beauty that industrialism properly produces is the beauty of bones; the beauty that radiates from the work of men is the beauty of holiness'. Gill is unique in having worked at both extremes with such success.

Given his socialist past it might seem inconsistent that Gill was producing vellum copies of *The Four Gospels* at eighty guineas, or *The Canterbury Tales* at £30. 5s for the rich specialist market of the private presses. As we have seen he had no illusions that widespread printing for profit would produce anything other than the despicable 'Daily Mail mind', and by the time of *Typography* he seems to have forgotten all about his early onslaughts on the Arts and Crafts Movement for their limited market amongst the rich. 'It is obvious that the number of possible buyers of expensive books is comparatively small. This will always be so, and rightly. That everybody should be "rich" is, in the nature of things, neither possible nor desirable. That everybody should be able to read or even wish to do so, is extremely doubtful. There is therefore no question of the limited production of expensive books involving any injustice, and, apart from the efforts of a few earnest enthusiasts, the production of cheap literature, whether daily newspapers or books, is without doubt the affair not of those interested in books but of men of business interested in money.'[26] Indeed *Typography* itself first appeared as 500 signed copies at 25 shillings each.

Once having analysed what the hand-press and mach-ine press owners ought to be doing, and then designing appropriate typefaces for each so they could get on with it, he proceeded to tell the whole industry what it had been doing wrong for years. Gill never lacked for self-confidence in any of his pronouncements on any subject whatsoever.

First what are letters? No one asks the maker of letters 'what's that represent?' – the eternal cry of the Philistine, because letters are things, not pictures of things. The typographer has no need to invent an A, all he has to do is find what constitutes the A-ness of A, the norm for A, and to discover this is an exercise of the rational mind. Of course the tool used to make a letter has some influence too, but that is secondary for, 'the mind is the arbiter in letter forms, not the tool or the materials'. The rational mind has fuller play in lettering than in any of the other arts Gill practised because letters are more or less abstract forms, so 'no one can say that the o's roundness appeals to us only because it is like that of an apple or of a girl's breast or of the full moon.'[27] He writes, 'Art and morals are inextricably mixed, but the art of lettering is freer from adulteration than most arts.' It is also a precise and a useful art, joining the fair and the fit: all features Gill looked for in any art, but could find nowhere so purely as in lettering. The bases of all lettering are legibility and readability, and if we are to pursue these with all the rationality we have available then it will lead us to some very radical reforms of typography and printing as we know it.

For example, there will be no more 'exact and scholarly resuscitations of letters whose virtue is bound up with their derivation from humane craftsmanship' (i.e. calligraphy). Italic letters are so derived, so why should modern ones still retain their exaggerated slope and cursive features? Justification (making a square page by making all lines of print the same length) grew from imitation of medieval scribes' rectangular blocks of illuminated writing, so why do we still need it? We accept an irregular right edge in blank verse and a typewritten letter, so why not in a book? Close, even spacing is much more important than line length for legibility, and if we need emphasis why not use spacing w i t h i n the word or words rather than using italics, which are best reserved for quotations and footnotes? Legibility might also benefit from the use of more contractions such as &, or ¶ to mark paragraphs rather than beginning a new line. While there is a certain reasonableness and plausibility in the current belief in 'allusive typography', that is that the style of typeface chosen should reflect the contents of the book, this is not the first consideration. Rather we should begin with the size of the book and the likely places it will be read, such as in the hand, at a table, on a lectern, or kept in the pocket as a reference book. Why could we not use one basic good type for all these, though in different sizes of course? Nor is it necessary for the title page to be 'the showing-off ground for the printers and publishers' when it could be simply set in the same style and size of type as the rest of the book, giving the title, author and list of contents only. If the publishers insist on getting in on the act then their name and address could appear on a page by themselves preceding the title page. Why too all that fake tooling on covers when books could be issued in sheets or simple paper wrappers? All these reforms are demonstrated in *Typography* itself, and in several other books from the Hague and Gill Press.

Finally, 'since reasonableness is the first necessity', why not scrap the whole 1800-year tradition of Roman lettering altogether and invent new letters which fit the sounds of English more rationally? Gill thought shorthand could be developed into a true phonology – and when that was done why could Gill not be asked to design a fount of phonological symbols? He is probably thinking of G.B. Shaw's campaign for the same kind of reform. To experts in linguistics any such attempt must seem laughably naïve. Then, as a final irony from one whose fame will probably rest upon his type designs, he complains, 'there are now about as many different varieties of letters as there are fools', far too many display letters, and too many book types, most of them rehashes of preindustrial designs. He concludes by biting clean off the hand that fed him.

Lettering has had its day, Spelling, and philo-logy, and all such pedantries have no place in our world. The only way to reform modern lettering is to abolish it.   Joanna typeface

Conclusion

How can one sum up a man so diverse in his skills, so wide in his interests, so prodigal in his energies and achievements – yet so human in his failings? One cannot, but Edward Johnston came near when he wrote, 'Swift was a good word for him. He lived swiftly . . . youthfulness of spirit commonly goes together with youthfulness of years. Eric's was less dependent upon actual age, and his best work has the spirit of Life itself.'

Gill committed himself dogmatically and often to paper so that all his beliefs in art, morals, politics and religion are out in the open for public debate. He also compulsively documented his own private life, down to the smallest errors, which makes it all the easier for us to see where he occasionally compromised on these widely proclaimed standards, either from expediency or from human weakness. But, as Walter Shewring writes, 'if a man is to be a prophet at all, he is to be judged primarily by the truth of what he says, not by the numbers of those who act upon it,' and that would presumably include the prophet himself. Nevertheless, Gill's life and work certainly did attain a coherence and integrity few people could aspire to, and he could with justice turn back on us Whitman's words from *Song of Myself*,

Do I contradict myself?
Very well then I contradict myself.
(I am large, I contain multitudes).

Gill *was* large, and he set himself correspondingly enormous tasks such as the analysis and reform of modern industrial society. It is not surprising that in the thousands of words he poured out on all aspects of that society the odd hole appears in the logic, or the evidence, or the practice. Nor is it surprising that his certainty about his own rightness should appear as arrogance to readers who lack certainty about anything themselves.

Some of the burning issues he tackled have now cooled; some of the reforms he advocated have been achieved; and others, such as his hope that every man would be an artist, or that small rural communities like his own would be widespread, or that the masses would rise up to demand the right to make fewer but quality goods, now look hopelessly romantic dreams in contemporary Britain. And yet, must we not admit the continuing pertinence of the questions he asked so often and so trenchantly? How can we live the life of reason ('few adventures are more honourable than an attempt to live by it')? How can quality goods be made available to a large population rather than cheap rubbish? How can we make workmen involved and responsible in an industrial society? How can we make work a privilege and not a drudgery? How do we wean the vast majority of people off sentimentality and the flattering reproduction of appearances in art? How do we get the modern artist out of his isolation and into useful contact with that majority again without him selling out? Behind all these questions, Gill reminds us, are the even bigger ones about man himself and his relationship to God.

As a writer about art Gill was making pronouncements as radical and modern as any of his contemporaries. When we come to look at his works, however, they look more like the end of a tradition rather than the start of a new one, and were seen to be so even in his own life-time. Their typical characteristics are a cool linear grace, figuration, permanence, optimism, accessibility, and a clear simple didactic intent. All these features the twentieth century has come to distrust or despise. His attempted revival of a tradition of public symbolism and his use of art as propaganda for a religious faith now seem hopelessly doomed in our secular age. In the era of the collage, the multiple, the throw-away, and the happening, his concern with craft skills and the slow deliberate making of a thing to last for generations seems irrelevant to people who may have no future. Even his all-pervading eroticism looks curiously innocent to our more 'kinky' times. But, as Gill pointed out, it is the times which are out of joint, not him. We live in a historical aberration and have gone off the rails. David Jones reports that Gill said, 'What I achieve as a sculptor is of no consequence – I can only be a beginning – it will take generations, but if only the beginnings of a reasonable, decent, holy tradition of working might be effected that is the thing.' Jones thought he did not sound very hopeful.

Woman bending (1926), wood-engraving, 6.3cm × 5.1cm

References

1. '*Man is matter and spirit: both real and both good*'

1 Count Harry Kessler, *The Diaries of a Cosmopolitan 1918–1937*, trans. C. Kessler (London 1971), p. 256.
2 David Kindersley, 'An Introduction and Memoir' in the catalogue to the Eric Gill exhibition, Kettle's Yard Cambridge, 20 October–18 November 1979.
3 Sir John Rothenstein, *Summer's Lease: Autobiography 1901–1938* (London 1965), p. 179.
4 David Kindersley, 'My Apprenticeship to Mr Eric Gill', *Craft* magazine, July/August 1979.
5 Letter to the author.
6 Priscilla Johnston, *Edward Johnston* (London 1959) p. 288.
7 *Letters of Eric Gill*, edited by Walter Shewring (London 1947), p. 111.
8 Copies in the Gill collections at The University of Texas in Austin, and the Richard A. Gleeson Library, University of San Francisco.
9 David Kindersley, 'My Apprenticeship to Mr Gill', *Craft* magazine, September/October 1979, p. 44.
10 *Diary* for 1906 in William Andrews Clark Memorial Library, Los Angeles.
11 *Letters*, p. 239.
12 Beatrice Warde, 'Eric Gill Typographer', in *Life and Works of Eric Gill* (pub. William Andrews Clark Library, 1968), p. 16.
13 Conrad Pepler, 'A Study in Integrity: The Life and Teachings of Eric Gill', in *Blackfriars*, vol. XXVIII, May 1947, pp. 198–209.
14 *Catholic Herald*, 29 November 1940, p. 8.
15 Robert Speaight, *The Life of Eric Gill* (London 1966), p. 136.
16 Speaight, p. 137.
17 John Rothenstein, *Summer's Lease*, p. 127.
18 Eric Gill, *Autobiography* (London 1940), p. 233.
19 *Autobiography*, p. 26of. Other captors he evaded were Art Schools, the Architect's Office, Scientific Rationalism, the Arts and Crafts Movement, Socialism, London, and the 'Art World'.
20 Speaight, p. 228.
21 Donald Attwater, *A Cell of Good Living: The Life, Works and Opinions of Eric Gill* (London 1969), p. 201.

22 Notebook, William Andrews Clark Library.

23 Speaight, p. 179.

24 See Notebook, William Andrews Clark Library.

25 From tape recording made at WAC Library, 20 April 1967, in which David Kindersley interviews Gill's brothers Cecil and Vernon.

26 *Autobiography*, p. 168.

27 *Letters*, p. 50.

28 *Ibid.*, p. 51.

29 *Autobiography*, p. 212.

30 *Ibid.*, p. 247.

31 For example in the Preface to *Drawings from Life* (London 1940) p.i.

32 *Autobiography*, p. 119.

33 *Ibid.*, p. 227.

34 See the chapter 'The Naked Christian' in *The Male Nude* by Margaret Walters (London 1978).

35 Speaight, p. 167.

36 Rayner Heppenstall, *Four Absentees* (London 1960), p. 40.

37 *The Necessity of Belief* (London 1936), p. 28.

38 *Autobiography*, p. 282.

39 Conrad Pepler, 'A Study in Integrity: The Life and Teachings of Eric Gill', *Blackfriars*, vol. XXVIII, May 1947, pp. 198–209.

40 Donald Attwater, *A Cell of Good Living*.

41 Cecil Gill, 'Reminiscences' in *Life and Works of Eric Gill*, WAC Library (Los Angeles 1968), p. 4.

42 Herbert Read, 'Eric Gill' in *A Coat of Many Colours* (London 1945), p. 6.

43 Richard Church, *New Statesman and Nation*, London, 22 March 1941.

44 Cecil Gill, 'Reminiscences' in *Life and Works of Eric Gill*, p. 6.

2. *Writing, crafts, clothes, and the modern woman*

1 Evan Gill, *Bibliography of Eric Gill* (London 1962).

2 In article on 'Stanley Spencer' in *The Guardian*, 29 April 1979.

3 John Rothenstein, *Summer's Lease*, p. 119.

4 D.H. Lawrence, 'Eric Gill's Art Nonsense', *Book Collector's Quarterly*, no. XII, Oct–Dec 1933, pp. 1–7.

5 'Slavery and Freedom' in *Art Nonsense* (London 1929), p. 1.

6 Review article on 'A Propos of Lady Chatterley's Lover' by D.H. Lawrence, *The Dublin Review*, no. 376, January 1931, pp. 161–2.

7   Speaight, p. 231.

8   *Beauty Looks After Herself* (London 1933), p. 5.

9   *Letters*, pp. 17–22.

10 *Ibid.*, p. 246.

11 *Ibid.*, p. 365.

12 *Ibid.*, p. 127.

13 *Ibid.*, p. 133

14 'The Revival of Handicraft', *Art Nonsense*, p. 118.

15 *Autobiography*, p. 270.

16 See H. Th. Fischer, 'The Clothes of the Naked Nuer' (1964), in *Social Aspects of the Human Body*, ed. T. Polhemus (London 1978).

17 *Art Nonsense*, p. 209.

18 Speaight, p. 168.

19 *Trousers and The Most Precious Ornament* (London 1937), p. 2.

20 'Dress', *Art Nonsense*, p. 22.

21 Speaight, p. 160.

22 Eric Gill, review of *Christianity and Sex* by C. Dawson, and *Comments on Birth Control* by Naomi Mitchison, in *The Dublin Review*, no. 374, July 1930, pp. 174–6.

23 *Autobiography*, p. 132.

24 Eric Gill, *Trousers & The Most Precious Ornament*, p. 15.

25 *Autobiography*, p. 241.

26 *Art Nonsense*, p. 54.

27 Margaret Walters, *The Male Nude*, p. 315.

3. *'But see how good are my leaders'*

1   *Autobiography*, p. 24.

2   *Ibid.*, p. 32.

3   *Essays* (London 1947), p. 171.

4   John Ruskin, *The Stones of Venice*, vol. 2 (London 1853), 'The Nature of Gothic', reprinted by William Morris on the Kelmscott Press, 1892, and here quoted from C. Harvie (ed.) *et al*, *Industrialisation and Culture 1830–1914* (London 1970), p. 305.

5   *The Stones of Venice*, vol. 2, *ibid.*, p. 308.

6   'The Veins of Wealth', in *Unto this Last* (London 1862), pp. 40–46.

7   Quoted by W.R. Lethaby in 'What Shall We Call Beautiful?', in *Form in Civilization* (Oxford 1922), p. 165.

8   For a detailed study of the relationships between Gill's ideas and Morris's see: *William Morris and Eric Gill* by Peter Faulkner (The William Morris Society, 1975).

9   *Autobiography*, p. 268.

10 In 'News from Nowhere', *William Morris: Selected Writings and Designs*, ed. Asa Briggs (London 1962), p. 266.

11 Eric Gill, *The Necessity of Belief* (London 1936), p. 304.

12 Beatrice Warde in *The Life and Works of Eric Gill* (Los Angeles 1968), p. 15.

13 'Town Tidying' in *Form in Civilisation* (Oxford 1922), p. 17.

14 'The Centre of Gravity' in *Form in Civilisation*, p. 229.

15 'Town Tidying', *ibid.*, p. 17.

16 'Arts and the Function of Guilds', *ibid.*, p. 205.

17 Walter Shewring, *Blackfriars*, vol. XXIX, no. 341, August 1948, p. 385.

18 M.D. Kirk, *The Esthetics of Eric Gill* (MA thesis, Loyola University of Los Angeles, 1959), p. 30.

19 Jacques Maritain, *The Philosophy of Art*, trans. Revd J. O'Connor, (Ditchling 1923). Introduction by Eric Gill.

20 See, Roger Lipsey, *Coomaraswamy: His Life and Work*, Bolingen Series LXXXIX (Princeton 1977).

21 *Viśvakarma: Examples of Indian Architecture, Sculpture, Painting, Handicraft*, chosen by Ananda Coomaraswamy. First Series, Sculpture, part VIII, (London 1914).

22 *Autobiography*, p. 174.

23 Quoted by Ian Bradley; *William Morris and his World* (London 1978) p. 95.

24 D. Attwater, *A Cell of Good Living*, p. 113.

25 *Engravings 1928–1933 by Eric Gill* (London 1934), pp. v–vi.

26 *Letters*, p. 253.

27 Attwater, p. 114.

4. *The artist in modern society*

1 *Beauty Looks After Herself* (London 1933), p. 216.

2 *Ibid.*, p. 226.

3 *Letters*, p. 178.

4 *Ibid.*, p. 180.

5 *Art Nonsense* (London 1929), p. 51.

6 Jacques Maritain, *Art and Scholasticism*, trans. J.F. Scanlan (London 1932), p. 47.

7 *Letters*, p. 422.

8 *Ibid.*, p. 424.

9 *Ibid.*, p. 143.

10 'Exhibitionism and Criticism', in *Form in Civilization* (Oxford 1922), p. 174.

11 A. Coomaraswamy, 'What Use is Art Anyway?' *Six Broadcasts Sponsored by Boston Museum of Fine Arts* (Newport, R.I., 1937), p. 2.

12 *Beauty Looks After Herself*, p. 243.

13 *Ibid.*, p. 54.

14 *Ibid.*, p. 228.

15 *Ibid.*, p. 230.

16 D. Ashton (ed.), *Picasso on Art: A Selection of Views* (London 1972), p. 48.

17 G.K. Chesterton, 'Eric Gill and No Nonsense', *The Studio*, vol. XCIX, no. 445, April 1930, pp. 231–4.

18 *Art Nonsense*, p. 65.

19 *Letters*, p. 179.

20 *Art Nonsense*, p. 28.

21 *Ibid.*, p. 73.

22 *Ibid.*, p. 123.

23 *Autobiography*, p. 274.

24 *Ibid.*, p. 177.

25 *Art Nonsense*, p. 53.

26 *Ibid.*, p. 205.

27 D. Attwater, *A Cell of Good Living*, p. 140.

28 Speaight, p. 228.

29 *Art Nonsense*, p. 321.

30 'The Nature of Medieval Art', reprinted from *Arts of the Middle Ages* (Boston 1940).

31 Raymond Williams, *Keywords* (London 1976), p. 34.

32 What Use is Art Anyway? *Six Broadcasts* . . ., p. 10.

33 'Art in Education', *Essays* (London 1947), p. 57.

34 *Letters*, p. 306.

35 Notably in such essays as 'Twopence Plain, Penny Coloured', 'Architecture and Machines', 'Plain Architecture', 'Architecture as Sculpture' (all in *Beauty Looks After Herself*); 'Architecture and Sculpture' (*Art Nonsense*), 'Sculpture on Machine-Made Buildings' (*Essays*).

36 *Art Nonsense*, pp. 159–91.

37 *Letters*, p. 373.

38 Speaight, p. 239.

39 *All that England Stands For*, pamphlet for The Peace Pledge Union (London, 5 January 1940).

40 An article on page 1 of the *Catholic Herald*, Friday, 13 October 1939, sets out these views very succinctly.

41 *Social Justice and the Stations of the Cross* (London 1939).

42 The naïvete of his social and political views was pointed out in two reviews of his posthumous essays: George Orwell, 'Return Journey', *The Observer*, Sunday, 9 July 1944; and Charles Morgan, 'Eric Gill', *The Sunday Times*, Sunday, 27 April 1947, p. 3.

5. 'The excess of amorous nature fertilizes the spiritual field'

1   *Autobiography*, p. 222.
2   *Ibid.*, p. 121.
3   *Ibid.*, p. 85.
4   Preface, *Twenty-Five Nudes* (London 1938), p. 3.
5   *Drawings from Life* (London 1940), p. xiv.
6   John Rothenstein, *Summer's Lease*, p. 184.
7   According to David Kindersley in a letter to the author. Its present whereabouts are unknown.
8   *Autobiography*, p. 53.
9   R. Heppenstall, *Four Absentees*, p. 99.
10 D.G. Bridson, *Prospero and Ariel: The Rise and Fall of Radio* (London 1971), p. 41.
11 A. Boyle, *Only the Wind Will Listen* (London 1972), p. 250.
12 Speaight, p. 179.
13 Kenneth Clark, *The Nude* (London 1960), pp. 1–4.
14 Speaight, p. 190.
15 *Autobiography*, p. 123.
16 *Ananga-Ranga or The Hindu Art of Love*, trans. by Richard Burton and Foster Arbuthnot (London 1885).
17 Count Harry Kessler, *The Diaries of a Cosmopolitan 1918–1937*, p. 330.
18 Speaight, p. 179.
19 *Autobiography*, p. 97.
20 'Art and Love', *Art Nonsense*, pp. 192–215.
21 *Art Nonsense*, p. 201.
22 *Ibid.*, p. 204.
23 *Letters*, p. 36.
24 J.G. Fletcher, 'Eric Gill', *The Arts* (London, February 1928), p. 95.
25 'Indian Sculpture' in *Art Nonsense*, p. 108.
26 *Art Nonsense*, p. 205.
27 *Ibid.*, p. 31.
28 I.M. Lippman, *Engravings of Eric Gill: A Study of 20th Century Hieratic Art*, M.A. Thesis, University of Texas, Austin, 1975.
29 *Art Nonsense*, p. 212.
30 A theme already treated in France by Felicien Rops (1833–98) in his blasphemous *Les Sataniques* drawings, and by Rodin in his 1894 marble of *Christ and the Magdalene*.
31 *Art Nonsense*, p. 213.
32 For a briefer and more scholarly account of how this transformation from love poem to religious allegory came about see Dr David Goldstein's Introduction to *The Song*

of Songs, translated by Peter Jay (London, Anvil Press, 1975).

33 *Art Nonsense*, p. 33.
34 *Ibid.*, p. 36.
35 *Letters*, p. 211.
36 *Ibid.*, p. 212.
37 Kessler, p. 331.
38 Speaight, p. 118.
39 Attwater, p. 100.
40 A. Garrett, *A History of British Wood Engraving* (London 1978), p. 226.
41 *Letters*, p. 212.
42 *Drawings from Life* (London 1940), p.i.
43 Speaight, p. 174.
44 *Art Nonsense*, p. 42.
45 Speaight, p. 176.
46 David Kindersley, 'My Apprenticeship to Mr Gill', *Crafts*, London, Sept/Oct 1979, p. 43.
47 P. and E. Kronhausen, *Erotic Art* (London 1971), p. 23.
48 *Ibid.*, p. 26.
49 *Autobiography*, p. 227.

6. Drawings

1   *Autobiography*, p. 73.
2   *Ibid.*, p. 83.
3   David Kindersley, 'My Apprenticeship to Mr Eric Gill', *Crafts*, July/August 1979, p. 40.
4   Speaight, p. 218.
5   *Art Nonsense*, p. 322.
6   Kineton Parkes, 'Eric Gill as Draftsman' in *Pencil Points*, vol. XIV, no. 12, December 1933, p. 528 (Stanford, USA).
7   *Twenty-Five Nudes* (London 1938), p. 1.
8   *Autobiography*, p. 162.
9   *Letters*, p. 413.
10 John Rothenstein, *Summer's Lease*, p. 183.
11 'Sculpture and the Living Model' in *Beauty Looks After Herself*, p. 110.
12 *Ibid.*, p. 112.
13 *Ibid.*, p. 113.
14 *Art Nonsense*, p. 83.
15 *Drawings from Life* (London 1940), p. vii.
16 Speaight, fly leaf.
17 *Ibid.*, p. 292.
18 *Twenty-five Nudes* (London 1938), p. 2.
19 *First Nudes* (London 1954), Introduction, p. 2.
20 Quoted in Roger Lipsey's *Coomaraswamy: His Life and Work*, Bolingen Series, LXXXIX (Princeton, 1977), p. 108.

7. *Wood engravings*

1 A fuller account of this history can be obtained from: H. Furst, *The Modern Woodcut* (London 1924); A. Garrett, *A History of British Wood Engraving* (London 1978); W. Chamberlain, *Wood Engraving* (London 1978).

2 Chamberlain, p. 66.

3 George E. Mackley, *Wood Engraving* (London 1948), p. 11.

4 Garrett, p. 327.

5 H.D.C. Pepler, 'Eric Gill', *The Aylesford Review*, Spring 1965, p. 37.

6 *Ibid.*, p. 38.

7 See Evan R. Gill, *Bibliography of Eric Gill* (London 1953).

8 C.F.T. Balston, *The Wood-Engravings of Robert Gibbings* (London 1949).

9 Gibbings reveals this, and their rather haphazard working methods in 'Memories of Eric Gill', *The Book Collector*, Summer 1953, pp. 95–102.

10 R. Heppenstall, *Four Absentees*, p. 103.

11 J.F. Physick, *The Engraved Work of Eric Gill* (London, HMSO, 1963).

12 R.J. Beedham, *Wood-Engraving* (Ditchling 1920) and re-issued (London 1946). Introduction by Eric Gill, p. 10.

13 *Ibid.*, p. 12

14 Preface to *Engravings by Eric Gill* (London 1929).

15 Appendix to R.J. Beedham's *Wood-Engraving*, p. 51.

16 'The Society of Wood Engravers', *The Architect* 1920: also in *Blackfriars*, vol. 1, no. 9, Dec. 1920, p. 555.

17 *Letters*, p. 187.

18 *Glue and Lacquer*: Four Cautionary Tales translated from the Chinese by H. Acton and Lee Yi-Hsieh (London 1941).

19 *Canticum Canticorum Salomonis* (Weimar 1931).

20 'Troilus & Criseyde', review by John Rothenstein, *Bibliophile's Almanack for 1928* (London 1928), pp. 75–9.

21 Speaight, p. 205.

22 R.A. Walker, 'The Engravings of Eric Gill', *The Print Collector's Quarterly*, vol. XV, no. 2, April 1928, p. 162.

23 Speaight, p. 178.

24 Garrett, p. 204.

25 B.N. Lee, *British Bookplates: A Pictorial History* (Newton Abbot 1979), p. 126.

26 Garrett, p. 329.

27 H. Furst, 'The Modern Woodcut', *Print Collector's Quarterly*, vol. VIII, no. 2, July 1921, p. 294.

28 H. Furst, *The Modern Woodcut* (London 1924), pp. 221–2.

29 *Letters*, p. 415.
30 Garrett, p. 149.
31 *Engravings 1928–1933 by Eric Gill* (London 1934), p. vi.
32 *Letters*, p. 400.
33 George Mackley, *Wood Engraving* (London 1948), p. 119.

8. *Sculpture and architecture*

1   *Autobiography*, p. 158.
2   *Ibid.*, p. 161.
3   William Rothenstein, *Men and Memories 1872–1938*, edited and abridged by M. Lago (London 1978), p. 159.
4   *Autobiography*, p. 162.
5   R. Wittkower, *Sculpture: Processes and Principles* (London 1977), p. 21.
6   P. James, (ed.), *Henry Moore on Sculpture* (London 1966), p. 190.
7   *Letters*, p. 262.
8   M. Batten, *Stone Sculpture by Direct Carving* (London 1957), p. 13.
9   Barbara Hepworth, *Carvings and Drawings* (London 1952), p. vii.
10 *With Henry Moore*, photographs by G. Levine (London 1978), p. 95.
11 Anthony Foster, *Blackfriars*, vol. XXII, no. 251, February 1941, p. 65.
12 Speaight, p. 78.
13 *Art Nonsense*, pp. 15–20.
14 *Autobiography*, p. 200.
15 D. Farr, *English Art 1870–1940* (Oxford 1978), p. 223.
16 T. McGreevy, 'Eric Gill: An Appreciation', *The Studio*, vol. CXXI, no. 574, January 1941, p. 6.
17 *Letters*, p. 318.
18 *Ibid.*, p. 319.
19 *Ibid.*, p. 323.
20 *Ibid.*, p. 369.
21 M. Holroyd, *Augustus John: The Years of Innocence* (London 1974), p. 363.
22 Ezra Pound, *Gaudier-Brzeska: A Memoir* (London 1916, reprinted 1960), p. 32.
23 *Ibid.*, p. 97.
24 *Letters*, p. 138.
25 Margaret Walters, *The Male Nude* pp. 81–2.
26 *Autobiography*, p. 219.
27 Speaight, p. 229.
28 Cf. D. Attwater *A Cell of Good Living*, pp. 128–9.
29 *Letters*, p. 247.

286 · References

30 *Ibid.*, p. 82.
31 *Ibid.*, p. 98.
32 P. James (ed.), *Henry Moore on Sculpture* (London 1966),
    p. 32.
33 *Art Nonsense*, p. 110.
34 *Letters*, p. 57.
35 *Ibid.*, p. 99.
36 Republished in *Art Nonsense* as 'A War Memorial', pp.
    110–14.
37 *Letters*, p. 170.
38 Speaight, p. 133.
39 *Letters*, p. 228.
40 See particularly 'Architecture as Sculpture', 'Architecture
    and Machines', 'Plain Architecture' (All in *Beauty Looks
    After Herself*), 'Sculpture on Machine-Made Buildings'
    (*Essays*), 'Architecture and Sculpture', 'The Future of
    Sculpture' (*Art Nonsense*) and variously throughout the
    Letters.
41 P. James (ed.), *Henry Moore on Sculpture* (London 1966),
    p. 97.
42 D. Farr, *English Art 1870–1940* (Oxford 1978), p. 251.
43 *Ibid.*, p. 251.
44 For more details and photographs of the building and
    sculptures *in situ* see *Architectural Review*, vol. LXVI,
    1929, pp. 225–41.
45 *Letters*, p. 256.
46 *Autobiography*, p. 248.
47 *Letters*, p. 266.
48 'Plain Architecture', *Beauty Looks After Herself*, p. 156.
49 *Letters*, p. 419.
50 *Autobiography*, p. 252.
51 *Letters*, p. 336.
52 Speaight, p. 259.
53 *Letters*, p. 96.
54 *Ibid.*, p. 35.
55 'What's it All Bloomin' Well For?' *G.K.'s Weekly*, 20 June
    1930.
56 *Letters*, p. 382.
57 *Autobiography*, p. 251.
58 Jacob Epstein, *An Autobiography* (London 1963), p. 204.
59 *Viśvakarma, Examples of Indian Architecture, Sculpture,
    Painting, Handicraft*. Chosen by A. Coomaraswamy
    (London 1914). E. Gill's Introduction, p. 4.
60 Stanley Casson, *The Technique of Early Greek Sculpture*
    (Oxford 1933), pp. 236–8.
61 Letter in the Albert Sperison Gill Collection, Gleeson
    Library, University of San Francisco.
62 David Jones, 'Eric Gill as Sculptor' (1941), *Epoch and
    Artist* (London 1959), p. 292.

63   *Ibid.*, p. 293.
64   P. James (ed.), *Henry Moore on Sculpture* (London 1966), p. 135.
65   *Letters*, p. 313.
66   David Jones, 'Eric Gill as Sculptor', *Artist and Epoch*, p. 290.

9. *'Absolutely legible-to-the-last-degree letters' in stone and ink*

1   Priscilla Johnston, *Edward Johnston* (London 1959), p. 100.
2   *Autobiography*, p. 118.
3   *Ibid.*, p. 119.
4   Paul Beaujon (pen-name of Beatrice Warde), 'Eric Gill: Sculptor of Letters' in *Fleuron Anthology* chosen by F. Meynell and H. Simon (Toronto 1973), p. 278. See also Kessler's description of Maillol at work on these (*Ibid.*), pp. 260–3.
5   Edward Johnston, *Writing & Illuminating & Lettering* (London 1906).
6   *Letters*, p. 304.
7   Evan Gill, *The Inscriptional Work of Eric Gill: An Inventory* (London 1964), p. ix.
8   Cf. *The Aylesford Review*, a literary quarterly issued by English Carmelites, Spring 1965, Hilary Pepler Memorial issue, p. 11.
9   Speaight, p. 186.
10   *Letters*, p. 188.
11   Robert Harling, *The Letter Forms and Type Designs of Eric Gill* (Westerham, Kent, 1976), p. 16.
12   *Ibid.*, p. 44.
13   Eric Gill, *An Essay on Typography* (London 1931), p. 127.
14   Harling, p. 48.
15   For an assessment of Morison's work see: James Moran, *Stanley Morison: His Typographical Achievement* (London 1971), and *The Monotype Recorder*, memorial issue, vol. 43, no. 3, Autumn 1968.
16   Beatrice Warde, 'Eric Gill: Master of Lettering', *The Monotype Recorder*, Vol. XLI, no. 3, Autumn 1958, pp. 10–11.
17   Roy Brewer, *Eric Gill: The Man Who Loved Letters* (London 1973), p. 14.
18   'Paul Beaujon', 'Eric Gill: Sculptor of letters', p. 286.
19   *Monotype Recorder*, vol. XLI, no. 3, p. 7.
20   'Five Hundred Years of Printing', in *Essays* (London 1947), p. 58.

21 *The Three Ridings Journal*, vol. 5, no. 1, published by the
     Yorkshire Alliance of Master Printers, *c*.1935, p. 10.

22 'Eric Gill: Typographer', a paper read at the symposium
     on 'The Life and Works of Eric Gill', 22 April 1967,
     William Andrews Clark Memorial Library, Los Angeles.

23 *Ibid.*, p. 26.

24 *Autobiography*, p. 220.

25 Beatrice Warde, 'Eric Gill: Typographer', p. 33.

26 *Typography*, p. 111.

27 *Autobiography*, p. 120.

Select bibliography

D. ATTWATER, *A Cell of Good Living: The Life, Works and Opinions of Eric Gill* (Chapman, London 1969)

P. BEAUJON (Beatrice Webb), 'Eric Gill: Sculptor of Letters', in *The Fleuron Anthology* (Benn, Toronto 1973)

R. BREWER, *Eric Gill: The Man who Loved Letters* (Muller, London 1973)

A. GARRETT, *A History of British Wood Engraving* (Midas, London 1978)

ERIC GILL, *Autobiography* (Cape, London 1940)

– *An Essay on Typography*, (Dent, London 1931)

EVAN R. GILL, *A Bibliography of Eric Gill* (Cassell, London 1953)

– *The Inscriptional Work of Eric Gill: An Inventory* (Cassell, London 1964)

R. HARLING, *The Letter Forms and Type Designs of Eric Gill* (Westerham, Kent, 1976)

D. KINDERSLEY, 'My Apprenticeship to Mr Gill', *Craft* Magazine, July–August 1979/September–October 1979 (Crafts Advisory Committee, London)

J.F. PHYSICK, *The Engraved Work of Eric Gill*, Victoria and Albert Museum (HMSO, London 1963)

– **The Engraved Work of Eric Gill*, Large Picture Book, no. 17 (HMSO, London 1977)

W. SHEWRING, *The Letters of Eric Gill* (Cape, London 1947)

R. SPEAIGHT, *The Life of Eric Gill* (Methuen, London 1966)

* This reproduces 221 of Gill's engravings and would form a useful supplement to my own book, as I have tried to avoid duplicating works already appearing there.

Index